Bulbs in the Basement
Geraniums on the Windowsill

BULBS IN THE BASEMENT GERANIUMS ON THE WINDOWSILL

How to Grow and Overwinter *165* TENDER PLANTS

Alice and Brian McGowan

Storey Publishing

The mission of Storey Publishing is to serve our customers by publishing practical information that encourages personal independence in harmony with the environment.

Edited by Carleen Madigan Perkins
Art direction and book design by Jessica Armstrong

Photography credits appear on page 200
Illustrations by © Beverly Duncan, except for page 28 by © Elayne Sears

Indexed by Christine Lindemer, Boston Road Communications

Printed in China by Dai Nippon Printing
10 9 8 7 6 5 4 3 2 1

LIBRARY OF CONGRESS CATALOGING-IN-PUBLICATION DATA

McGowan, Alice.
    Bulbs in the basement, geraniums on the windowsill /
    Alice McGowan, Brian McGowan.
        p. cm.
    Includes bibliographical references and index.
    ISBN 978-1-60342-042-6 (pbk. : alk. paper)
    1. Perennials—Massachusetts. 2. Plants, Ornamental—
    Massachusetts. 3. Greenhouse gardening—Massachusetts.
    I. McGowan, Brian, 1952— II. Title.
SB434.M383 2008
635.9'32—dc22
                                                2008022440

We dedicate this book to our daughters,
Leah and Emma, in the hope that they will
continue to enjoy plants despite a surfeit of
early exposure to them.

CONTENTS

A Little History

LIKE SO MANY THINGS IN LIFE, the road that led to our discovery of tender perennial plants was not a particularly well-marked one. It's hard to pinpoint exactly when we began our journey upon it, but we would never have arrived at our eventual destination if we hadn't begun with the dream of operating a diversified fruit and vegetable farm. This was the road we thought we were headed down in the early 1980s, when we grew vegetables for the wholesale market — lettuce, early tomatoes, and red peppers for specialty outlets.

We had always grown flowers too, and when, in 1981, we moved onto the long-abandoned Magdycz farm in Montague, Massachusetts, it included a neglected perennial bed. We enjoyed reviving it and discovering new plants hidden in the weeds. For years we had eyed the potential market for ornamental plants and concluded there was already an abundant supply of them. But in the spring of 1988, when our daughter Leah was three and Emma was six months old, we planted flowers among the six-packs of lettuce in the greenhouse.

Quiet Beginnings

That first spring, we set up a tent on the side of the road. If you never visited the nursery, you probably can't imagine what an out-of-the-way spot our location was. In those days, our neighbors were all residential or wholesale farming operations. No vehicle went by that we didn't know, and, in fact, very few went by at all.

Even that first quiet season, we noticed encouraging signs — one of which was that people traveled out of their way for well-grown plants they couldn't find elsewhere. And that when they shopped for flowers, they were happy to pay more than they did for tomatoes and lettuce. Our plant selection that year was a simple one. We grew standard annuals in six-packs, and then a few that no else seemed to bother with, like cosmos and lobelia. We already had a thriving wholesale sideline in herbs grown in four-inch pots, so we sold those too. We listened to our customers' requests for plants they couldn't find. Alice had a good memory then, so she didn't have to take notes.

The next year, Brian built a simple stand near the road, with a plywood counter, a lattice roof, and some wooden shelves for flats of plants. That summer we erected our first aluminum hoop house to overwinter perennials. That spring Emma compliantly rode on Alice's back in a frame carrier most of the day. A sun hat kept her face in the shade, but she had very well-tanned limbs. Fortunately, she was not only a light baby, but also a cheerful one.

Early on, it became clear to us that if we were going to survive as a retail business in a remote location, we were going to have to offer something unusual. A small newspaper ad we ran during the late 1980s said simply: "We're not on the way to anywhere, but you'll be glad you came." We spent winters combing catalogs for plants we'd never grown, many we'd never heard of.

Early Gardening Friendships

It wasn't long before we became intrigued by the many annual plants no one seemed to grow anymore. Our friendships with several veteran gardeners were instrumental in the development of this interest.

Esther Colburn grew up in the hills of Shelburne Falls, then married and settled with her husband in our valley for the remaining 70 years of her life. An accomplished painter and amateur naturalist — our daughter Leah still remembers her demonstrations of how to stand very still with birdseed on your outstretched palms to attract chickadees — Esther was also an accomplished gardener who was curious about the world around her to the very end of her life.

Despite the challenges of visiting with two children under three, visiting Esther brought alive a period in gardening history that Alice had previously known nothing about. Esther remembered decades before, when perennial plants had been popular, and pointed out her *Macleaya cordata* romping happily in the shade. That shade was simply the result of small trees she had once planted in her yard. While batches of hazelnut cookies baked in the oven, she introduced Alice to stacks of old catalogs from Logee's Greenhouses dating back to the 1920s. Esther had always started her own moonflowers indoors, and recounted planting obscure plants for dried flowers in the forties.

Our friendship with Esther was a brief one — she died soon after her 90th birthday — but the influence of her friendship was enormous. We began to collect old seed catalogs, especially those from the Victorian era, when the populations of both England and the United States were smitten with botanical diversity and everyone wanted pieces of the newly discovered world in their own backyard.

At about the same time, we met Elsa Bakalar, a well-known gardener and the author of *A Garden of One's Own*. Alice enrolled in Elsa's Introduction to Perennial Gardening class, a workshop that involved visiting her established gardens in nearby Heath. Alice learned a tremendous amount from Elsa, whose gracious generosity is legendary. Elsa transformed a hilly, rock-filled field into a magnificent series of English borders. Her gardens were a testament to her finely tuned sense of color and design and a lively interest in plants.

Planting on the Road

From the beginning, some of our most successful promotions consisted of planting what we were growing where others could see. It was a simple and highly effective strategy. As difficult as it is to believe now, in 1989 we were having trouble selling our customers an obscure annual called cleome. We had noticed a single plant of it a few years before while on a Sunday drive. That June, when we were left with several flats of transplants, Brian decided to plant a hedge of cleome by the road. By August it was a traffic-stopping sight — 250 continuous feet of bright pink cleome plants, four feet high. The following spring, nearly everyone who came to the nursery was looking for it. If customers hadn't seen what cleome looked like in high summer, we probably never would have sold all those spiky, odd-smelling seedlings.

In an industry that famously avoids selling its product "green" — pushing dwarf, pack-sized marigolds to bloom quickly so they sell — we were trying to convince customers to buy on faith. It took time, but eventually many did. One of the ways we achieved this was to plant extensive display gardens.

We began with perennial borders in the sun, first small beds in front of that original lathe structure. In 1989, Elsa designed a long perennial border that enclosed an entirely new garden area. We first planted an herb garden at its center, but by the early 1990s, inspired by our first visits to Wave Hill in the Bronx, New York, we replaced that with four rectangles featuring annuals — and later included tender perennials. We planted every daylily on our list in a crescent-shaped bed toward the back of the field. In 1997, when we took down the old farmhouse, we planted a woodland garden in its stead. Elsewhere, we established a heath and heather bed and additional perennial borders — and a rock garden had come and gone. The nursery included a full acre of gardens by the time we closed it in 2005.

The Tender Question

So first we grew annuals, then perennials — but where do tender perennials fit in? Answering this question isn't easy, in part because it was a process that happened gradually, almost in stages. Our early involvement with herbs led quite naturally to overwintering tender stock in the greenhouses. For years we kept scented geraniums and bay laurel and lemon verbena indoors for the winter. Initially, like many herb enthusiasts, we kept them in our sunny kitchen. Then, as they grew beyond that space, we heated a limited portion of our smallest greenhouse.

Looking back, it was serendipitous that among the generous gardeners we met in those years was Rob Nicholson, at that time the manager of the Botanic Garden Greenhouses at Smith College, in Northampton, Massachusetts. He met Brian during a visit to the nursery one spring day in 1994. The most important development to result was the arrival of Ida Hay, Rob's wife, as a member of our nursery's permanent staff the next year. But Rob played another decisive role: as the facilitator of our first acquaintance with the tender members of the genus *Salvia*. In one of the routine house cleanings that any greenhouse must periodically have, he passed along a group of plants the Smith greenhouses didn't need — older stock that had outgrown its pots, leggy or woody specimens superseded by fresh cuttings.

Among these was a group of tender salvia species. They had arrived at Smith through another twist of fate, having been given to the college by Richard Dufresne, a specialist collector and breeder of salvias from North Carolina. He visited the area on a regular basis, and eventually, he too, became an annual visitor to the nursery, eventually acquiring many of our own salvia introductions, disseminating them in turn to a wider audience. But in 1994, only a handful of salvia species were grown by northeastern gardeners, and we were fortunate to encounter this exciting group of plants.

Brian planted them out in the field along with rows of hardy perennial stock, and we watched them that summer. As they bloomed with abandon through heat and drought, we were impressed. Brian potted them up in the fall, and moved them into the greenhouse. That was probably the beginning of our serious involvement with tender perennials — certainly with salvias. By 2004, our final spring season, we offered 74 species and cultivars of salvia in print, and Alice is fairly certain that a few more never made the list. Salvias remained, to the end, one of the plant groups our nursery was known for, but we soon became involved with tender perennials of all kinds.

Choosing Plants

The plant selection for this book was made in much the same way that we regularly chose what to grow at the nursery. And because the plants included here are mostly ones we actually grew, the book is based upon our nursery experience.

Often selection was based on past success. In this fashion, we assembled collections of favorite genera, like *Ipomoea* and *Nicotiana*. We continued to grow a given plant because it was particularly floriferous, had interesting foliage, presented a strong or attractive form, or — best of all — boasted all of the above. We exercised a preference for plants that were easy to grow and avoided fussy ones, especially those that had problems with insects or diseases when cultivated under our growing conditions. We completely avoided growing plants that required regular spraying. We found that often choosing what to grow was a matter of finding the right cultivar or selection — some cultivars are just inherently weaker than others. Experience taught us that the way to find the best is to try growing as many as possible.

We've used the phrase "common pest problems" to indicate pests that may be a problem for a particular plant. Given the right conditions, any plant can succumb to or attract nearly any pest. The problems noted here, however, are ones that the plant in question is particularly susceptible to under average growing conditions.

Exhaustive? No

The longer we've grown plants, the more we've realized that there'll always be more to try. This book is not, by any means, exhaustive. It is a compendium of plants that we have enjoyed and recommend. We encourage readers to be adventurous and try new plants.

Consider mail-order nurseries as a way to obtain exciting new specimens. These nurseries are in a position to specialize or to grow a wide variety of plants they might never sell on a local basis. One that specializes in tropicals or succulents, for example, might offer more of these than you've heard of.

If such a resource is located near where you live, support it. A good nursery offers gardeners a great deal more than just the plants for sale. Its proprietors may share information about plant culture based upon their experiences and preferences. Nothing compares with the opportunity to observe plants before you buy them, particularly planted out, where you can appreciate their mature size and habit.

Expanding Horizons

We also encourage you to visit interesting gardens both in your immediate area and whenever you travel. Observing other gardens is one of the best ways to expand your horticultural horizons. Take a notebook and ask questions.

When we first began growing Blue Meadow Farm, we didn't entirely appreciate that we were both, in different ways, oddly suited to this undertaking. Born in Sligo, Ireland, Brian spent his early years helping his mother in their backyard vegetable plot before his family made the move to the suburbs of Cincinnati, Ohio. Alice had been introduced to the world in Tokyo, and spent a peripatetic childhood moving every few years from one country in Asia to another before ending up in New England for high school. We both knew firsthand about other climates and cultures — we still kept in touch with our countries of birth. Perhaps this equipped us with a more-than-average sense of adventurousness, and our imaginations were grounded in real memories of people and plants in distant places. In hindsight, it's easy to see how these factors contributed to the establishment of Blue Meadow Farm.

Brian's plant and soil science training provided a scientific foundation for our endeavor and the springboard from which he created an oasis of plants and gardening where none had existed before. And although Alice took it entirely for granted at the time, assembling and cataloguing collections, as well as writing descriptions of individual specimens, were processes familiar and enjoyable due to her training in art history.

Our nursery was a unique fusion of our personal histories and passions. During the 18-year span of its life, we learned much — about plants, about ourselves, and about the wide world in which we all live and grow.

— *Alice and Brian McGowan*

GARDENING WITH TENDERS

Tender perennials are an amazingly adaptable and diverse group of plants.

Because they've arrived in our gardens from so many different corners of the world, tenders introduce wonderful complexities and variations — of texture, bold color, and sheer drama. Caring for them is surprisingly simple when you consider all that they offer the gardener. The diversity of tender perennials lends them to a marvelous variety of uses — these are plants that range from delicate twiners to those that make bold statements, exceeding 10 or 12 feet in height. We suggest that you use your imagination and take your cues from the plants themselves.

LEFT How better to emphasize the bright orange spines of *Solanum pyracanthum* than to pair it with orange-flowered lantanas?

ABOVE *Canna* 'Striata' is considered tender in most climates north of Zone 10, but is easy to overwinter in a cool basement.

What Is a Tender Perennial?

Directly behind the cash register in our sales greenhouse at Blue Meadow Farm — the nursery we operated for 18 years in western Massachusetts — we hung a large sign that supplied a definition for the term *tender perennial.* But in all the time we grew and sold these plants, the sign seemed to fall short in its mission. Many visitors would point at our featured display, an exuberantly blooming specimen of the blue-flowered *Convolvulus mauritanicus* or an arrangement of anisodontea and fuchsia standards, and ask, "Now is *that* perennial?"

"Well, yes and no," we might have replied. "It's not a *hardy* perennial in this climate. Here, it's a tender perennial." Such a funny concept, one that most people seem to find challenging the first time they hear it.

What *is* a tender perennial, anyway? Put simply, it's a plant that, though hardy in its original habitat, will not survive the winter outdoors in the climate of the gardener. Tender perennials in one zone may be perfectly hardy in a different location. But for gardeners in any location other than a truly tropical one, chances are that some plants are tender perennials.

Some tender perennials are, in fact, tropical. But many others come from relatively moderate climates where winters just don't get as cold or, perhaps, as wet as they do where you live. From the temperate climates of the Mediterranean come marvelous gray-leaved plants — like helichrysum and santolina — that require dryness in winter. From New Zealand there are trees and shrubs, even grasses and sedges like *Carex comans,* that make delightful indoor plants. Both South Africa and the South American continent have wonderful plants that simply won't survive outside year-round in other locales, but which (we think you'll agree) can enrich your gardening experience tremendously.

Will tropical and semitropical plants look out of place in your garden? We've spoken with gardeners who worried that might be the case. We suggest you experiment — you might be surprised. After all, the geographic origins of most hardy perennials are already quite diverse. In our experience, the visual characteristics of plants — their form, texture, and color — are far more important in creating a visually unified and satisfying garden picture.

Location Makes a Difference

The word *tender* suggests that these plants will not survive frost. But many tender perennials tolerate light or sometimes even heavy frosts. They are called tender in a particular place simply because they are unlikely to survive an entire winter in that climate. This distinction may be confusing, but it really needn't be. Even hardy plants respond to freezing temperatures in different ways. Any plant's tolerance of frost and cold is influenced by a variety of factors: hydration, stress, and the plant's recent history. In general, only plants that originate where frost is a common occurrence will withstand it consistently, and even this is not always the case.

Perennial vs. Annual

SOME GARDENERS in cold climates think any plant that dies in winter is an annual. The term *annual,* though, refers specifically to a plant that blooms, sets seed, and dies in a single season. Annuals are usually grown from seed. Lettuce poppy (*Papaver somniferum*) and signet marigold (*Tagetes tenuifolia*) are examples of annuals.

To obtain maximum show (bloom) from most annuals, it is essential to deadhead, thereby tricking the plant to create new blooms. Once it has set seed, the plant no longer has a reason to continue blooming. Many annuals will self-sow in your garden; these do, in effect, return each year. This does not make them true perennials, however; they are therefore outside the scope of this book.

In general, perennial plants do not bloom until their second year, and then they live on. Biennials bloom in the second year and then die. Of course, plants don't follow rules very well, and there are exceptions to these definitions, many of which are either short-lived perennials or biennials. Daylilies (*Hemerocallis*) and peonies (*Paeonia*), for example, are perennial plants; sweet William (*Dianthus barbatus*) is a biennial that usually blooms in its second season.

Most gardeners have noticed that the ubiquitous hosta, though reliable and quite hardy in a Zone 5 garden, is prone to react extremely to late-spring frosts. In years when these occur, hostas will generally grow an entirely new set of leaves to replace those that succumbed. Although a plant's appearance may be affected for the duration of the season, this doesn't mean that it's not hardy. It's just an indication of the structure of hosta leaves and stems, and shows that once they've begun to grow, hostas are sensitive to frost, despite being hardy to much colder temperatures while in a dormant state. It's also an indication that in their Japanese homeland, frosts rarely occur once the plants have leafed out.

Other plants seem unaffected by cold nights. Some salvias, for instance, will continue as before, generally blooming and carrying on as if nothing has happened. This is a reminder that frost does occur in the desert, where salvias originate, and also that though most tender salvias cannot survive the winter in many colder zones, they are well adapted to life in the spring, summer, and fall in those places.

ORIGINS ARE IMPORTANT

Tender perennial plants come from every corner of the world, and — as the hosta and salvia examples illustrate — it is important and also remarkably helpful to consider a plant's origins in order to understand the best conditions for growing and overwintering it. A desert plant will be happiest in sunny, well-drained conditions of low humidity; one from the Amazon may require both protection from the sun and extra humidity, along with temperatures well above freezing.

Having grown tender plants over the years, we find it fascinating to learn more about their origins. Gardening is one of the most tangible ways there is to gain a deeper appreciation and sense of place through interaction with your very specific plot of land. But it is also a wonderful way to travel imaginatively through both time and space — and to contemplate where in the world a particular plant grew before it arrived in your own garden.

BELOW The aptly named Kangaroo paws (*Anigozanthos*) are hardy in their Australian homeland but tender in most parts of the United States.

Which Plants to Keep?

MOST HOUSE INTERIORS tend to be warmer and drier than is ideal for many plants in containers. Are you willing to adjust the thermostat down to 55 or 60°F? Will you remember to water your containers once a week? (Don't forget to provide saucers for all the pots.) These are basic but important questions to consider before you start hauling around those heavy pots!

As tempting as it may be to save everything from the summer patio, be realistic about the storage space you have. A smaller number of plants with more space around them will be easier to keep healthy than a jungle of plants crammed into an area that's too small to accommodate them all.

Your available space for plants is an important factor in determining what will be manageable for you. Assuming that you're considering only those plants that have performed well, begin your selection with ones that would be difficult to replace. A plant might be expensive or relatively rare where you live. Perhaps you grew it from seed that took a long time to germinate or was difficult to obtain. Or maybe the plant was given to you by a close friend or relative and has sentimental value. Everyone has his or her own reasons for wanting to keep a particular plant.

Some plants are so inexpensively and readily available that it doesn't make sense to keep them from one season to another. When such a plant is winter blooming, however, or has particularly attractive foliage and form, it may be worth keeping, especially if it is also easy to care for. Most kalanchoes, cacti, succulents, durantas, many convolvulus, and anisodontea fall into this category.

How you define *low-maintenance* is highly personal and depends quite a bit on the specifics of your space. In a cool sunroom or porch, keeping rosemary happy should be easy. But overwintering the same plant in a warmer, heated living area is guaranteed to be a challenge. In the dry, warm air of most homes, it's easy to miss the early signs that this plant needs to be watered, and serious damage may occur before you notice its distress. In a warm space without good air circulation, conditions will also be ripe for the development of mildew or for the proliferation of pests like aphids. By the same token, keeping a brugmansia healthy in a cool, sunny space might not be so difficult — but try it in a warm room and you'll be inviting an infestation of whiteflies. The decision of what to keep for the winter and where to situate it will be informed by many factors. Give each plant some thought well before you need to take action. Remember that when they're happy, plants have a way of growing, and will, in time, occupy more space than they were originally allotted.

Choosing Plants

With all the wonderful plants available to gardeners today, our selection in this book is necessarily an arbitrary one. We have focused primarily on those tender perennial plants that we have had experience growing and that we have found worthwhile. Some of them may winter over outdoors in your climate — we have included them here because we found successful methods for growing and storing them because they were not hardy in our zone. Gardeners have many reasons for overwintering certain plants indoors rather than out in the ground.

For example, we knew a very knowledgeable and determined rock gardener who potted up the majority of her alpine plants so that they could escape the wet, and also very cold, winters of southern New Hampshire. She was amazingly matter-of-fact about the enormous amount of work this entailed each season. Her story illustrates that the extraordinary effort we put into gardening can sometimes be justified only by the pleasure we derive from growing plants. She was quite proud — and justifiably so — of her large, impressive, zone-defying alpine garden. Compared to her efforts, saving a few tender plants on the windowsill, or in whatever way makes the most sense for you, should be a relatively small investment in your gardening future.

Why Grow Tenders?

"Oh, I grow only hardy plants," we've been informed by more than one gardener. And there are certainly arguments to be made for doing this. In general, despite the occasional winter that decimates much of the perennial garden, planting exclusively hardy plants simplifies gardening activities.

But it does limit your options. Even your grandmother probably grew plants in her garden or on her windowsills that were neither annual nor hardy. If she hung her geraniums in the cellar for the winter or kept a sweet-smelling heliotrope in a pot on a windowsill, she was simply overwintering her tender perennial plants. Many gardeners a century ago were familiar with a far greater variety of plants than most are today. One reason is that European and American gardeners of earlier

ABOVE *Convolvulus cneorum* and *Pelargonium sidoides* are two of the many fascinating plants you can observe in bloom if you bring them indoors for the winter.

LEFT Colorful tenders like bananas, cannas, and coleus expand your options for gardening.

ABOVE This handsome basil has been trained to a columnar form during its winter storage. Now it adds foliar distinction to the summer garden.

periods were terribly curious about the many distant places that were still being opened to the eyes of the Western world by plant collectors. Growing the exotic plants that resulted from expeditions to those lands was a tangible way to share in the latest discoveries.

SAVE MONEY

In our own consumer culture, plants are viewed as replaceable commodities. Many gardeners simply rely on garden centers and catalogs to supply them with plant products to fill up their gardens each season. These merchandisers produce only those plants that will provide instant and predictable results, regardless of the skills of the gardener. Overwintering tender perennial plants can be a way to save money and to achieve a measure of independence from commercial marketers at the same time. And saving money by not buying the same plants year after year will extend your gardening budget.

GIVE AND RECEIVE

Tender perennials make great gifts for friends and neighbors. Winter bloomers, such as the stunning white-flowered *Convolvulus cneorum,* will remind them of you each winter when their buds open. Or if the summer garden is the plant's moment to shine, your friends will remember your kindness at the height of the seasonal spectacle.

Giving away plants is practical, too. It's common wisdom among professional propagators that you never know when you'll need to ask for a piece of something back. What if you forget to water during a critical time or the power goes off during a prolonged cold spell? If your friend still has the plant you shared with her, she'll be more than happy to return the favor.

LEARN NEW SKILLS

In the process of learning to grow tender perennials, you'll acquire new propagating skills as you maintain original plants and increase your stock. Saving any kind of plant also increases the amount of control you have over the selection of plants you're growing and of those you will perpetuate for the future.

You may have more time to notice your plants when they're indoors, too, and there aren't the million distractions of the summer outdoors. You'll learn more about the varying needs of plants, which change with a specific plant's place in its own life cycle as well as with the season.

SEE PLANTS AT THEIR BEST

Saving and storing tender perennials also gives the plants more than one season to mature. Aside from the brevity of the growing season in a place like Zone 5, where we live, many plants just don't reach their full potential in a single season. Some withhold bloom until their second year, and others simply require time to grow large and impressive. Some plants are actually herbaceous in their first season and woody in the next. The young growth of many tender perennial plants — such as salvias, strobilanthes, and durantas — is soft and herbaceous, turning woodier in time. You'll probably learn more about insects, too, as you monitor your plants and keep them healthy. In their second season, they will be ready to create an altogether different and dramatic effect in the garden.

FILL IN THE GAPS

Many tender plants bloom during those famous gaps in the hardy-perennial bloom cycle. Tender salvias, daturas, and tibouchinas: these and other plants kick in just when most of the perennial border is giving up the ghost. You may be surprised at how much more interesting the August/September garden is when tender perennials are added to your plantings. Their contributions don't necessarily end with the first frost, either. In the chapters that follow, we will show you how to grow and save your favorite plants, and in many cases, how you can continue to enjoy their beauty even through the coldest months of winter.

Who wouldn't want a room full of sweet-smelling flowering plants to enjoy in the dead of winter? No matter where you live, and no matter what your budget, if you choose carefully and consider realistically the conditions of your living space, you'll be pleasantly surprised by the possibilities of your own indoor winter paradise.

ABOVE 'Blackie' sweet potato vine (*Ipomoea batatas* 'Blackie') helps fill out the summer garden when other perennials are on the wane.

Container Combinations

Probably the first way most of us think of planting tender perennials is to combine several in one container. When considering mixed containers, first take into account the cultural requirements of each plant, and then combine plants that will be happy in similar conditions. Contemplate their light requirements and whether they prefer moist or dry soil. Combining plants that will be happy in similar conditions greatly simplifies the care of the whole container, and will also help to ensure that it is a successful one.

Choosing Partners

The most obvious thing to consider when you place multiple plants in a single container is how they combine from a visual perspective. Place them side by side and see how they look together. Often, the texture of a plant's foliage is just as important to the success of a combination as its flower or leaf color. Another consideration is the shape and scale of each plant element. It is generally good to have a balance of taller and shorter plants, some with large leaves and others that are more delicate, and to include both colorful and less strident elements. If your plants are already in bloom, you can easily gauge how your selections will appear in a shared space throughout the season. If they're not in bloom, do your research and try to imagine the flower color as part of the composition. This is usually more challenging, but if the foliar combination is a good one, you can probably pull it off.

Design Considerations

Perhaps you'd like to have something hang over one edge of your container. Remember to balance large-leaved plants with those that are more finely textured. Some variation in height also makes combinations more interesting. It may help you to choose one or two plants with bold architectural form or a strong color. Then fill in the spaces with others that contrast and complement them.

RIGHT *Dahlia* 'Bednall Beauty', potted up with *Dichondra argentea*, serves as a colorful neighbor for the unusual chartreuse blooms of pineapple lily (*Eucomis*) and lily-of-the-Nile (*Agapanthus*).

BELOW Backed by the strappy foliage of lily-of-the-Nile (*Agapanthus*), *Cuphea cyanea* and *Helichrysum argyrophyllum* 'Moe's Gold' are the perfect combination for the gray-green patina of this tall urn.

Choose one or two plants with bold architectural form or strong color

Dahlia 'Bishop of Llandaff'

Pineapple lily (*Eucomis bicolor*)

Dicondra argentea 'Silver Falls'

Lily of the Nile (*Agapanthus africanus*)

Your container design should also take into account the pot itself. What type of container is it? What influence does its size and color have on your selection of plants? Will the pot be viewed from all sides or just from the front? Also consider the weight of the container. Filled with soil, it will become much heavier. This is especially critical if you're planning eventually to move the entire thing inside. Lightweight plastic, which is now available in some surprisingly attractive forms, could be your best option.

Experiment with unusual containers when planting tender perennials. We don't always remember that hanging baskets often make a good home. And in the sun, some of the more prostrate abutilons and kalanchoes are ideal for basket culture. In the shade, there are bromeliads and the more recumbent begonias. All kinds of out-of-the-ordinary containers can be used to house your tender perennials, and how you place them can be arresting. Hang some on an exterior wall of your house or place them along lower freestanding walls in the yard. Have fun!

Pay attention to individual plant requirements. Remember that if all the plants in a container are drought tolerant, you may be able to plant them in a relatively shallow container. But if you're situating a thirsty banana or canna, you'd better choose a large, deep pot and fill it with plenty of rich soil mix.

These are all questions to consider as you put together a combination container. Just remember that there is no one right answer. Have fun with this opportunity to create a combination that is uniquely pleasing to you.

The Solo Specimen Approach

Another approach to growing tender perennials — one that has become quite popular in recent years — is to place each one alone in its own container. Situated singly as a specimen, one plant to a pot, a tender perennial such as an agave or a begonia can make a handsome, simple statement. The container you choose to plant it in can complement the plant's color or shape or even a relatively small detail like the pattern

LEFT Sue Webel's terrace garden at Idyll Haven shows how a gathering of solo plantings can create an entire outdoor living area.

BELOW Here, the annual *Verbena × hybrida* weaves together tender perennial participants, including a pelargonium and *Phormium tenax* 'Atropurpureum'.

along the edge of its leaves. When selecting a container for a plant that has prominent or long-lasting blooms, do take the flower color into account as well.

Color combinations can emphasize contrast — you can place silver foliage against deep brown- or red-glazed containers, for instance — or they can complement more subtle harmonies. Not only can you work with the glazes and textures of container surfaces, but the actual shape of a container can emphasize different characteristics of the plant as well. For example, a long trough can be planted with something that trails down its elegant sides, like dichondra, or it can house something more upright, even a standard. Sometimes the simple texture of a plain terra-cotta pot is the perfect way to showcase a plant. A funkier, more eye-catching container will highlight that same plant in an entirely different manner.

Grouping these containers is a great way to create visually compelling areas on your patio or in the garden. The contrast

Tips for Planting and Care

WHEN COMBINING PLANTS in a container, it's important to give each plant adequate space to enlarge over time, even when you're attempting to create a more immediate effect of overall fullness. Also consider where the sun is coming from — will everything receive enough light? Would some of your container candidates prefer a little shade? Those with a trailing or weaving habit should be situated with some anticipation of their eventual growth. Also, make sure to cut off most of the flowers after you pot them; this will encourage the plants to put their energy into growing roots and getting established in their new home.

Deadheading is an opportunity to visit with your containers. This "quality time" spent interacting with your plants is one of the best ways to learn more about their preferences, and it's an excellent time to take notes. As you remove spent blossoms, you're likely to notice the relative vigor of each plant and whether any pest populations are present. Use this time to monitor whether the container is providing adequate fertility, and remove old leaves, too.

For more information about soils, fertility, and watering suggestions, see page 28.

of tall, upright specimens with wider, shorter, or more trailing plants will invite garden visitors to examine each one more closely. Groups of containers can create a new garden area on their own. Don't forget to consider the containers, as well as the plants, in combination. Some contrast — between light- and dark-colored containers, smooth and rough surfaces, even tall and short or round and square shapes — will keep things interesting. Sometimes a variation in the height at which containers are displayed, such as that created by placing some on top of flat rocks or low tables, increases their visual interest. Move things around until you like what you see. In our experience, if you've got some nice plants to work with and a few complementary pots, it's not difficult to come up with a satisfying arrangement.

Choosing a Container

Most plants grow equally well in plastic or porous containers. Keep in mind that the soil in different types of containers dries out at different rates. If your plants are well developed and do require large containers, consider some of the new lightweight, synthetic terra-cotta look-alikes; your back will thank you. If you are a purist, then nothing but the real — more difficult to move — thing will do. A variety of containers in a number of colors, textures, and shapes can be pleasant to look at in your living space (and also outdoors) and will complement the various forms and textures of your plants. Try to balance aesthetic considerations with the practical — generally a plant will grow happily in almost anything as long as it has a drainage hole. The latter is an important point; you may discover that many containers on the market these days don't have any holes for drainage. These containers, called cachepots, may be used to hold smaller pots that have drainage, but don't plant directly into them. You can attempt to compensate for nonperforated containers by cautious watering, but most plants, with the exception of true water plants and those that grow in bogs, really do require drainage.

ABOVE Terra cotta is a traditional choice for containers and can be found in a variety of shapes and sizes.

Soils

The best soil to use for any container planting is one that drains well. Nothing kills as many plants in pots as waterlogged soil. Make sure your mix incorporates sufficient materials for aeration; this will improve its drainage capacity and ability to hold oxygen — essential for the plant's roots.

In many ways, gardening is like cooking. Acquiring a feel for mixing potting soils is similar to the process of learning essential kitchen skills. These suggestions for what to incorporate in your soil mix should be regarded as merely a baseline recipe, and can be adjusted to fit the needs of the specific plant in a particular situation. Materials available in one location may also vary from those available in others.

All or some of these ingredients will be part of almost any prepackaged soil mix. The simplest approach is to find a bagged potting mix that is formulated especially for containers. Then, additional ingredients like Turface and compost can be added to improve it. Experiment — get a feel for how much of what to incorporate in the mix, and keep records.

Your ultimate goal is to develop a recipe that absorbs and holds water, yet drains and maintains pore space, enabling the soil to hold oxygen at the same time. Remember that organic amendments such as peat and compost break down over time, causing the soil to compact and thus lose space for oxygen. You will then see the volume of soil shrink — a sure sign that it's time to repot with fresh soil or at least top off the container with a layer of compost.

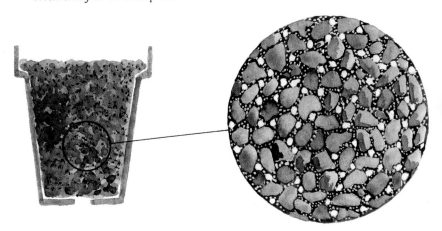

RIGHT Good soil mix should have a loose, open structure for proper drainage.

Potting Mix Ingredients

COARSE SAND

Also known as angular sand, sometimes referred to (in the Northeast, anyway) as winter sand (because it's used on roads here in slippery winter weather), coarse sand will add weight (desirable in tall or top-heavy containers), as well as considerable drainage capacity, to your mix.

PERLITE

Perlite is volcanic glass that, when heated, expands due to the water trapped inside it. It has good water- and air-holding capacity, and is another ingredient for the improvement of drainage. Because it's dusty, make sure to wear a dust mask if you include it, and also wet it down before handling it.

TURFACE

This material may be available at feed and garden supply stores. It consists of calcined clay, which is clay that has been heated, in a process similar to the firing of clay pots, until the moisture is removed. In their texture, the small, angular bits of baked clay resemble kitty litter; the color is of terra-cotta pots. We have found it to be remarkably useful for improving the drainage of any mix, and it also makes a fine mulch on top of the soil.

PEAT MOSS

Peat moss absorbs and holds moisture and contributes organic matter to the mix. Peat has extraordinary water-retaining and water-repellent qualities. If dampened well before use, however, it will not repel water. Because its pH is acidic, adding a dash of lime is recommended. Alternatives to peat, such as coir (coconut fiber), are sometimes suggested as a growing medium in the debate concerning the sustainability of peat moss. There is evidence that peat is, in fact, renewable at the pace of current horticultural consumption.

COMPOST

Unlike peat, compost can be rich in beneficial microbial activity, and has nutritional benefits besides. These are both important contributions, particularly helpful in fighting soilborne diseases, but also important for the general health of your plants. Compost usually contains the major plant nutrients — nitrogen, potassium, and phosphorus — and micronutrients such as calcium and magnesium. Without testing it, though, you cannot know exactly what levels of these nutrients it contains. Probably the greatest benefit of using compost is that it helps to introduce a broad range of beneficial microorganisms into the soil.

HOT SHOTS FOR LATE-SUMMER BLOOMS

- ❋ *Bessera*
- ❋ *Dahlia*
- ❋ *Ipomoea*
- ❋ *Plectranthus*
- ❋ *Salvia*

BELOW, LEFT TO RIGHT
Dahlias really come into their own in late July and August. *Bouvardia ternifolia* is hard to beat for show-stopping color in the dog days of summer. Morning glories bloom over a long season. Here the flowers of *Ipomoea × imperialis* 'Chocolate' unfurl in the early hours of morning.

In the Garden

Perhaps less familiar to many gardeners is the idea of incorporating tender perennials into the heart of the garden by planting them directly into the ground. This prospect may be intimidating, but it's similar to planting dahlias or cannas, which you may have done. Planting tender perennials does require attention to details, such as when outside temperatures are warm enough to plant them. Later in the season, you'll need to monitor when it's cool enough to consider digging them up for the trip indoors. Although timing is an important consideration when you plant tender perennials into the garden, it shouldn't prevent you from trying this approach.

Dog Day Rescue

Certain tender perennials, such as some salvia species and the agastaches — plants that we grow primarily for their flowers — happen to bloom at the peak of our summer, when there is sufficient heat to remind them of their original habitat. As many perennial gardeners are well aware, keeping the garden interesting can be challenging at this point in the summer season. The majority of hardy perennials we grow in North American gardens originate in the more moderate climates of Europe, places like Great Britain, where the temperature rarely exceeds the 70s, and where there is also regular rainfall. No wonder our gardens look fried by August.

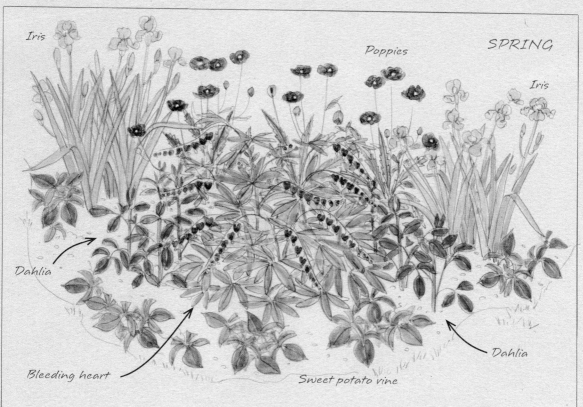

Iris

Poppies

SPRING

Iris

Dahlia

Bleeding heart

Sweet potato vine

Dahlia

Agastache

LATE
SUMMER

Iris

Iris

Dahlia

Sweet potato vine

Many of the stars of June are not nearly as attractive by August. The early
introduction of smaller tender perennial plants can pay off by summer's end.

Large tender perennials introduce bold architectural elements to your garden landscape.

'Carmencita' castor bean
(*Ricinus communis* 'Carmencita')

Plectranthus
(*Plectranthus argentatus*)

'Purple Duckfoot' coleus
(*Solenostemon* 'Purple Duckfoot')

There is good reason for the sentiment held by many northeastern American gardeners that their plantings look best in June. But you can fundamentally change this situation by complementing those beds of campanulas and delphiniums with plants that actually love the hot weather of July and August in North America. Viewed this way, planting more tender perennials is simply facing reality.

And Do Drop In

Even if you didn't have the foresight to plant them out in your beds in the early spring, tender perennial plants can come to the rescue when the garden becomes dull later on. Try the time-honored technique commonly referred to by British gardeners as "dropping in." This consists of growing plants in a holding bed or in ordinary plastic containers, and then planting them in areas of the garden that need some livening up. Use these plants to replace tired specimens that have either finished their show for the season or have succumbed to the vagaries of weather and pests. Don't be afraid to prune and train them before they're actually needed. And once they've been moved into their new positions in the garden, water them as you would any other new addition, until they have had an opportunity to settle in.

Opportunities in Scale

There are many benefits to having tender perennial plants mixed into the garden. Certain plants, especially tropical ones, sport large leaves, even in the sun. This is somewhat unusual; as a general rule among hardy perennials, most of those with large leaves grow only in the shade — likely an adaptation to limited sunlight. These plants have developed increased surface area to maximize opportunities for photosynthesis; in the shade, they don't have to conserve moisture, as they would have to in full sun. But cannas, colocasias, and bananas provide the same type of structural element in full, hot sun that hostas do in shadier corners. In addition, many of them, like the 12-foot *Canna musafolia,* provide considerable height.

ABOVE The large, flexible leaves of *Colocasia esculenta* 'Illustris' dramatically emphasize the finely textured presence of *Amsonia hubrichtii.*

LEFT 'Carmencita' castor bean plant (*Ricinus communis*) pairs with silvery *Plectranthus argentatus* and 'Purple Duckfoot' coleus (*Solenostemon*) for a bold foliage display.

Some Tips for the Shade

Many tender perennial plants supply boldly colored foliage, even where color can be a challenge, as is usually the case in the shade. By planting coleus or begonias, you can create broad swaths of color in areas of the garden where once the only option for color was impatiens. These plants also contribute an exceptionally long season of interest with minimum maintenance.

Coleus leaves come in a wide range of colors, from bright pink to chartreuse and cream. The patterning of color on their leaves also provides considerable texture. A few coleus have flowers that are interesting in their own right, with spikes of blue and violet brightening those shadier spots. Some of our own favorites are: the glowing rosy 'Alabama Sunset'; the large-leaved and tropically colored 'Anini Sunset' (a Blue Meadow Farm introduction); the small chocolate to plum, elegantly jewel-edged 'Arabian Nights' (also known as 'Trailing Red'); the chartreuse-edged purple-black 'Inky Fingers'; the dusty salmon 'Inky Pink', with its mossy, chocolate overlay; and the petite, web-footed maroon 'Purple Duckfoot'.

Begonias offer a tremendous selection of textures and colors to the shaded garden. From the finely textured, glossy green leaves of the species *Begonia foliosa* var. *miniata* to the round and massive, dusky maroon leaves of the rhizomatous 'Selph's Mahogany', begonias offer a world of visual excitement for partial to full shade.

BELOW, LEFT TO RIGHT
Begonias, like 'Escargot', 'Iron Cross', and 'Fireworks', also thrive in the shade.

Those Challenging Places

Tender perennials can sometimes provide a solution for difficult sites, those that are terribly hot in summer or subject to winter abuse. That spot under the eaves, just beyond the reach of rainwater all summer, then buried by a pile of snow for the winter, is the kind we're thinking of. Drought-tolerant tender perennials — helichrysums, euphorbias, and agaves, for example — might be exactly the plants to thrive under conditions guaranteed to kill a year-round resident.

The edge of a sun-baked driveway and a garden next to a parking lot present a similar challenge. Many tender perennials are ideal used as a screen — such as one placed between two driveways — that will be present only for the summer season. Some of the taller cannas and brugmansias and many of the tender vines are splendid plants to use this way.

Adapting to Climate Conditions

JUST AS PLANTS DEVELOP large leaves to maximize photosynthesis in shade, many drought-tolerant plants that grow in full sun have relatively small leaves. Some of these plants have further adaptations designed to conserve moisture, such as fine hairs, which prevent evaporation of moisture from the leaf surface. Silver foliage is the ultimate expression of this efficiency; it actually reflects sunlight away from the leaves. Many South African plants are superbly adapted to drought and unrelentingly sunny growing conditions. *Helichrysum petiolare* 'Variegatum' (right) is one of these.

ABOVE Tender abutilon, planted directly into the garden, fronts a mass of hardy goldenrod to great effect in late summer.

Quick Shows and Slow Spectacles

Some tender perennials grow so quickly that they provide drama and flash in a single season. For instance, cuttings taken from an overwintered stock plant of *Salvia* 'Indigo Spires' in early spring will enlarge considerably and put on a colorful show by late summer. (See From Cutting to Blooming Plant, page 37.) Other plants to use in this fashion are alternantheras, coleus, and *Salvia involucrata,* all of which will grow quickly from spring cuttings and literally rise to the occasion when you plant them out in midsummer. Then, even more amazingly, they will continue the show nonstop right into hard frosts.

There are other salvias — generally ones with woodier stems — that grow more slowly. These floriferous plants supply a dramatic show in their second season, which is why overwintering them is so worthwhile. This group includes most cultivars of *Salvia greggii* and *Salvia discolor* among others, like *Convolvulus cneorum.*

Design Considerations

This is not to say that planting tender perennials will solve all your gardening challenges effortlessly. You will still need to ask the same design questions you would when engaged in any other kind of gardening. It is just as important to consider the texture and color, the height and bloom time of each addition as you would when situating any other new plant in the garden. One factor that makes the process a little easier from a visual standpoint when situating cutting-grown tender perennials is that the plant in your hand more nearly resembles what it will eventually grow into.

It is always important to take into account the nature of the existing setting when you add a new plant. Planting tender perennials into beds of annuals is altogether different, say, from incorporating them into established perennial gardens, or from placing them in a shaded woodland setting. Tender perennials can be quite happy in all these places, and perform well in them, too. But each type of garden setting presents its own questions and considerations.

From Cutting to Blooming Plant

SOME TENDER PERENNIALS, like *Salvia* 'Indigo Spires', grow so quickly that cuttings taken in early spring and planted into the garden will become full, blooming plants by late summer.

1. TAKE TIP CUTTINGS from an overwintered salvia in early spring.

2. GROW THE CUTTINGS in individual pots, ready to be planted out into the garden after the last frost date.

3. BY LATE SUMMER, the cuttings will have become full, blooming plants.

Coleus, fuchsias, and begonias create broad swaths of color in shady areas.

'Big Red' coleus
(*Solenostemon* 'Big Red')

'Sum and Substance' hosta
(*Hosta* 'Sum and Substance')

'Versicolor' fuchsia
(*Fuchsia magellanica* 'Versicolor')

'Pineapple' coleus
Solenostemon 'Pineapple'

If you are incorporating tender perennials into an annual planting, your questions may be somewhat different. Because annuals by their very nature bloom most of the summer and provide a lot of color, the tender perennial plants you add in with them will probably offer other benefits — they can add drama because of their size, for example, or complement the flower colors of plants that are already there. In a woodland setting, tender perennials like coleus and begonias offer color where other options for it are limited.

Larger tender perennials introduce bold architectural elements to your garden landscape. Few other plants grow so quickly and assume such dramatic proportions in a single season. Cannas, bananas, melianthus, and some of the larger begonias are just a few that make an arresting statement in any setting. Plants like amorphophallus and colocasia accomplish this simply because of their exotic appearance. Other plants bring interest and a dramatic focal point because of their scale or eye-catching colors.

LEFT Hosta, fuchsia, and coleus are a fine trio for moist shade.

Where in the World?

LEARNING ABOUT the climatic backgrounds of tender perennials can help gardeners give plants the conditions they need to thrive.

Mediterranean: Many plants from this region have silver leaves, and all are extremely drought tolerant. In most of this area, very hot, dry summers are followed by moderate but still dry winters.

Tropical Rain Forest: Warm temperatures and high humidity encourage fecund vegetation, leading to some of the greatest plant diversity on earth.

Southwest United States: Arid and very warm in summer, followed by equally dry but surprisingly cold winters, the desert has given rise to wondrous plant forms adapted to extreme conditions.

South Africa: We think of Africa as hot and humid, but the geography of South Africa is a great deal more varied than that. Much of the terrain is mountainous, and the hot, relatively humid summer weather gives way to cool and dry winter weather in much of the country.

OVERWINTERING YOUR PLANTS

With all the various ways to overwinter plants, there's sure to be an option that will work for every gardener.

We hope that by now you're convinced that overwintering your tender perennials is worthwhile. You'll save money when you buy plants next year, because you'll already have several to put out into the garden. Many of these plants will have become much larger — ready to be either impressive specimens in the garden or some of the striking elements of your containers.

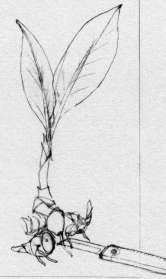

LEFT *Salvia guaranitica* is one of the most reliable performers in the mid- to late-summer garden. It's one of the easiest plants to overwinter.

ABOVE A scented geranium and small-leaved coleus share a sunny windowsill.

Overwintering 101

The key to successfully bringing a plant through the winter indoors is understanding its natural dormancy cycle. Some plants continue to grow during their indoor vacation and thus need a warm, sunny location. Others enter a stage of partial dormancy and are more suited to a spot that's sunny but cool. Some plants go completely dormant and simply need to be properly stored for the winter.

What Kind of Space Do You Have?

Anyone can overwinter tender perennials, but your available facilities will limit and define the possibilities. The options you choose will then depend on how elaborate you want to get and also on your personal preferences.

There are three basic ways to store tender perennials. Each is best suited to certain types of plants. This doesn't mean there is only one way to store each plant, however — just that there may be only one *best* way.

A SUNNY WINDOWSILL

Some tender perennials — many of them tropical plants like begonias and alternantheras — will be perfectly happy on a sunny east-, west-, or south-facing windowsill. Treat these as you would a houseplant, watering and fertilizing on a regular schedule. If you keep the thermostat between 65 and 70°F, the temperature inside your house will remind these plants of winter in the tropics. This may cause their growth rate to slow slightly, but for the most part, the plants will continue to be in active growth. They will need every bit of sunlight you can supply. Lacking sufficient sun, you might keep them happy with a supplemental source of light, like the fluorescent lights that many gardeners use for vegetable seedlings.

A COOL, BRIGHT SPOT

Another group of tender perennials benefits from a period of relative dormancy in winter, and would be happiest in a very cool but sunny part of your house, such as an unheated porch or a rarely used bedroom. These plants originate in parts of the world that experience dry, cool winters, such as the high elevations of South Africa and parts of the Mediterranean region. They are happiest in a temperature range between 40 and 50°F, accompanied by bright sunlight. The greatest number of tender perennial plants will find these conditions agreeable.

A DARK BASEMENT OR CLOSET

Some plants prefer the dark and will survive the winter in your basement. Most of these can be classified as corms, bulbs, and tubers. Others, such as cannas, like their darkness on the damp side. Still others, like dahlias, will fare better if the conditions are drier. Certain plants from other groups can survive a period of dormancy in the dark almost as well as they might in bright sunny conditions. Some salvias, brugmansias, four o'clocks (*Mirabilis*), bananas (*Musa*), lemon verbena (*Aloysia*), *Sinningia,* and *Bouvardia ternifolia* can overwinter in the basement just in their pots.

A subset of the bulbs-and-corms group can be left in the pots they grew in all summer or can be transferred into paper bags. Because they will tolerate warmer temperatures and will not grow until watered, move them into a closet, where conditions will be dark and dry enough to maintain their dormancy. This group includes bessera, *Begonia sutherlandii,* amorphophallus, and certain oxalis.

Overwintering Techniques

In addition to where a plant is stored, it's also important to consider the proper technique for bringing it in for the winter. To find additional overwintering information about a particular plant, turn to the Tender Palette on page 83.

Sunny & Warm

PREFERRED TEMPERATURE: 60–70°F

POSSIBLE LOCATIONS: south-facing window in warm living area, heated greenhouse or solarium

PLANTS THAT LIKE IT SUNNY & WARM

* Acalypha
* Adromischus
* Agave
* Aloe
* Alternanthera
* Ananas
* Aristolochia
* Begonia*
* Cissus discolor
* Colocasia*
* Crassula
* Echeveria
* Gasteria
* Gynura aurantiaca
* Haworthia
* Hibiscus
* Impatiens
* Juanulloa mexicana
* Kalanchoe
* Kleinia
* Lantana
* Manihot
* Musa*
* Mussaenda
* Neoregelia
* Pachyphytum
* Pentas

Continued at right

The first, and perhaps easiest way, to keep plants is to place them inside your living space, where they'll receive the maximum amount of both warmth and light.

This is the best way to store many tropicals, like alocasias, colocasias, and coleus — plants that flourish in seriously warm temperatures. These plants would love best to be above 60°F, in a moist, sunny place — recall the climates they originally come from. It would be safe to say that for this group of plants, the cooler the temperature, the drier the soil conditions should be. In warm temperatures, they'll have much higher requirements for moisture. They will also require extra space to be happy because, under warm and sunny circumstances, the plants will be in active growth, and it's likely that over the course of the winter, they'll increase somewhat in size. It's sometimes difficult to imagine when you look at a relatively small plant, like a seedling or a cutting, how much bigger it will be in just a few months. But even many older plants will increase their dimensions considerably — remember that the winter season will be at least five months long.

If your living space has windows with southern, eastern, or even western exposure, there are many tender perennial plants that you can successfully overwinter in containers. Because of the relative weakness of winter sunlight, southern exposure will give you the most choices, because when they are indoors, the majority of plants benefit from basking in shafts of sunlight.

Succulent plants, which provide a wonderful variety of shapes and textures, are just one group of tender perennials that would enjoy a southern exposure. Most require infrequent watering and make ideal houseplants. Another group that is

Bringing the Sun Indoors

ARTIFICIAL LIGHTING can be beneficial when storing tender perennial plants in either cool or warm conditions. Even when they are placed in south-facing windows, the intensity or duration of winter light does not equal that of the spring and summer, and the growth of plants at this time of year is necessarily affected by the difference. Use supplemental fluorescent lighting either to augment the intensity of available light during winter daylight hours or to create additional hours of light in order to extend those shorter winter days.

surprisingly happy in south-facing windows is the begonias. Although southern exposure might be too strong for them in the summer, it seems to be just right when combined with the lower intensity of winter light.

Pots placed in an eastern or western window will necessarily receive more-limited light. But the early-morning sun afforded by an eastern windowsill is ideal for some plants, like abutilons and fuchsias. And in winter, even a western exposure, which might be too harsh and hot in summer, can work out well for a collection of begonias or succulents. If you pay attention to the needs of your plants, and maybe even consider adding supplemental light where necessary, you'll find a suitable spot for a wide variety of tender perennial plants inside your living space.

Just as you benefit from increased humidity in the winter, so will your plants. Although succulents and cacti are not fussy,

Plants That Like It Sunny & Warm, *continued.*

＊ *Rhodochiton atrosanguineus*
＊ *Saccharum officinarum*
＊ *Solenostemom scutellarioides*
＊ *Strobilanthes*
＊ *Thunbergia*
＊ *Tibouchina*
＊ *Xanthosoma**

*May also be stored dormant.

Taking Cuttings

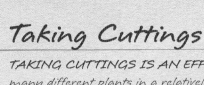

TAKING CUTTINGS IS AN EFFICIENT WAY to keep many different plants in a relatively small amount of space. Larger plants require considerable room to overwinter. They use more water, and also must be pruned and checked for pests more frequently. Overwintering smaller cuttings from a large plant is actually a lower-maintenance alternative.

1. EXAMINE THE PLANT CAREFULLY, and select longer stems with healthy leaves. The length of your cuttings will depend on the plant, but make sure to choose young growth, three to four inches long. Using a sharp implement like a clean razor blade, make a clean cut just below a leaf node.

make cut just
below leaf node

2. STRIP THE LOWER LEAVES.
Dip at least half an inch of the stem into rooting hormone.

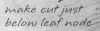

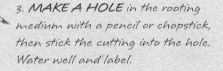

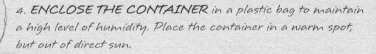

3. MAKE A HOLE in the rooting medium with a pencil or chopstick, then stick the cutting into the hole. Water well and label.

4. ENCLOSE THE CONTAINER in a plastic bag to maintain a high level of humidity. Place the container in a warm spot, but out of direct sun.

* Monitor cuttings frequently, to ensure that the medium is adequately moist.
* Check to see if cuttings have rooted after three to four weeks by tugging very gently on them. When sufficient roots have developed, the cutting will not pull up easily out of the rooting medium. At this point, it may be potted up with a well-draining mix and moved into brighter light.

Turn to **Propagation 101**, page 73, for more information on taking cuttings.

LAVANDULA 'GOODWIN CREEK GREY'

the majority of other plants will be far happier if the air they grow in is not excessively dry.

Even if you are unable to offer them this relatively convenient and easy winter setting, there are other ways to hold on to your plants from one season to the next. Don't despair, then, if you live in a cold, drafty house or if your only windows face north. Just keep reading.

MOVING IN FROM THE GARDEN

When overwintering plants in a warm, sunny space, consider all the options before bringing the plants indoors. One method is to overwinter cuttings from a plant (see Taking Cuttings, page 46). This works especially well with plants that grow quickly and may threaten to monopolize the indoor overwintering space. Softwood cuttings should be taken well before the end of the growing season, so they have time to become established before the low light of winter.

Container-grown plants that are potted up as individual specimens can simply be moved indoors (after being inspected for insect pests). Combination plantings should be dismantled and each plant should be potted up individually before being taken indoors. Those that have been planted in the ground also need to be potted up (see Trim It, Dig It, Spray It, page 48).

SPACING AND TEMPERATURE

Once the plants have been moved indoors, try to leave plenty of space around each of them. When plants begin to touch one another and their stems start to tangle, take notice. Either move their pots farther apart or prune the plants so that they are smaller. Close physical proximity will usually encourage a plant's new growth to reach upward, resulting in growth that is ungainly and spindly. Lack of air circulation can contribute to the development of diseases like mildew and botrytis, and also enables insect pests to spread among plants. The ideal temperature range for this group of plants is between 60 and 70°F.

Trim It, Dig It, Spray It

BALLOTA

PHYGELIUS

ALTERNANTHERA

CUPHEA

ANISODONTEA

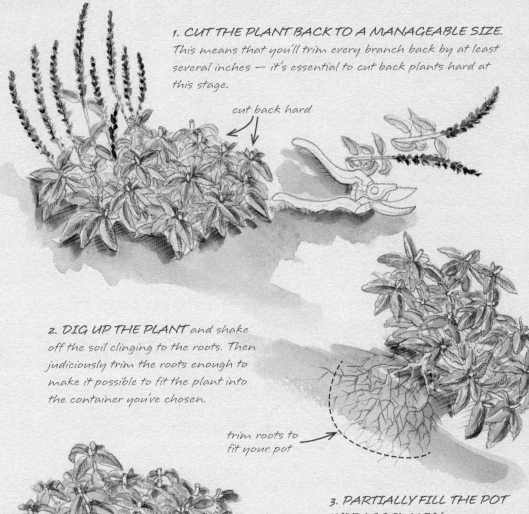

1. CUT THE PLANT BACK TO A MANAGEABLE SIZE. This means that you'll trim every branch back by at least several inches — it's essential to cut back plants hard at this stage.

cut back hard

2. DIG UP THE PLANT and shake off the soil clinging to the roots. Then judiciously trim the roots enough to make it possible to fit the plant into the container you've chosen.

trim roots to fit your pot

3. PARTIALLY FILL THE POT WITH SOIL MIX (see page 28 for information about soil mixes) and set the plant firmly within it. Fill the pot with mix to within half an inch of the rim, gently tamp it down, and water it thoroughly. Check for insects, and spray with horti-cultural oil.

* Keep a watchful eye on your transplant for a week or two after planting. It may require more water and some shade until it has resumed its composure.

PRUNING AND GROOMING

If plants are sharing your living space with you, it's likely that you'll want to groom them occasionally. This can consist of nothing more complicated than cleaning off dead leaves or flowers as they appear. But it can also involve some cosmetic pruning.

A few minutes spent trimming off spindly growth can be quite rewarding. Not only will the plant immediately look better, but its future growth should be affected positively as well. Thoughtful pruning will result in more attractive, compact specimens. Try to cut close to the last leaf node and remember that cuts made at an angle are less obvious than those that are made straight across. Especially as the days get close to spring, do not hesitate to prune off quite a lot. It may look drastic temporarily, but plants really do respond favorably to pruning, and the increase in their vigor will surprise you.

WATER AND FERTILIZER

We've said this before, but it bears repeating: if there is one key to the successful overwintering of tender perennials, it's that it is usually better to underwater rather than to overwater plants. And make sure to let the containers dry out between watering.

At some point during the winter, think about putting some of your plants in the shower. They'll really appreciate the extra humidity, and their leaves will emerge with a much shinier appearance. Alternatively, take a wet cloth or paper towel and wipe larger leaves individually. It is easy to forget how dusty the interiors of our heated houses can get in winter.

As the days begin to lengthen (in late February in Zone 5), start feeding plants lightly with a balanced soluble fertilizer, such as 5-10-10, to encourage growth and flower bud development (see page 76 for more information on fertilizer).

PESTS

Aphids, whitefly, and scale are likely to be the major pest issues that occur on plants in these conditions. For more information, see page 64.

Cool & Bright

PREFERRED TEMPERATURE: 45–55°F

POSSIBLE LOCATIONS: unheated sunporch or guest room, cool greenhouse

PLANTS THAT LIKE IT COOL & BRIGHT

* Abutilon
* Agapanthus africanus
* Agastache
* Aloysia triphylla
* Angelonia angustifolia
* Billardiera longiflora
* Bouvardia
* Brachyglottis
* Carex
* Ceanothus
* Centaurea
* Citrus
* Convolvulus
* Cordyline
* Cuphea
* Datura
* Dichondra micrantha
* Dicliptera suberecta
* Duranta
* Eucomis
* Euphorbia
* Fuchsia
* Gardenia
* Gunnera manicata
* Heliotropium arborescens
* Hibiscus
* Iochroma
* Ipomoea
* Jasminum
* Juncus

Continued at right

For the majority of tender perennial plants, the ideal overwintering situation is a cool space with bright, natural light. This relatively large group of plants includes salvias, phormiums, pelargoniums, fuchsias, most Mediterranean plants, and/or those with gray foliage. In older or more spacious houses, accommodations for plants like these can often be found in unheated extra rooms or a glassed-in porch or in an attached greenhouse that receives minimal heat or that at least can be kept at a cooler temperature than the rest of the house through the winter. If the space can be maintained above freezing — preferably in the range of 45 to 55°F — and has abundant natural light, it could be a perfect spot for storing many tender perennials. Don't forget that although these spaces cool off at night, they may require ventilation when the sun heats things up sufficiently in the middle of the day. Temperatures much above 55 or 60°F should be avoided. Particularly as the season moves to late winter, the increased length of daylight combined with the greater strength of the sun will cause temperatures in this type of space to increase; do what you can to keep temperatures cool or your plants will shift into active growth.

The goal, when storing this group of tender perennials, is to prevent them from growing for most of the winter or, alternatively, to let them continue to grow but very slowly. Even though most will retain their leaves, cool conditions — around 45°F, with bright light — will induce a period of rest that is beneficial. What this means is that they are really pretty low-maintenance for the winter.

Our neighbor and good friend Bobbi Rosenau has successfully stored her salvias and tibouchina for many seasons in just this fashion, using an unheated upstairs bedroom. Of course, if the space is cool and dark, rather than bright, you could con-

Can You Dig It?

IF YOU'RE GOING TO DIG UP A PLANT, it's best to do it as early as possible or when there is a month or so of warm growing conditions left — the roots of the disturbed plant will require at least that long to become reestablished. This is a good time to prune the plant for a number of reasons. By pruning, you will be cutting back on the amount of stem and leaf it has to support, making the transition much easier for the plant. The process of digging will inevitably reduce the size of the plant's roots; the shock of this change will be reduced if its top growth is likewise decreased. It will also diminish the area available for insects to inhabit. Cutting back a plant makes it more manageable to move and care for down the road. It will also encourage compact new growth, which may be advantageous in its more restricted indoor quarters.

sider adding supplemental light, as many gardeners do when growing their spring seedlings. If the available overwintering space is too warm, the plants will continue to grow. Depending on the plant, this can be undesirable — at the very least, it will complicate matters. When any plant is in active growth rather than a semi-dormant state, it will require more water and more attention in general. If it's something that blooms only once a year, like agapanthus, the warmer temperature could encourage it to bloom while it's indoors, rather than later when it's out in the garden.

Additionally, cool storage conditions will tend to discourage insect problems. Any professional grower will tell you that in the large-scale greenhouse environment, insect problems that are negligible early in winter will suddenly and predictably escalate when conditions warm up and day length increases. Put simply, insects that feed on plants respond favorably to the same conditions that plants do. By discouraging your plants from growing abundantly during their winter storage, then, you will also be minimizing the numbers of insects that feed on them.

Plants That Like It Cool & Bright, *continued.*

* *Kniphofia*
* *Lavandula*
* *Leonotis*
* *Lupinus albifrons*
* *Mandevilla*
* *Marrubium*
* *Melianthus*
* *Nerium oleander*
* *Nicotiana*
* *Ocimum americanum*
* *Ophiopogon planiscapus*
* *Origanum*
* *Osmanthus fragrans*
* *Osteospermum*
* *Oxalis*
* *Passiflora*
* *Pelargonium*
* *Polianthes tuberosa*
* *Rosa chinensis*
* *Rosmarinus officinalis*
* *Salvia*
* *Santolina*

MOVING IN FROM THE GARDEN

If the plants in question are already growing in containers, check them carefully for insects before bringing them indoors. If you're digging and potting plants, do so well ahead of really cold nights, so that they have time to settle into their new containers. Many plants benefits from being cut back hard and sprayed with dormant oil before being taken indoors for the winter. (See Trim It, Dig It, Spray It, page 48, and Can You Dig it?, page 51).

SPACING AND TEMPERATURE

One of the most important aspects of spacing is maintaining the ability to actually see how your plants are doing. When conditions are crowded, small plants can easily be lost, due to their lack of visibility. Even though this type of storage is relatively low maintenance, it's important to keep checking for potential insect and disease issues — they're far easier to control when they're just beginning. Keeping temperatures between 45 and 55°F is ideal.

PRUNING AND GROOMING

Unless the plant is becoming unmanageable, it's best to postpone serious grooming projects until the spring. Remove dead leaves and spent flowers from both the plant and its surroundings, but refrain from pruning. Pruning at this time will encourage new growth, which is not always desirable.

WATER AND FERTILIZER

Because the plants are growing very little during this time, they shouldn't be using much water. Feed little, or not at all, between October and most of February. As the days begin to lengthen (in late February in Zone 5), start feeding lightly with a balanced soluble fertilizer, such as 5-10-10, to encourage growth and flower bud development (see page 76 for more information on fertilizer).

No Trimming Needed

A NUMBER OF TENDER PERENNIALS do not require any pruning. Along with the usual candidates — those with evergreen foliage, such as agaves — there are less obvious ones, such as many perennial grasses. Tender scirpus, carexes, and most of the restio family should never be trimmed by cutting. Instead, pull out the dead leaves periodically to reveal newer growth. Unfortunately, trimming these plants can result in their death.

Another group of plants that don't require much pruning are the slow-growing woody ones, such as punica, sericea, and coprosma. You may want to shape them slightly or thin out weaker growth, but it doesn't make sense to prune these slow-growing plants very substantially; keep it light.

The last group of plants you shouldn't prune before you move them inside is made up of those that bloom in winter, such as bouvardia, ceanothus, citrus, and kalanchoe. You wouldn't want to cut off any developing buds before they have a chance to blossom!

PESTS

The same potential exists for pest and disease problems, but infestations and outbreaks will be less severe because of the cool temperature.

Dark & Damp

PREFERRED TEMPERATURE: 35 to 50°F

POSSIBLE LOCATIONS: unheated cellar or garage, crawlspace, cool closet

PLANTS TO STORE DARK & DAMP

* Canna
* Colocasia
* Cosmos atrosanguineus
* Dahlia
* Gunnera manicata
* Ipomoea
* Manihot
* Pennisetum setaceum
* Xanthosoma

Older houses often have a cool basement, and this can be handy for the storage of various kinds of tender perennials. As long as the pipes don't freeze, your plants shouldn't either. Over the years, we've heard from many of our customers who regularly put their salvias and other tender perennials in the dark cellar, pots and all. Lacking some of the other overwintering options we've discussed, they've found that a dormant period in the basement works surprisingly well for plants that we had assumed required light to survive. We encourage you to experiment with the plants and conditions available to you. The results may surprise you.

Just make sure you remember that the ideal cellar storage for plants and tubers is a *cool* one. Be forewarned that if your cellar is warmed by the furnace and stays at a cozy temperature, this method will probably not work for you. Temperature is critical when it comes to storage in the dark. The ideal range for these plants is between 35 and 50°F. A good rule of thumb is that the darker the storage space, the cooler it should be.

You won't be watering these in the usual way, but it's still a good idea to check on the relative moisture of your storage conditions. Don't allow cannas and other tubers and corms to completely dry out, or their spring viability may be affected. If they seem dry, sprinkle a *little* water on them. Excessive moisture can lead to problems too. Here, it's key to differentiate between *damp* and *moist*. If the medium within the container is damp enough, it should not dry out all winter; you should still check periodically, however. If the conditions you find are overly wet, open the container to air out a bit to avoid rotting.

Storing Tubers

1. DIG UP PLANTS carefully and gently shake off the soil.

2. TRIM off herbaceous growth, so that just the tuber is left.

3. ALLOW PLANTS TO CURE for one or two days in a warm, dry location.

4. PLACE TUBERS in damp (but not wet) peat moss, inside a storage container that will exclude light, such as a black plastic garbage bag or an old ice chest.

store with damp peat moss

5. PUT THE CONTAINER in a cool, dark place, like a cellar.

* Check tubers periodically through the winter and spray lightly with water if needed.

* Discard any tubers that have rotted.

DAHLIA COCCINEA

DAHLIA   IPOMOEA   CANNA   CURCUMA

Dark & Dry

PREFERRED TEMPERATURE: 35 to 50°F

POSSIBLE LOCATIONS: unheated cellar or garage, crawlspace, cool closet

PLANTS TO STORE DARK & DRY

* *Amorphophallus*
* *Begonia sutherlandii*
* *Bessera elegans*
* *Gladiolus*
* *Mirabilis*
* *Salvia*
* *Sinningia*

Finally, there are those tender perennials that will wait out the winter in the most unpromising conditions. These are mostly corms and tubers, which — like *Bessera elegans* and *Begonia sutherlandii* — can be left in a dry pot inside a dark closet for the duration of the winter. They will tolerate a warmer temperature than the plants that require dark and damp conditions. As long as they do not come into contact with water, they will simply remain dormant. It is not necessary to wrap them or put them into bags, although if it is more convenient for you, you certainly can. Corms and tubers stored in this way should remain quite dry. This would be an excellent time to separate a few to give away to friends, because bessera, in particular, multiplies like crazy, and you will have more than you can possibly use within a few gardening seasons. Just left to sit in a dry pot of soil or emptied into a simple paper bag, these amazing tubers will keep quietly all winter and not demand a bit of attention.

When the days begin to lengthen, bring them back into the light and begin cautiously to water them. Perhaps, like us, you remember those magical paper flowers of childhood, which came to splendid three-dimensional life as they gracefully unfolded in an ordinary glass of water. Although bessera won't bloom until later in the summer, much like those Oriental wonders, upon hydration these little tubers will begin to swell and come to life for another season.

Storing Dry Corms and Bulbs

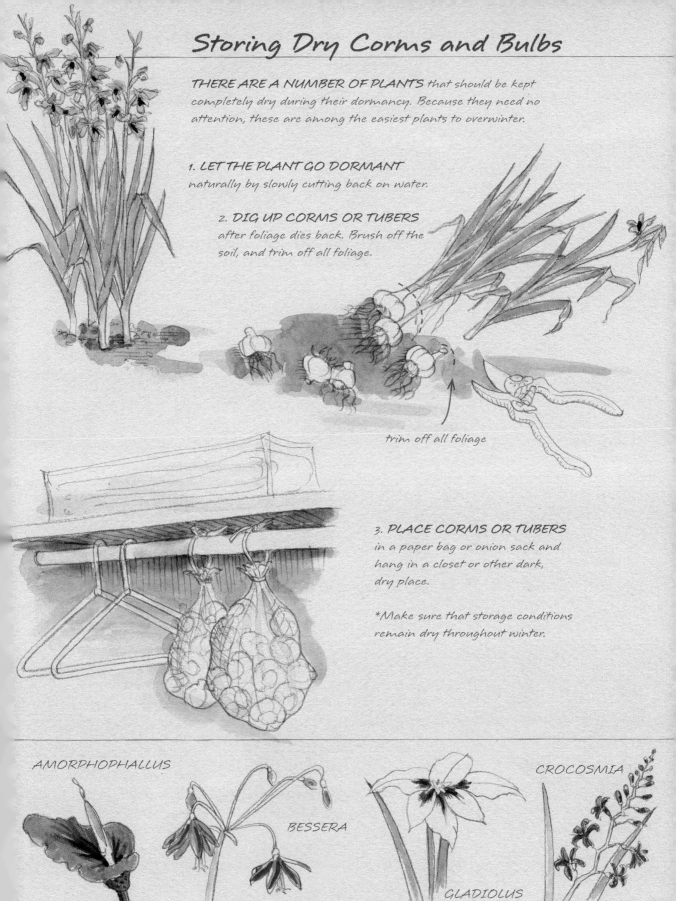

THERE ARE A NUMBER OF PLANTS that should be kept completely dry during their dormancy. Because they need no attention, these are among the easiest plants to overwinter.

1. LET THE PLANT GO DORMANT naturally by slowly cutting back on water.

2. DIG UP CORMS OR TUBERS after foliage dies back. Brush off the soil, and trim off all foliage.

trim off all foliage

3. PLACE CORMS OR TUBERS in a paper bag or onion sack and hang in a closet or other dark, dry place.

*Make sure that storage conditions remain dry throughout winter.

AMORPHOPHALLUS

BESSERA

GLADIOLUS

CROCOSMIA

Storing Dormant Woodies

MIRABILIS

MANY TENDER WOODY PLANTS, like fig trees, can simply be stored dormant in their pots. At the end of the summer, wait for a light frost to occur before bringing plants into a dark, cool space.

MANY WOODIES — like fig and lemon verbena — will lose their leaves. In order to encourage dormancy, do not repot the plant. Soil in the pot should be damp but not wet. Be sure to check for any obvious signs of pests, as well.

BRUGMANSIA

LANTANA

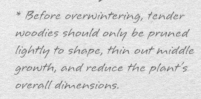

* Before overwintering, tender woodies should only be pruned lightly to shape, thin out middle growth, and reduce the plant's overall dimensions.

CHECK THE PLANT periodically during the winter, and water lightly if soil dries out completely.

IOCHROMA

The Importance of Temperature

If plants are sharing your living space, the ambient temperature is likely to be determined by what is comfortable for humans, not necessarily by what is best for plants. Examine your plants carefully to determine whether the current overwintering arrangement is working out. Elongated growth and thin, pale foliage can be a sign that conditions are too warm, and that actively growing plants aren't receiving enough sunlight. Perhaps another, cooler area is available that you could move them to, or maybe it's simply time to turn down the thermostat and tell your partner to put on a sweater.

If a plant shows signs of stress from overly cool temperatures, you will have a different set of issues to consider. Does it appear to be losing its leaves? Each plant has its own tolerance for cold, and this threshold is a combination of the actual minimum temperature and the duration of the period that temperatures are below what the plant can handle. Such a plant may have wilted, pale leaves that droop despite adequate moisture and fertility. Plants suffering from marginal cold can be difficult to diagnose because their symptoms have involved a long period of exposure. By the time the plant loses its leaves, it might be too late.

Judging whether your plants are in trouble is one of those things you'll learn from experience, and the cause of their distress is not always clear. Just like the symptoms of overwatering and underwatering, sometimes plants lose their leaves and are still fine. The annual behavior cycle of lemon verbena (*Aloysia triphylla*) is just such a case. Defoliation is part of its normal dormant behavior. After sitting with bare branches the entire winter and looking, well, dead, your lemon verbena plant will revive quickly once the temperatures warm and you begin to water it again. On the other hand, if a coleus loses all its leaves, you probably have cause for serious concern. You could attempt to rejuvenate it by moving the plant to a very warm area — one that does not go below 55°F at night and stays in the 70s during the day. If the pot is at all damp, do not water. Just wait and monitor. Times like these are

PLANTS THAT CAN BE STORED DORMANT IN THE POT

* *Aloysia*
* *Brugmansia*
* *Buddleia*
* *Ficus carica*
* *Iochroma*
* *Lantana*
* *Mirabilis*
* *Musa*

What to Do in a Frost Emergency

WE ALL HAVE THE BEST INTENTIONS of getting to the last garden chores in the final days of summer, and it seems like there's never enough time for everything we need to do. So even if you never had the chance to sit down and consider all your overwintering options, and the first frost came before you had an opportunity to move your favorite pots indoors, it may not be too late to act.

A garage or shed can provide a temporary holding area for tender plants when the weather changes abruptly. Even if your plants get damaged by frost, you can sometimes revive them by pruning them back — for many plants, this is something you were going to do anyway. As long as the temperature hasn't dropped too low, they may survive. If, after a few days, there still seems to be damage to the stem tissue beyond where you cut, the damage may be irreversible. Remember, though, there is an enormous range in minimum temperatures that tender perennials can withstand, and many plants that look terrible now may still bounce back.

often when we learn the limits of a given winter storage/growing space. If plants are sitting in front of a window that can be opened, make sure that all who might open it on a warm, sunny day understand the minimum-temperature tolerance of your plants! We've heard sad stories from gardeners who've forgotten the window was open when the outside temperature dropped suddenly or the sun moved away. It doesn't take very long at freezing temperatures to do serious damage to some tender perennials.

Setting Up Your Site

The time to think about all this is in July or early August (in Zone 5), well before the end of the summer. When the weather forecasters predict a hard frost, you'll be much better off if you've already taken care of moving all those pots indoors. And cuttings taken in the dark of an autumn evening are rarely as useful as those you select carefully in broad daylight well before the last minute.

After you make a list of plants you want to save and consider your options for overwintering, it's time to prepare the area you've chosen. Evaluate whether you need to change or augment the existing conditions.

ABOVE An assortment of succulents can easily adapt to winter life in most home interiors.

Making Space in the Living Area

If you would like to move plants into your living space, will you need shelves in front of a window to accommodate all of them? Do you have enough trays or dishes to put under all their containers? If you have many small containers, consider setting them on large trays constructed of either sheet metal or plastic. This will enable you to water them easily, as long as you remember to place plants with similar moisture conditions in the same tray. The water that collects in the tray will also contribute to the ambient humidity, which is desirable in heated spaces. For that matter, how dry is the heat in your living area? This may be a good time to purchase a humidifier if you don't already have one. Tropical plants prefer conditions that are warm, but also quite humid.

When setting up a cool, bright location in which to overwinter plants, make sure that temperatures can be moderated. You should be able to prevent freezing or alternatively keep it from overheating. Some form of ventilation is necessary for sunny days. Is additional light required? Even though the space is cool, there should be good light.

Down Below

Perhaps you've decided to use part of your basement for plant storage. Although an unheated basement is generally better for this purpose than a heated one, you could also adapt part of the existing space within a heated basement area. One method is to create a small, separate room adjacent to one of the basement windows. Section off the area with some type of wall — the more insulated, the better — and then open the window just a crack, and you have a workable storage area.

If you don't require access to the basement through the bulkhead door, you can turn it into an excellent storage area for bulbs, tubers, and semi-dormant plants (those that have died back for the winter). First, thoroughly insulate any surface that is directly exposed to outside temperatures, especially the metal doors. The ideal temperature range for this type of storage is between 35 and 40°F.

A Word about Saucers

ALTHOUGH ALICE LOVES TO COLLECT old dishes and is therefore happy to put them to use under planted pots when they're indoors for the winter, Brian suggests that deeper saucers are more convenient when watering time comes around. Shallow plates simply don't leave you the same leeway if you like to apply water with abandon. Your preference may depend on your watering technique.

As we've noted before, keeping pots in trays, whether of plastic or metal, is a sensible overwintering practice for several reasons. In addition to eliminating spills on the floor and furniture, their use increases air humidity.

A wide pebble-filled tray will reduce spills and increase the ambient humidity around a plant.

Preventing Pest Problems

Experience will teach you which plants are insect bait. Those prone to infestations may not be worth the time and trouble. Look carefully at each plant — if, like us, you're over the age of 40, use your reading glasses to make certain that the plant is clean. Concentrate particularly on a plant's growing points, the undersides of its leaves, and in the leaf axils. When insect populations are building up on a plant, these are the locations where their presence will be most obvious. If there are problems, take the time to deal with them now, before you move the plant into an enclosed space, where any insects will quickly multiply and spread to other plants. Plan on making a regular inspection of your plants — once a week would not be too often.

Aphids tend to congregate in the leaf axil of a plant — the point where the leaf meets the main stem.

Spraying with Oil

We have had good success controlling most insect problems with either horticultural oils (such as Sunspray) or insecticidal soaps. Look for summer oil, a type of horticultural oil that can be applied to actively growing plants. It's critical to follow the product directions and to test a small amount first; these substances can still harm some plants. These materials work by smothering insects but are nontoxic to people and animals, which makes them an excellent choice for plants in your living space. To minimize the amount that you inhale, we recommend that you wear a mask while spraying them.

If you do find an infestation, spray at least twice before moving the plant indoors. This is simply a good preventive measure — even if you have well-trained eyes, it's easy to miss a small number of tiny insects.

Remember that application will be most effective if you recognize a problem and treat it in its early stages. Later, it will be more difficult to conquer, as many a gardener has discovered to her dismay. To avoid damaging your plants, don't apply dormant oil when plants are stressed for moisture. It's also important to avoid periods of high humidity, because the oil must dry quickly after it has been applied.

Spraying plants with summer oil before overwintering them is a good way to avoid pest infestations indoors.

Specific Pests and Diseases

The first and most important step in coping with pests is correct identification. It is amazing how rarely most gardeners bother to do this before attempting a solution. Each type of pest requires its own treatment, so take the time to figure out exactly who your unwelcome guest is.

Diseases

The most common diseases that pose problems for the indoor gardener are mildew, botrytis, damping-off, and root rot. It is possible to prevent their occurrence by employing a combination of temperature control, air circulation, correct watering, and adequate sanitation. Although they are in widespread use within the greenhouse industry, fungicides are something we have never used in the 20 years we've grown greenhouse crops.

BOTRYTIS is also referred to as "gray mold," which is a pretty good description of its appearance. Its most common manifestation is on dead leaves and flowers, which explains why removing these from a plant and taking them away — otherwise referred to as sanitation — is important. Because the spores of this mold require moist conditions for a period of 8 to 12 hours with temperatures between 55 and 65°F, sufficient air circulation is another key to its prevention and control. The mold may actually be present on dead and decaying plant parts and not bother healthy, living tissue if conditions are not optimal for its growth.

Botrytis can announce its presence through the appearance of brown and gray zones on live plant tissue.

DAMPING-OFF and ROOT ROT are caused by a variety of fungi. Both cause plants to wilt, droop, and eventually die. In the case of damping-off, you will see a specific weakening point in a plant's stem as the disease advances, and once it establishes a toehold, it will travel from plant to plant quickly, particularly among seedlings. Evidence of root rot is clearest below the soil. Affected roots will discolor and have a foul odor. The plants themselves will lose vigor and may wilt even when the soil is moist.

You should be able to avoid both of these diseases by using a well-drained soil mix and watering properly. Water only when the pots are dry, and then water thoroughly. Be especially careful during periods of cool, cloudy weather. Plants use considerably less water under these conditions, making it much easier to overwater at these times.

Once either disease is present, you should dramatically cut back on watering, and also consider changing your soil mix. In the case of root rot, it might also be helpful to trim the affected roots. After cutting, let them dry until they form callus tissue on the cut areas. None of these approaches can guarantee saving your plant, however.

Recent research indicates that the use of compost in soil mixes may offer particular benefits when it comes to preventing and managing soil-disease problems. Compost is generally rich in beneficial bacteria and fungi that take up space and feed on nutrients — the same nutrients that disease-causing microbes might otherwise make use of. Their presence makes it more difficult for disease organisms to become established (remember that nature abhors a vacuum). Much about the microbial and chemical activity of soils is still unknown to us — soil is a mysterious and highly complex environment, and exciting information concerning the interaction of plants and soil microbes continues to be discovered.

A plant with root rot will emit a foul odor. A dark root color is sometimes a tip-off as well.

POWDERY MILDEW differs from these other fungi in that it does not require water for infection to occur. Water may actually kill its spores and inhibit the growth of this disease. Powdery mildew has the appearance of a fine white powder, and although not all plants succumb to it, those that do generally have a specific type of powdery mildew to which only they are susceptible. For example, the powdery mildew that affects lilac bushes will not spread to the rest of a garden. Likewise, the powdery mildew that covers your summer phlox will remain confined to the phlox plants you unfortunately included in the border. Warm temperatures and high humidity are both prerequisites for its growth — on both indoor and

Among plants often wintered indoors, rosemary is infamous for attracting powdery mildew.

outdoor plants — but the temperature range varies with the specific mildew.

Among plants often wintered indoors, rosemary is infamous for attracting powdery mildew. We have found that keeping the plant in a cool space with bright light is key to the avoidance of powdery mildew — and also results in a happy, healthy plant. Another way to control powdery mildew is by selecting individual plants within vulnerable groups that seem to have better resistance than is usual. This is the type of characteristic that professional breeders watch and select for. On plants where powdery mildew has been discovered, repeated applications of summer oil, or baking soda mixed with water, may reduce or stop its spread.

Insect Pests

APHIDS are probably the most common problem gardeners encounter when they bring plants indoors. In the garden, aphids are part of the larger ecosystem. If the environment is diverse, and if you have not used insecticides, you should have a resident population of insect predators and parasites that will keep the aphid population under control. When you move plants indoors, however, some aphids will surely travel with them.

Using Oil and Soap

IN OUR EXPERIENCE, insecticidal soap is somewhat less effective than horticultural oil, but it may be safer for use in some cases because of the adverse reactions certain plants — like succulents — can have to horticultural oil. If you're trying to control insects without using more toxic materials, insecticidal soaps may be useful.

Because insecticidal soap is a relatively benign product, thorough and adequate coverage is critical, as is the repetition of applications. Mix the soap according to the instructions on the label and spray in a fine mist on to the foliage and stems. Spray plants at least twice to ensure adequate coverage.

Aphids are small, slow-moving, soft-bodied insects that tend to appear in groups on the undersides of leaves and on the tips of plants. They also have a brief stage in their life cycle when they can fly. Curling leaves on a plant may be a sign that you have them. Individual aphids vary quite a bit in size and color, depending on the species. Often their body color seems selected to match the host plant — shades of green are common — but it's also possible that their color is affected by the juices of the plant on which they are feeding. We have always found the bright orange aphids that usually situate on butterfly weed (*Asclepias*) fascinating in this regard. In warm conditions, aphids reproduce very quickly, causing their populations to increase dramatically.

Cutting back the plants before moving them inside will help to reduce populations. Spraying with summer oil after cutting the plants is also effective. If your storage conditions are cool enough, you probably won't have an overwhelming problem. The most challenging period will be in spring, when the temperature warms up. If aphids are on your plants, keep a close eye on them and consider spot treating with insecticidal soap or summer oil.

If your plants are spending the winter in a greenhouse, consider using beneficial insects to control aphid infestations. Over the years, we have developed management plans for our greenhouses that use insect predators and parasites almost exclusively. (See Suggested Reading, page 199, for more information about this subject.)

FUNGUS GNATS are small, mosquito-like gnats that lay their eggs in soil, which is where the small worms hatch. Although the adult gnats are bothersome, it is the larvae that do the serious damage, feeding on roots and stems near the soil. Their presence can also enable the introduction of decay organisms.

We've found that a combination of careful watering and reasonable sanitation practices is the best way to avoid fungus gnats. The grubs feed on decaying plant debris, so

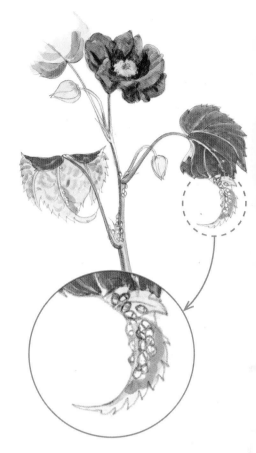

Curling leaves may be a sign that your plant is harboring aphids.

Once a population of fungus gnats (and their larvae) is established, there are a few options for eliminating them: letting the soil dry out thoroughly, watering the plant with a Bt solution, or simply repotting with fresh mix.

it makes sense to eliminate their food; then they'll be less inclined to stop by. Applying a coarse, dry mulch on top of the soil, such as calcined clay, can also help to prevent infestations. Mulching containers establishes a dry surface on top of the soil; this creates an environment that is inhospitable to fungus gnats.

Once a population of fungus gnats (and their larvae) is established, there are a few options for eliminating them. Start simply by allowing the soil to dry out completely, and water only sparingly afterward. If this isn't successful, you might try repotting the plant with fresh potting mix (Remember that prebagged mixes may not have adequate drainage, and may therefore have the potential to become breeding grounds for fungus gnats. You might be better off making your own well-drained mix.) As a last resort for tackling a widespread or particularly stubborn infestation, you might treat the plant with beneficial nematodes (which will eat the gnat larvae) or drench the soil with a dilute dose of *Bacillus thuringiensus* (Bt). Predatory mites (generally available through mail-order companies; see Resources, page 200) may also be effective.

MITES are so small that if you are of a certain age, you may not be able to focus on the individuals with your naked eye. You can generally recognize their presence, however, by a telltale mottling of the affected leaves. In severe infestations, white webbing will also be present. If you look at mites with a magnifying lens, they resemble tiny spiders, and come in a wide range of colors, from bright red (this tends to be a winter coloration) to very pale yellow and tan.

Horticultural oil works well on mite infestations after they have been discovered, but continued monitoring is essential and repeat treatments may be necessary. There are also many species of predator mites that feed on the mites that attack plants. They work well in greenhouse situations and are worth trying even inside your house if you have a lot of plants in combination with a mite problem.

Mites are so small that if you are over 45, you may not be able to see the individuals with your naked eye. Their webbing, however, is quite apparent.

SCALE and MEALY BUGS are small sucking insects that spend most of their time stationary on the plant, although there is a youthful "crawler" stage when they move around a bit. Some scales are "armored," which means they have a hard shell; others are soft-shelled. Mealy bugs are covered with a white, wax-like material.

Insecticidal soaps and horticultural oil are effective controls, but your plants will probably require several treatments. Scale and mealy bugs can be particularly stubborn; after spraying, you'll want to wipe the plants with a cloth to ensure that you remove all the insects.

THRIPS are small, soft-bodied insects that are longer (about 1/16 inch) than they are wide. Their color varies: brown, yellow, and black are most common. When the weather is warm, they will crawl rapidly. You can see them with the naked eye if your vision is good, but they are easiest to recognize by the damage they inflict. They feed primarily on plant buds, both flower and shoots, but also enjoy the undersides of leaves. These feeding patterns result in a characteristic appearance that should alert you to the presence of thrips on a plant. The leaves they feed on will appear streaked with white and the buds will be deformed.

Some control is possible by spraying with dormant oil. In our experience, though, for severe infestations, the most long-lasting control is the introduction of predator mites (*Amblyseius cucmeris*).

WHITEFLIES are very small insects that appear whitish in color. The adult flies lay eggs on plants, from which nymphs hatch, and these nymphs feed on the plant. We have never had a problem with whiteflies, in part because they prefer warm temperatures between 70 and 75°F, and we kept the plants in our greenhouses at much cooler temperatures during the winter. But we were also very lucky, and Brian has always quarantined new plants for observation before introducing them into the larger greenhouse environment. This

Scale and mealy bugs are small, sucking insects that spend most of their time stationary on the plant, although there is a youthful "crawler" stage when they are mobile.

You can see thrips with the naked eye if your vision is good, but they are easiest to recognize by the damage they inflict.

Whiteflies are a fairly challenging problem to control; if you notice them on a plant, you may want to reconsider your decision to overwinter it.

is a recommended practice; it is surprising how often plants are commercially distributed with problems like whitefly in evidence.

If you are keeping tenders in the warm part of your house, you may run into problems with certain plants. Whiteflies seem to have a particular attraction for specific groups of plants, such as the Solanaceae and the Verbenaceae. If you notice them on a plant, reconsider your decision to keep that particular plant, because whiteflies are a fairly challenging problem to control. Oil will kill the nymphs and may smother the eggs, but you must continue to monitor and spray again if necessary. Some growers effectively use beneficial insects to control whiteflies; if you have an infestation, we encourage you to learn more about this possibility. (See Resources, page 200.)

Tips for Avoiding Indoor Pests

✳ Prune back and carefully check plants for insects before bringing them indoors, and quarantine new purchases for at least two weeks before putting them in close quarters with other plants.

✳ Be vigilant: conduct weekly inspections.

✳ Keep temperatures on the cool side, and water plants only when soil is dry.

✳ Place blue or yellow sticky traps among the plants in order to monitor whitefly and thrips populations.

✳ Be open to the idea that you may not be able to save plants that are frequently problematic in your storage conditions. Plants susceptible to whiteflies, for instance, will be challenging to store on a warm windowsill.

Spring: The Transition

When spring weather arrives, you can begin to move plants back outside, as the temperature permits. Most of the hardier plants, such as salvias, buddleias, agaves, abutilon, agapanthus, gazanias, haloragis, and lavender, can go out fairly early (April in Zone 5). The tropical plants, like cannas, dahlias, begonias, abelmoschus, alternanthera, and *Hamelia patens* should be kept indoors longer. Keep an eye on the weather. Any extreme conditions could set back tender herbaceous growth.

Potting and Pruning

If you plan to keep the plant in a container or to use it as an element in a combination container planting, this is an excellent time for a transition. Before the plant enters this period of increased growth, it is important to make sure that all the conditions within your control are optimal. At the very least, this means giving the plant new soil; chances are that most of the nutrients you added to last summer's mix have been depleted over the season and the structure of the soil has been compromised.

When repotting a plant, take it out of its old pot and refresh the roots, either by teasing smaller root systems with your fingers or with a cultivator. In the case of larger, tougher roots, cut through them in a few strategic spots with your pruning shears.

Now is also the best time to prune plants — before they begin spring growth. Select weak and damaged growth for pruning. If the plant is a woody one, prune to open up the center. If your tender perennial was growing under less-than-ideal conditions, it's a good idea to prune this weak growth in order to promote better form and structure. Don't be afraid of cutting back; remember that pruning promotes new growth. At the same time, don't cut too much from woody plants — after all, you've stored them all winter in order to give you this much more substantial plant.

Some overwintered plants become leggy because of low light conditions indoors. It's a good idea to prune this weak growth in order to promote better form and structure.

prune weak growth

After trimming, place the plant in a container of freshly mixed potting soil and tamp it in. Make sure the soil line is at the same height on the plant's stem as it was previously. At the same time, leave at least half an inch of space between the soil and the upper edge of the pot to facilitate watering. If you are combining it with other plants in a single container, try to imagine (and then allow enough space for) each plant's eventual spread. Consider, too, the growth habit of the plant and the orientation of the pot.

To prevent the spread of disease, it's important to pot up only solid, blemish-free corms.

POTTING UP BULBS AND CORMS

This is a good time to bring out any bulbs or corms you stored for the winter and pot them up in the containers you have chosen for their summer lives. Discard any bulbs or corms that have become rotten or have questionable spots. Plant them root-side down in fresh potting mix and water them in. Place them in a sunny place that's not too warm; they'll grow best in a relatively cool location until you can move them outside.

POTTING UP PUPS

A few plants, among them agaves, alocasias, aloes, bromeliads, and musas, produce basal offsets, or miniature new plants. These are commonly referred to as "pups" and might be defined as new plants that form on underground shoots or rhizomes of their mother plants. If you have a mature plant that is surrounded by a ring of babies, it may be time to liberate them from the central plant and to pot them up individually.

Spring is a good time to divide and pot up canna offsets.

Spring is probably the best time to do this, but if it is more convenient for you to do it in fall, there's no reason you can't. If the plant is a prickly one, wear gloves to protect your hands. Use sharp blades to disconnect pups from the parent plant. Plant them in well-drained soil mix, and place them in partial shade for a short time, until they have rooted well. Whether or not a pup has visible roots, repot it so that the bottom makes good contact with the soil. Roots will form eventually. Plants have to be drought resistant to multiply in this manner! Water only occasionally.

Propagation 101: Taking Cuttings

CUTTINGS ARE A SIMPLE WAY to propagate plants. Some plants simply can't be grown from seed, either because they're sterile, and therefore don't set seed (often the case with hybrids) or because they wouldn't come true from seed — that is, the resultant seedlings would not have the same characteristics as the parent you're trying to propagate. If it cannot be reproduced in other ways, the best way to get multiple plants of a selected variety may be to take cuttings from it.

Propagating plants by cuttings is also speedy. By the end of its first growing season, a rooted cutting will be, in most cases, predictably larger than a seedling of the same plant grown for the same amount of time. Additionally, the cutting will generally result in a flowering plant within the first season.

Increasing plants by taking cuttings is one of the most useful gardening skills. Don't be intimidated by it — many plants, especially tropicals and tender perennials, are surprisingly easy to root. Having said this, there are some tips to consider: whenever possible, take cuttings early in the season, before plants have begun to bloom; taking cuttings at the end of the season can be somewhat more challenging than doing so early in the spring. Once bud initiation and bloom have begun, the plant will be concentrating on those processes, and is less likely to put energy into the formation of new stem and leaf growth and, perhaps most critically, is less likely to contribute energy to the formation of roots.

SOFTWOOD CUTTINGS

Non-woody, tropical plants like coleus are some of the easiest to propagate by cuttings. When plants have growth that becomes woody with age, it is necessary to plan more carefully. Cuttings should be taken when the growth is still soft and the plant is not yet flowering.

In the case of brugmansias, you must plan ahead in this respect. Because of their large size and slow growth rate, we've found that the best time to take brugmansia cuttings is in the early part of the summer for the following year. In other words, you must propagate it before the plant begins to concentrate its primary energy into the formation of flower buds. But even later in the season, plants such as *Mussaenda frondosa* and the phygelius cultivars should be propagated while the plant is still in active growth. It should

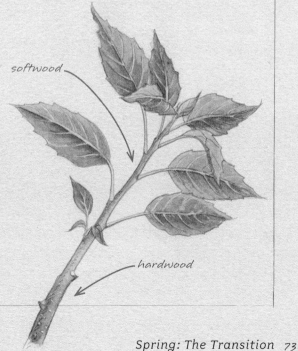

softwood

hardwood

not be losing many leaves and should still look good. The plant's nonflowering shoots are the best ones to gather for cuttings.

Using sharp tools will enable you to be precise in your cuts. Brian prefers a pair of Felco pruners that he uses only for cuttings, so that the blades always remain sharp. But a small paring knife or even a good pair of scissors can do the job too. And be prepared to sharpen any of these when they lose their edge.

In the past, gardeners simply took cuttings, stuck them in a glass of water or in a jar, and kept them on an east-facing windowsill. This has worked well for many plants and many gardeners over the years. Alternatively, however, you can use a purchased rooting hormone. Although it is possible to encourage the growth of roots on new cuttings without it, the application of rooting hormone will improve your chances of success, especially with plants that are more difficult to root, such as those that have woody stems.

Cuttings from large-leaved plants should be cut in half to prevent moisture loss.

If you decide to use some, mix it with water if it requires dilution, and put the solution into a fairly small container, so that you can dip the cut stems easily into either the liquid or powder. Rooting hormone is available in different strengths — those for use with woody plants are generally of greater strength than those needed for herbaceous tropical plants. Some require dilution to achieve the desired strength. After you've used a batch of rooting hormone, it is best to discard it.

After dipping the stem in rooting hormone, stick it into some perlite, where it can remain until it is well rooted. You can use small pots or flats to hold the perlite, depending on the space you have set aside for this project. Tamp down the perlite into the container. Use a pencil or a chopstick to create vertical spaces that are narrower than the diameter of your cuttings before sticking them.

Once you have stuck all the cuttings, water the container well and place it in a warm spot out of direct sunlight. Placing the cuttings on a low-energy heating mat (rubber-coated and specifically designed for propagation) will encourage rooting. Keep the perlite moist; enclosing the plant and its container in a plastic bag will help maintain a high level of humidity. This will decrease the amount of moisture lost through the leaves and stem tissues of the plant while it is busy creating roots. Once the cuttings are stuck, they will grow roots most quickly where conditions are fairly warm. When propagating big-leaved plants, like larger coleus, it may be beneficial to cut the leaves in half. This approach is not necessary for smaller-leaved plants such as rosemary and lavender.

Be patient, and take careful note of the cutting's appearance. Once it has rooted, it will begin to grow more vigorously — an excellent visual clue. After two or three weeks, give the plant a gentle tug to determine whether it has developed roots. Once the roots have developed, pot the cutting in a three-and-a-half- to four-inch container and dispose of the plastic bag. Resist the urge to overpot. A small plant in a large pot will result in soil that stays wet too long. The plant will grow faster and be healthier in a pot that dries out periodically. After root formation, most plants benefit from being moved to a cooler location. Remember not to let them dry out at this vulnerable stage.

LEAF CUTTINGS

Begonias are an excellent example of a plant best propagated by leaf cuttings. Cut a leaf into sections, with the edge of the leaf forming the top of the cutting. The base of the cutting should be longer than the top and include one of the leaf's larger veins. One of the best rooting mediums to use is perlite, because of its excellent capacity for drainage. Using a knife or other slender tool, make a narrow opening in the perlite that corresponds to the length of the cutting's base. Dip the base of the leaf cutting into rooting hormone, then stick it vertically into the perlite. Water well and enclose in a plastic bag. Monitor the humidity — you shouldn't have a great deal of condensation inside the bag, because begonias are prone to rot. Keep cuttings out of direct sunlight; an eastern window is ideal.

Succulent cuttings root in flats of perlite in our nursery's propagation greenhouse.

Many succulents can be propagated from their leaves. With these water-storing plants, it is not necessary to cut a leaf into sections. Simply place the base of the leaf into the perlite. Eucomis is another plant that can be propagated from leaf cuttings. Cut the long, straplike leaves of eucomis into one- or one-and-a-half-inch sections, making sure you keep the basal ends of the cuttings oriented similarly. Slice the perlite with a knife and insert the basal end of each cutting into it.

Water

Because their rate of growth has increased dramatically in the spring, you should expect that your plants will require substantially more water than they did during the winter. Especially on warm, sunny days, they will go through a surprising amount of water. It's still good to let the containers dry out between watering, however.

Do yourself a favor and buy a watering wand for your garden hose. A "water-breaker" that fits on the end of the extension makes it even more useful. This simple gadget is a large nozzle with numerous holes that facilitate the delivery of copious amounts of water to pots without washing away their soil.

Fertilizer

Longer daylight hours will encourage plants to increase their rate of growth, but additional fertility will influence its quality. As the days grow longer, begin adding some nutrients either to the water you give the plant or to the soil in which it is planted.

Fertilizing Tips

* Remember that small amounts applied frequently are more valuable to a plant than large amounts provided less often. You can always adjust the fertilizer dose and add more, if this seems necessary.

* Synthetic fertilizers are a form of salt, and in excess, they will harm the roots of plants. Once a plant has been burned, it will take some time to recover. Keeping records is particularly useful here as you discover what works and what doesn't work in caring for your plants.

* We've found that including a dilute concentration with every watering is an easy way to avoid mistakes.

SOLUBLE FERTILIZER

One of the great conveniences of soluble fertilizers is that they can be used each time you water or at weekly intervals. Follow the recommendations on the package, and keep records of what works well for various plants under specific conditions. The amount you use will depend on the formulation — a higher percentage of N, P, and K (nitrogen, phosphorus, and potassium) will require a smaller amount to be efficacious. For example, 20-20-20 delivers twice as much fertilizer as the same amount of 10-10-10.

If you use a hose for watering, especially when the plants are outdoors, consider investing in one of the readily available devices that inject concentrated fertilizer solution into the hose. The strength of the dosage can be controlled either by the mechanism itself or by the concentration of the fertilizer solution in your bucket. These injection devices range from fairly expensive and complex models to simple siphons that are very affordable. Designed for professional use, the more expensive injection systems do provide greater precision and are adjustable, but their cost is probably prohibitive for most gardeners. The siphon models should be perfectly adequate.

Another piece of equipment that is worth considering when fertilizer is injected into the water supply is a back-flow preventer. In the event that there is a momentary loss of water pressure, this will prevent fertilizer from draining back into the water source.

SLOW-RELEASE FERTILIZER

Many gardeners and professionals prefer slow-release fertilizers, in part because they eliminate the necessity for repeated applications. These fertilizers release to the plant relatively small doses of balanced nutrients through a permeable membrane. Simply sprinkle some on top of the soil; the granules will release small amounts with each watering. Alternatively, incorporate the fertilizer granules into the soil mix when it is first being prepared. Like many other fertilizers, these are available

Slow-release fertilizer is sprinkled directly on top of the soil.

What Does That Yellow Leaf Mean?

THE YELLOWING OF A PLANT'S lower leaves may be a sign that it is not getting sufficient nitrogen. This can be confusing, however, because the same symptoms might be caused by either too much or not enough water. Generally speaking, if overwatering or underwatering is your problem, there should be yellow leaves distributed over an entire plant. This is where there is no substitute for being in tune with your plants — older leaves will also naturally yellow and fall as they age. Particularly when you first move many plants indoors, they are likely to spend some time losing leaves. This is a natural response to both the shock of transition and the ending of the outdoor growing season. Try to resist overwatering when this happens; it may be that all a plant needs is some time to adjust. Reading the responses of plants will become easier the more time you spend with them.

The normally blue-green fronds of *Melianthus major* will naturally turn yellow as they age.

in a variety of concentrations. Once again, follow the directions supplied by the manufacturer. And bear in mind that though the effects of these fertilizers can last for a year, they are temperature dependent — this means that the cooler the ambient temperature, the more slowly nutrients will be released. They are also available in a range of time durations, so some will continue to perform over a longer period than others.

ORGANIC OPTIONS

From a chemical standpoint, the main difference between organic fertilizers and their synthetic counterparts is that the synthetic fertilizer is more readily available to a plant. The immediate availability of synthetic fertilizers is a positive factor, but the downside is that it is much easier to overfeed plants with synthetic fertilizers; and excessive amounts can also be harmful to soil microbes. The N, P, and K of an organic fertilizer are not as readily available to plants, and the concentrations tend to be lower, which means you'll have to apply greater quantities in order to deliver sufficient nutrients to them. But its slower release can be beneficial, both to plants and to soil microbes.

These days, any well-supplied farm and garden center stocks an overwhelming selection of fertilizers. Take time to read the labels, and then keep notes on what works well for you. When they are successful, try to stay with the same formulations and similar products. Remember, too, that not all types of plants require the same level of fertility. Many tropical plants — because they grow quickly, have large leaves, and bear abundant flowers — will need more fertility than those from the Mediterranean region, which have developed characteristics that conserve moisture and nutrients under their native harsh growing conditions.

Pest Issues

Just as the longer days of spring encourage plants to grow, this increase in day length is also an important trigger for insect populations. Be vigilant and carefully monitor insect presence on your plants — catching any infestation early is your best defense. Most insect problems, as long as they are not too severe, will improve automatically when a plant moves outside. Cooler temperatures and the availability of other host species will usually cause a decrease in the population on any one plant. This may constitute a significant enough relief that a plant will be able to rebound and repel further infestations.

If you are fortunate enough to have a greenhouse or a large sunroom dedicated to plants, you may want to consider the use of beneficial insects. This approach is not necessarily an easy one, but it will result in an environment for both you and your plants that is free of toxic chemicals.

Once your plants move outdoors, the world of naturally occurring, beneficial insect parasites and predators will become a factor. If you don't use toxic sprays, your garden should already contain a healthy population of these. Remember that a few aphids here and there is a sign that your insect predators won't go hungry!

Hardening Off

As weather permits, help your plants acclimate to outside conditions gradually. Even if they have spent all winter in a southern window, the much greater amount of sunlight outside will be a severe shock if plants move out all of a sudden. Similarly, after months spent in the shelter of your house, they are unprepared for the buffeting winds and fluctuations of air temperature that are a normal part of any spring day outside. This is why most gardeners engage in a process commonly referred to as hardening off.

Tender 911

ACCIDENTS HAPPEN, and every once in a while, tender plants will be hit by frost. Here are a few tips to help an affected plant recover:

✽ Don't do anything rash. Give a plant time — wait and watch.

✽ Don't overwater. Keep it in the shade. If temperatures remain cool, move it to a warmer location.

✽ After a few days, if the leaves do not recover, trim them off. If the growing points of the plant are damaged, prune back branches or stems to healthy tissue.

✽ Keep the plant in a warm location and water normally (avoiding overwatering) until it begins to put out new growth.

Hardening off usually involves moving a plant, or selectively protecting it from outdoor conditions, in order to prepare it for full-time life outside. It generally takes place over a week or two. Ideally, the weather will be cooperative and give you daytime temperatures above 50°F with relatively little wind. Some rain is fine as long as it's warm and not accompanied by high winds.

The most important thing is not to leave the plants unattended to fend for themselves at night, when the temperatures are much lower. In the evening, either move the plants back under some cover or, if they are too large to move easily, have some substantial covers ready to arrange over them. After three to five days of this process, plants will generally be ready to handle the outdoors on their own. But remain vigilant about the weather — if temperatures dip considerably, you may need to take precautions.

ABOVE Tender plants should be gradually acclimated to outdoor conditions in spring. For the first few days, place them in a sheltered, shaded location during the day, and move them indoors at night.

THE TENDER PALETTE

The first step toward success with tenders is selecting the right plant for the kind of overwintering space you have.

Much of our experience with the storage of tender perennials has taken place inside our nursery's greenhouses, but we've also stored them in our home — both in our living space and in the unfinished basement. We've also learned a tremendous amount about the storage of tender perennials from conversations with our customers, who have devised some ingenious methods for holding on to their favorite plants through the decidedly unfavorable conditions of the average New England winter.

Minimum Hardiness   Common Name   Latin Name   Overwintering Site(s)

Aloysia triphylla

Aloysia triphylla
Lemon verbena
HARDY TO AT LEAST 25°F

Lemon verbena grows into a nine-foot shrub in its native Argentina and Chile. Its distinctive narrow leaves emit a powerful lemon scent and are probably the chief reason this plant is so popular. In comparison, lemon verbena's small white flowers are not especially memorable.

DESIGN IDEAS. We normally grow lemon verbena in a container by itself, but it can also be paired with small summer-flowering bulbs.
OVERWINTERING. Cool and bright, although some gardeners have had luck storing dormant lemon verbena in a dark, cool basement. Prune back to live growth in the spring.
PROPAGATING. Cuttings.
COMMON PEST PROBLEMS. One of the best reasons to let lemon verbena go dormant in winter is to avoid insect infestations — particularly those of spider mites and whiteflies. This is a good example of how dormancy can benefit some plants. When they're hard up, aphids can also become interested in lemon verbena. (See Specific Pests and Diseases, page 64.)

Alternanthera
Alternanthera, Joseph's coat, joyweed
HARDY TO AT LEAST 25°F

Alternanthera is in the same family as amaranth, and its various species originate in Brazil, Argentina, and Mexico. The variety of its highly colored leaves and its tolerance of hot, humid conditions led to the popularity of Joseph's coat in Victorian bedding schemes.

SPECIES AND CULTIVARS. Some cultivars we've enjoyed are *A. bettzichiana* 'True Yellow', with its narrow, curled lemon-yellow leaves, and the contorted, cream-splashed green-leaved *A. ficoidea* 'Snowball'. *A.* 'Red Thread' and 'Brilliantissima' have intriguing linear leaves in a sumptuous shade of burgundy and are vigorous growers, guaranteed in the month of August to outpace any companion you plant it with.
DESIGN IDEAS. We've had a lot of fun arranging alternantheras into paisley and other patterns to create Victorian-inspired "carpets," but they're equally wonderful in containers, where their love of heat inspires them to impressive displays in midsummer. Brian says he's always wanted to carpet his car with them.
OVERWINTERING. Warm and sunny.
PROPAGATING. Cuttings.
COMMON PEST PROBLEMS. None.

Alternanthera bettzichiana 'Brilliantissima'

Sunny & Warm, page 44   Cool & Bright, page 50   Dark & Damp, page 54   Dark & Dry, page 56

How to Use This Guide

OVERWINTERING SITE These icons indicate the best site or method for overwintering each plant. Often, there is more than one way to overwinter a plant. For example, lemon verbena can be overwintered as an actively growing plant or in a dormant state. Many plants suffer less from pests when they're overwintered dormant. For more information, turn to the overwintering section on page 42.

🌿 Sunny & Warm   🌱 Cool & Bright

🌾 Dark & Damp   🌰 Dark & Dry

LATIN NAME A plant's botanical Latin name comprises a genus name (*Abutilon*), a species name (*pictum*), and sometimes a cultivar name ('Thompsonii'). Hardiness varies widely not only within a single genus of plants (some lavenders, for example, are hardy to −10°F, while others are hardy only to 10 or 15°F), but also from one species or cultivar to the next. Also, many plants within a genus — regardless of their individual hardiness minimums — have similar overwintering requirements. Because of this, it's helpful to learn both the botanical Latin and the common name of a plant.

COMMON NAME Some plants have many common names. We've tried to list those that are most widely used. Often, a plant's genus name is also used as a common name; in these cases, the name is not capitalized or italicized (e.g., abutilon).

MINIMUM HARDINESS What we call *hardiness* is affected to a surprising degree by a variety of factors, such as water, fertility, light, and, of course, temperature. Although stated hardiness ranges give us a starting point in estimating a plant's cold hardiness, never underestimate the importance of your specific site and actual conditions to a plant's tenderness or hardiness for you.

Generally speaking, the "hardy to" number here indicates the temperature that would kill this plant after prolonged exposure. But sometimes the exposure need not be very long — the duration necessary to cause death in a plant is highly individual. Often, a higher temperature can still damage the leaves and flower buds of a plant, although the plant itself survives.

SPECIES AND CULTIVARS These are just a few of our favorites. If you have difficulty finding a particular cultivar, try ordering online (see Resources, page 200) or experiment with what's available at your local nursery.

DESIGN IDEAS This section offers just a few planting suggestions and combinations we've tried over the years. We encourage you to experiment with putting plants together!

OVERWINTERING These notes are intended to give you an overview of how to overwinter a particular plant, and to refer back to the techniques mentioned in Overwintering 101 on page 42. We've also noted certain cases in which special care is needed to successfully overwinter a plant.

PROPAGATING Although plants often can be started from seed, many of them require special techniques to induce germination. Because we expect that most people will be propagating by taking cuttings (either to make more plants, or simply to overwinter a plant) we've included extensive information in Propagation 101: Taking Cuttings on page 73.

COMMON PEST PROBLEMS Whenever we've had problems with a particular pest we've noted it here. For solutions to pest problems you might encounter, turn to page 64.

Quick Tips for Overwintering

EVERY GARDENER faces somewhat different growing and storage conditions. Your own conditions are a unique combination of light, temperature extremes, and the type of potting mix you've used. Because of this, it's difficult to give general instructions that apply to everyone in every situation. We firmly believe that a gardener can learn much of what he or she needs to know about how to care for a plant simply by observation. To avoid problems, we recommend that you check on your plant frequently throughout the winter, even if it's tucked away in the basement or an unused part of the house.

TO PRUNE OR NOT TO PRUNE. This is a question that continues to perplex gardeners of every stripe. Throughout this section of the book, we've indicated when a plant can be cut back hard, either before it's been brought indoors or during the winter. Except for a few exceptions (see page 53), most plants will tolerate being cut back. Plants that grow very quickly can be cut back drastically.

WATERING THROUGH THE WINTER. A plant's water requirements are affected by its age, size, and whether or not it's actively growing. When plants grow outside, the humidity, light, and temperature all affect how much water a plant uses — these conditions determine how much moisture evaporates before it reaches the plant's roots. When a plant is grown indoors, the amount of water it needs to receive is dependent on these same conditions. Whether you keep your living space very warm, heat with a woodstove (which dries out the air), or live in a house that's built into a hillside makes a difference in your indoor ambient humidity and thus affects how often you need to water your plants while they're sharing your home. Developing a sense of how to give plants what they need is going to keep you in much better stead than if you were following the arbitrary directions of someone who isn't familiar with your surroundings.

Inserting your finger into the soil to test for moisture — or the lack of it — is a perfectly good way to assess whether a plant needs to be watered. You can often gauge dryness just by looking at the color of the soil at the top of the pot. If you study your plants, you'll also observe subtle changes in leaf color when they become dry. You'll also notice when they begin to wilt. Slight wilting is not necessarily a bad thing. It is far better for the plant than keeping the soil saturated with water — the resulting lack of air space in the soil may lead to disease.

FEED ME? In general, fertilizing plants is appropriate when they are in a period of vigorous growth, and most plants that are being overwintered indoors should need little or no fertilizing through the winter. No matter what kind of fertilizer you use, when you pot up a plant, you may find it helpful to label the plant with information about when it was potted, what amendments you added, and whether you incorporated a slow-release fertilizer.

Abutilon
Flowering maple, parlor maple
HARDY TO AT LEAST 35°F

With leaves shaped like those of maple trees and flowers that resemble dangling miniature hibiscus, abutilons are engaging plants that earn their keep indoors; in a cool, sunny spot, they will bloom most of the year. Popular as parlor plants during the Victorian era, they were collected and developed in a dazzling array of foliage and flower types. The genus comprises shrubby annuals, perennials, and trees. Abutilons are native to Central and South America.

SPECIES AND CULTIVARS. For their foliage alone, *Abutilon* 'Savitzii' and *A. pictum* 'Thompsonii' are both outstanding. With coral and yellow petals encased in deep plum calyces, 'Vesuvius' boasts the most dramatic flowers, and the soft peach and coral flowers of *A. megapotamicum* 'Kentish Belle' are among the loveliest.

DESIGN IDEAS. Upright abutilons are useful at the back of containers, especially large ones. Trailing types, like 'Aurora' and 'Lemon Drops', work well in hanging baskets.

OVERWINTERING. Cool, sunny window. Abutilons bloom profusely in winter and should be fertilized lightly. They can get scraggly, especially in less than full-sun conditions, so don't hesitate to prune leggy branches back hard.

PROPAGATING. Cuttings can be taken at most times of the year.

COMMON PEST PROBLEMS. Aphids are fond of abutilons. (See Specific Pests and Diseases, page 64.)

Abutilon 'Savitzii'

Acaena
New Zealand bur
HARDY TO AT LEAST 5°F

This low-growing, trailing, shrubby plant is particularly useful in containers, where its drought tolerance is a plus. Acaenas are native to the southern hemisphere, primarily New Zealand.

SPECIES AND CULTIVARS. *Acaena* 'Blue Haze', with its finely cut leaves the color of oxidized copper, makes an especially fine addition to gardens and containers.

DESIGN IDEAS. The textures and colors of acaena foliage make it a great plant to use in mixed containers for contrast. It is compatible with succulents; try *A.* 'Blue Haze' with *Echeveria* 'Blue Curls'.

OVERWINTERING. Cool with bright light; allow plant to dry out between waterings. These low-growing plants will never require a hair cut.

PROPAGATING. Cuttings in midwinter.

COMMON PEST PROBLEMS. None.

Acaena 'Blue Haze'

Acalypha wilkesiana

Acalypha
Jacob's coat 🖾

HARDY TO AT LEAST 45°F

This colorful species can attain shrub size in its tropical home, but the smaller selections we tend to grow in this hemisphere channel that vigor into an exuberant production of foliage. Members of the spurge family (Euphorbiaceae), acalyphas thrive in hot, humid conditions, and provide handsome tall accents in mixed containers. Native to Fiji, they were introduced to European gardeners in the 1870s.

SPECIES AND CULTIVARS. *Acalypha wilkesiana* 'Macrophylla' was first introduced in 1876. With large russet leaves glazed in shimmering bronze and copper, it makes an impressive focal point.
DESIGN IDEAS. Larger-leaved types contrast nicely with plants that have strongly colored flowers. Try *Acalypha wilkesiana* 'Macrophylla' with *Salvia discolor.*
OVERWINTERING. Warm and sunny. Acalyphas are slow-growing, so prune gently if you want to shape your plant.
PROPAGATING. Cuttings should be taken during periods of active growth but before the plant blooms.
COMMON PEST PROBLEMS. None.

Adromischus
Adromischus 🖾

HARDY TO AT LEAST 35°F

This South African genus belongs to the crassula family (Crassulaceae). The succulent leaves of many adromischus have a curious pinched appearance, and are generally arranged in loose clusters. They are extraordinarily undemanding as houseplants.

SPECIES AND CULTIVARS. *Adromischus cooperi* has plump, tubular leaves that are spotted. *A. cristatus,* also known as crinkle-leaf plant, has grayish leaves spotted with purple.
DESIGN IDEAS. Most succulents are best combined with plants that have the same requirements. Look for similarities or differences among the plants to make for a visually interesting combination, and keep their eventual size in mind.
OVERWINTERING. Warm and sunny; at room temperature in your living space is fine.
PROPAGATING. Leaf cuttings can be rooted at any time.
COMMON PEST PROBLEMS. None.

Adromischus cristatus

Aeonium
Aeonium 🜂

HARDY TO AT LEAST 35°F

Nearly all species of this distinctive succulent originate in the Canary Islands, although a few come from Madeira, Yemen, and North Africa. Some of the Canary Islanders are found on only one island. They tend to grow on cliffs and prefer dry conditions, in either full sun or partial shade. Most have yellow flowers.

SPECIES AND CULTIVARS. *Aeonium arboreum* 'Zwartkop', with its shiny black to crimson rosettes, is a particularly dramatic cultivar of a species that grows on cliffs and rocks on the coast of Gran Canaria. *A. tabuliforme* is low-growing, and forms particularly flat rosettes on shady cliffs along the north coast of Tenerife. The monocarpic, green rosette of *A. urbicum* situates itself on rocks, mountain ridges, and old roofs in Tenerife, and has pink to white flowers. Most species bloom spring to summer. Because aeoniums are relatively slow growing, only prune lightly to shape.

DESIGN IDEAS. Although there is no reason that you couldn't combine aeoniums with other succulents, they're just so visually entertaining on their own that we've never been tempted to. Try underplanting *A.* 'Zwartkop' with *Leptinella* 'Platt's Black' for a particularly dramatic combination.

OVERWINTERING. Cool and bright. Water sparingly.

PROPAGATING. Cuttings should be made in midwinter to early spring.

COMMON PEST PROBLEMS. None.

Aeonium arboreum 'Zwartkop'

Agapanthus africanus
Lily of the Nile 🜂

HARDY TO AT LEAST 25°F

This South African plant is surprisingly well adapted to our seasons when grown in a pot. The large, starry blue or white umbel-shaped flowers make this popular as both an indoor and outdoor plant.

SPECIES AND CULTIVARS. 'Elaine' has buds of deep ultramarine that open to eight-inch umbels of the richest cobalt blue we have yet to see in the genus. 'Lilliput' is a charming dwarf form with smaller, deep blue umbels held on 15-inch stems above grassy mounds of foliage. Cut back flower stems when bloom is over, and remove unsightly older leaves as necessary.

DESIGN IDEAS. Agapanthus is best grown one to a container, because it will become remarkably pot-bound in time — that

Agapanthus africanus

is, by the time it blooms. This raises an important consideration in choosing containers; the process of eventually dislodging this particular plant from its container in order to divide or repot it can be injurious to the pot. Try to use something inexpensive.

OVERWINTERING. Cool, with bright light. The cooler the conditions, the later agapanthus will bloom. When stored at 40°F, in Zone 5 it is possible to delay bloom until June or July.

PROPAGATING. Division. This method requires considerable exertion, but is also a necessity as the plant matures. Agapanthus does have a preference for being pot-bound — tight confines encourage it to bloom. You can also grow it from seed, but this will be a much lengthier process.

COMMON PEST PROBLEMS. Scale. (See Specific Pests and Diseases, page 64.)

Agastache 'Summer Breeze'

Agastache
Giant hyssop ⬛

HARDINESS VARIES; THOSE LISTED BELOW ARE HARDY TO AT LEAST 5°F

Aromatic members of the mint family, these are remarkably long-blooming, and their small, colorful flowers are attractive to bees and butterflies. There is considerable variation in hardiness within the genus — a few species are hardy in Zone 5, but most are not. What they all share is extraordinary drought tolerance. Agastaches are native to the southwestern United States and Mexico.

SPECIES AND CULTIVARS. 'Summer Breeze' is a particularly fine selection, with flowers in a shimmering combination of tangerine, coral, and orchid shades; these all contrast nicely with the gray-green foliage. 'Tangerine Dreams' is a Ginny Hunt selection, with flowers of a sensational orange Creamsicle shade on a plant with a tall, upright habit.

DESIGN IDEAS. Combine the flower colors of an agastache like 'Summer Breeze' with related shades like those in the foliage of 'Kingwood Critter' coleus (*Solenostemon*).

OVERWINTERING. Cool, with bright light. Good air circulation is key to successful storage. Prune the plant back hard initially for winter storage. If conditions are sufficiently cool, it will remain a rosette. If not, prune when the plant becomes too large for your space.

PROPAGATING. Many agastache varieties do come fairly true from seed and are quick to grow on from the seedling stage. But to duplicate the characteristics of any given plant, it is best to take cuttings. If taken early in the spring, when the young shoots are between two and three inches long, agastache cuttings root very easily.

COMMON PEST PROBLEMS. Aphids, mildew. (See Specific Pests and Diseases, page 64.)

Agave
Century plant 🌿 🌱

HARDINESS VARIES; THOSE LISTED BELOW ARE HARDY TO AT LEAST 25°F

Native to Mexico and the southwestern United States, agaves make us think of the desert. Magnificent container subjects in any climate, they are, naturally enough, happiest in dry conditions. Because the sharp tips of their leaf extremities can cause considerable discomfort upon contact, give careful thought to your agave's position in the landscape.

SPECIES AND CULTIVARS. *Agave americana* 'Mediopicta Alba' forms a handsome, large rosette of blue-green leaves, each leaf striped by a central wide cream band. *A. schidigera* is a distinctive Mexican species with upwardly cupped, deep green leaves rimmed in white and tufted with threadlike tassels. Its leaves end in especially brutal dark brown tips.

DESIGN IDEAS. We think most agaves are best potted up as single specimens. But young plants of the smaller species could be combined to interesting effect with other succulent plants.

OVERWINTERING. Agaves are equally happy in cool or warm conditions, as long as they receive plenty of light. Some gardeners prune off the sharp tips of certain agave leaves, to make them more companionable housemates.

PROPAGATING. Division of the pups that eventually surround the mother rosette. If your species agave blooms, you can also collect seed, but growing them this way is a slow process.

COMMON PEST PROBLEMS. Occasionally, scale can pose a problem indoors, especially when conditions are very warm. (See Specific Pests and Diseases, page 64.)

Agave americana 'Mediopicta Alba'

Aloe striata

Aloe
Aloe 🌿 🌱

MOST SPECIES HARDY TO AT LEAST 35°F

This large and diverse genus of succulent plants includes members that come from all regions of Africa, as well as from Madagascar and the Cape Verde Islands. Many of these are treelike or shrublike in form, and nearly all have showy and colorful flowers when they bloom. Adapted in their native habitats to periods of extended drought, they make undemanding container subjects — although it is humbling to see what they are capable of when established under hospitable conditions in the ground.

Aloe ferox

SPECIES AND CULTIVARS. *Aloe ferox* is a handsome, stout, and shrubby plant with glaucous leaves jaggedly edged by spots of orange and vermillion. When in bloom, it produces a large candelabra of bright scarlet flowers. *A. harlana* has very smooth and shiny, red-toothed leaves intricately spotted and streaked by white. *A. striata* forms a stemless rosette of substantial gray leaves. Its pendulous, bright pink flowers hang from multiple branched, three-foot flower stems.

DESIGN IDEAS. We prefer planting aloes as single specimens in containers. But while they are small, you might want to plant them in combination with other succulents, such as tender sedums.

OVERWINTERING. Room temperature and bright light. Cool and bright conditions work well, too.

PROPAGATING. Aloes are easy and quick to grow. Many species do not *reproduce* particularly quickly, however. Be patient and eventually you'll have offsets you can divide.

COMMON PEST PROBLEMS. None.

Alonsoa
Mask flower

HARDY TO AT LEAST 45°F

Related to *Antirrhinum, Nemesia,* and *Diascia,* the charm of *Alonsoa,* with its delicately cupped florets, is similar to that of its cousins. Most species originate in the region that ranges from Mexico to Peru. It is especially lovely in containers, and is also useful as a cut flower. Given favorable conditions, mask flowers seem to bloom continuously.

SPECIES AND CULTIVARS. *Alonsoa meridionalis* is a very floriferous species with delicate, rosy salmon flowers. We've also enjoyed the cinnabar-red blooms of *A. warscewiczii.*

DESIGN IDEAS. Alonsoa's trailing ways make it a natural choice for weaving around other plants in containers. It is lovely in combination with plants that have strong blue or purple flowers, such as *Salvia cacaliifolia.* Or combine it with *Angelonia* 'Blue Horizon', which has a flower form that echoes the cupped petals of the alonsoa.

OVERWINTERING. Cool and bright. This rangey grower benefits from frequent and fairly hard pruning.

PROPAGATING. Both cuttings and seeds. Cuttings are best taken in late winter.

COMMON PEST PROBLEMS. None.

Alonsoa meridionalis 'Shell Pink'

Aloysia triphylla
Lemon verbena

HARDY TO AT LEAST 25°F

Lemon verbena grows into a nine-foot shrub in its native Argentina and Chile. Its distinctive narrow leaves emit a powerful lemon scent and are probably the chief reason this plant is so popular. In comparison, lemon verbena's small white flowers are not especially memorable.

DESIGN IDEAS. We normally grow lemon verbena in a container by itself, but it can also be paired with small summer-flowering bulbs.
OVERWINTERING. Cool and bright, although some gardeners have had luck storing dormant lemon verbena in a dark, cool basement. Prune back to live growth in the spring.
PROPAGATING. Cuttings.
COMMON PEST PROBLEMS. One of the best reasons to let lemon verbena go dormant in winter is to avoid insect infestations — particularly those of spider mites and whiteflies. This is a good example of how dormancy can benefit some plants. When they're hard up, aphids can also become interested in lemon verbena. (See Specific Pests and Diseases, page 64.)

Aloysia triphylla

Alternanthera
Alternanthera, Joseph's coat, joyweed

HARDY TO AT LEAST 25°F

Alternanthera is in the same family as amaranth, and its various species originate in Brazil, Argentina, and Mexico. The variety of its highly colored leaves and its tolerance of hot, humid conditions led to the popularity of Joseph's coat in Victorian bedding schemes.

SPECIES AND CULTIVARS. Some cultivars we've enjoyed are *A. bettzichiana* 'True Yellow', with its narrow, curled lemon-yellow leaves, and the contorted, cream-splashed green-leaved *A. ficoidea* 'Snowball'. *A.* 'Red Thread' and 'Brilliantissima' have intriguing linear leaves in a sumptuous shade of burgundy and are vigorous growers, guaranteed in the month of August to outpace any companion you plant it with.
DESIGN IDEAS. We've had a lot of fun arranging alternantheras into paisley and other patterns to create Victorian-inspired "carpets," but they're equally wonderful in containers, where their love of heat inspires them to impressive displays in midsummer. Brian says he's always wanted to carpet his car with them.
OVERWINTERING. Warm and sunny.
PROPAGATING. Cuttings.
COMMON PEST PROBLEMS. None.

Alternanthera bettzichiana 'Brilliantissima'

Alyogyne
Lilac hibiscus ❄

HARDY TO AT LEAST 45°F

This relatively small genus consists of four shrubs, all originating in Australia. Although there is some variation in their leaves, the flowers of *Alyogyne* species bear the distinctive form of their malvaceous identity, forming a toothed cup, and range in color from pale yellow to mauve or deep purple. They bloom in late winter through spring.

SPECIES AND CULTIVARS. *Alyogyne hakeifolia* is a lax shrub and has distinctive, almost threadlike leaves. In order to open, the rarely pale yellow, mostly mauve flowers require very hot sun. *A. huegelii* 'Mood Indigo' has dramatic flowers of lovely deep purple (not indigo) and forms an open, shrubby plant with rough, deeply lobed leaves.
OVERWINTERING. Cool and bright. Alyogynes are quite happy in a winter greenhouse.
PROPAGATING. Cuttings.
COMMON PEST PROBLEMS. Aphids can be a problem indoors. (See Specific Pests and Diseases, page 64.)

Alyogyne hakeifolia

× *Amarcrinum* 'Pauline Oliver'

× *Amarcrinum*
× Amarcrinum ❄

HARDY TO AT LEAST 25°F

Resulting from an intergeneric cross between the amaryllis of South Africa and the pan-tropical crinum (sometimes also called ×*Crinadonna*), this interesting, tender bulbous plant has proved easy to grow in a large pot. It inherits the long-necked habit of crinum and has a flower shaped much like that of the standard amaryllis, although these upturned trumpets are bright pink and filled with a sweet perfume. It blooms from August until frost.

DESIGN IDEAS. ×*Amarcrinum* is best in a container by itself.
OVERWINTERING. Cool and bright.
PROPAGATING. Will produce bulblets that are easily separated from the parent plant and potted up.
COMMON PEST PROBLEMS. None.

Amicia zygomeris
Amicia 🌱

HARDY TO AT LEAST 35°F

This shrubby member of the pea family originates in the Andes, and has pleasing gray-green foliage reminiscent of the *Lathyrus* clan. The relatively large — one-and-a-half-inch — bright yellow flowers emerging from plum-colored calyces also remind us of pea flowers. Amicia blooms from summer into autumn.

DESIGN IDEAS. The soft texture and gray color of amicia's foliage make it a valuable addition to perennial borders. Alternatively, plant it in a large pot, where both flower and leaf will complement many other container companions. Try it with *Hibiscus acetabulosa* 'Red Shield' or *Ipomoea batatas* 'Ace of Spades.'
OVERWINTERING. Cool and bright. The loose growing habit of this plant benefits from hard pruning now and then.
PROPAGATING. Seeds, cuttings.
COMMON PEST PROBLEMS. None.

Amicia zygomeris

Amorphophallus
Devil's tongue, voodoo lily 🌑

CORM IS HARDY TO AT LEAST 45°F

Originating in the warmer regions of Southeast Asia, the corms of certain species of this perennial member of the Arum family are considered edible there. This plant provides possibly the most entertainment for your tender perennial buck in shadier parts of the garden.

SPECIES AND CULTIVARS. *Amorphophallus konjac* is unquestionably a dramatic plant, from the moment its spotted, dark purple petiole first appears through the emergence of its eventually malodorous, deep maroon flower spathe (which is pollinated by flies). Bloom time depends on when the corms are planted as well as subsequent growing conditions.
DESIGN IDEAS. We thought it charming in combination with *Aristolochia littoralis,* whose deep brown, veined flowers resemble certain aspects of the female anatomy, but that planting prompted the comment, "And I thought this was a family place!"
OVERWINTERING. Store corms where it is dark and dry, either closeted in their pot or placed in a paper bag. Try not to eat them all — they are edible and quite tasty.
PROPAGATING. Amorphophallus corms will produce numerous offsets. It takes three to four years for offsets to reach blooming size.
COMMON PEST PROBLEMS. None.

Amorphophallus konjac

Anagallis
Pimpernel

HARDY TO AT LEAST 15°F

Members of the primrose family, there are approximately 20 species of anagalis. These cosmopolitan plants grow in many parts of the world.

SPECIES AND CULTIVARS. *Anagallis monelli* 'African Sunset', with flowers of a brilliant shade of cobalt blue, is a plant we never could have enough of when it bloomed at the nursery. The cultivar 'Orange', probably selected from *A. arvensis* (the scarlet pimpernel), is also a noteworthy, highly floriferous plant. Anagalis is a summer bloomer.
DESIGN IDEAS. Anagalis is a good weaver; use it accordingly to soften the edges of containers and to blend together more-upright companions. 'African Sunset' is lovely with *Agastache* 'Tangerine Dreams' or *Angelonia* 'Pink.' The cultivar 'Orange' is stunning with any phormium — try it with 'Atropurpureum' or 'Maori Sunrise.'
OVERWINTERING. Cool and bright. This plant's scraggly habit is much improved by occasional hard pruning.
PROPAGATING. Roots easily from cuttings taken in late winter; also can be grown from seed.
COMMON PEST PROBLEMS. None.

Anagalis monelli

Ananas
Pineapple

HARDY TO AT LEAST 35°F

We don't usually think of the edible pineapple as an ornamental, but it can be an exciting plant off the plantation. All species of *Ananas* are native to South America.

SPECIES AND CULTIVARS. Breeders have focused on producing some gorgeous foliar variations, resulting in the cream-striped leaves of *Ananas* 'Ivory Coast', a variant of the edible pineapple, *Ananas comosus*. Other species are also strikingly beautiful, such as *A. bracteatus* var. *striatus*. Summer fruiting (but only in sufficiently warm and humid conditions), their foliage is a major contribution year-round.
DESIGN IDEAS. These are sizable plants for the most part, but can be combined with other elements in sufficiently large containers. The creamy, multicolored foliage and fruits of 'Ivory Coast' make a thrilling component in pairings with bold and contrasting plants such as *Lantana* 'Orange' and *Tradescantia* 'Purple Queen'.
OVERWINTERING. Warm and sunny with high humidity.
PROPAGATING. Division of pups.
COMMON PEST PROBLEMS. Whitefly and scale. (See Specific Pests and Diseases, page 64.)

Ananas 'Ivory Coast'

Angelonia 'Angelmist'

Angelonia angustifolia
Summer snapdragon 🝙

HARDY TO AT LEAST 35°F

A Mexican native with nonstop spring to fall blooms for sunny gardens and containers, summer snapdragon is remarkably tolerant of both heat and drought.

SPECIES AND CULTIVARS. We have grown a number of angelonia cultivars. *Angelonia* 'Blue Horizon' is the classic selection, and its flowers present a cheery combination of sparkling white and bright purple. One year, we found a white-blooming sport that occurred on one of our blue-flowered plants, and it was by far the most vigorous of the angelonias we grew. 'Angelmist' is another popular cultivar.
DESIGN IDEAS. Angelonia is a superb mid-sized choice for containers in a hot location. Combine *Angelonia* 'White' with *Alonsoa meridionalis* for a refreshing look at the height of summer.
OVERWINTERING. Cool and bright. Cut back hard at end of summer.
PROPAGATING. Cuttings.
COMMON PEST PROBLEMS. None.

Anigozanthos
Kangaroo paw 🝙

HARDY TO AT LEAST 35°F

This is native to western Australia, where it grows in sandy, well-drained locations, and is the floral emblem of that country. Its odd, woolly flowers are arranged in pawlike formations (hence the common name), and are set off by handsome, swordlike, deep green leaves. Nectar-seeking birds are attracted to the summer flowers, which are remarkably long lasting, both in the pot and when cut for arrangements. Some anigozanthos species and cultivars can reach six feet tall.

SPECIES AND CULTIVARS. Most selections of *Anigozanthos* are forms of *A. flavidus,* which has striking chartreuse flowers. 'Burnt Orange' is a particularly choice Ginny Hunt seed strain.
DESIGN IDEAS. We prefer to plant up kangaroo paws individually.
OVERWINTERING. Cool and bright. It is especially important not to overwater these in the winter; water only sparingly. In summer, when they are in active growth, they require much more water.
PROPAGATING. We have usually grown our kangaroo paws from seed, however it is also possible to divide plants with especially desirable characteristics.
COMMON PEST PROBLEMS. In the garden, kangaroo paws attract slugs. Slugs may be discouraged by copper barriers, but the most reliable way to eradicate them is through cultural practices that encourage air circulation and good soil drainage.

Anigozanthus manglesii

Anisodontea × *hypomadara*
African mallow

HARDY TO AT LEAST 35°F

Although its exact parentage is unknown, this hybrid form of the South African genus makes a charming container subject. Perpetually covered with small, rosy pink, mallowlike flowers, it can be grown either as an exuberant bush or trained into an elegant standard. In our experience, African mallows bloom most of the year if they are kept deadheaded.

SPECIES AND CULTIVARS. We've enjoyed growing the straight species for many years, but the new selection 'Elegant Lady', featuring much larger flowers, is worth growing too.
DESIGN IDEAS. African mallow is great in the back of a large container. For contrast, combine it with plants that have large leaves, like 'Inky Pink' coleus or *Acalypha wilkesiana* 'Macrophylla Mahogany'.
OVERWINTERING. Cool and bright conditions should ensure winter bloom. Shearing of the plant, or more fine-tuned deadheading on a regular basis, is also recommended. They respond well to pruning.
PROPAGATING. Cuttings.
COMMON PEST PROBLEMS. Aphids. (See Specific Pests and Diseases, page 64.)

Anisodontea × *hypomadara*

Antirrhinum majus 'Tequila Sunrise'

Antirrhinum
Snapdragon

HARDY TO AT LEAST 15°F

Although commonly regarded as annuals in Zone 5, snapdragons are in fact hardy perennials throughout much of Europe, and can be overwintered. Undemanding through the winter, the resulting substantial plants will be ready to bloom first thing in the spring.

SPECIES AND CULTIVARS. 'Tequila Sunrise' is a dwarf seed strain of *Antirrhinum majus* that we have found particularly useful in containers, with its remarkable heat tolerance and 15-inch stems sporting bright, tropical-looking flowers. The species *A. multiflorum* (sometimes referred to as *A. roseum*) is a splendid plant with rounded, glossy, deep green leaves and soft pink flowers on trailing stems. It is hardy in Zone 6.
DESIGN IDEAS. One particularly successful window box we once planted consisted of 'Tequila Sunrise' fronted with the low-growing, yellow-leafed *Sedum* 'Ogon.'
OVERWINTERING. Cool and bright.
PROPAGATING. *Antirrhinum majus* selections and hybrids grow easily from seed and cuttings. With the species, it is best to take cuttings.
COMMON PEST PROBLEMS. Aphids. (See Specific Pests and Diseases, page 64.)

Arctotis × hybrida
African daisy

HARDY TO AT LEAST 35°F

With their felted silver foliage and brilliantly colored, daisy-type flowers, African daisies do well in sunny containers and borders. They originate in the region that includes both South Africa and Angola.

SPECIES AND CULTIVARS. We have grown a number of the Harlequin hybrids, which are generally named for each flower's color — 'China Rose', 'Flame', and 'Wine', for example. African daisies bloom from late winter through the summer. They all have impressive vigor and heat tolerance.

DESIGN IDEAS. African daisies are well suited to the edge of a container and the front of the border. Their showy flowers and elegant foliage combine nicely with artemesias and phormiums.

OVERWINTERING. Cool and bright.

PROPAGATING. Cuttings.

COMMON PEST PROBLEMS. Aphids. (See Specific Pests and Diseases, page 64.)

Arctotis × hybrida 'Flame'

Argyranthemum
Marguerite, Paris daisy

HARDY TO AT LEAST 35°F

Many present-day cultivars are descendants of *Argyranthemum frutescens* (formerly *Chrysanthemum frutescens*), a native of the Canary Islands. They have the advantage of being winter bloomers, as well as durable and handsome container subjects. Marguerites are frequently trained into standards.

Argyranthemum frutescens

SPECIES AND CULTIVARS. 'Starlight', with its elegant lemon and white flowers, and 'Butterfly', a consistent performer with lovely yellow daisies, are valuable plants in containers.

DESIGN IDEAS. Marguerites lend themselves to all kinds of pretty combinations. Combine the white-flowered forms with carpeting plants like *Alternanthera ficoidea* 'Filigran'; try planting 'Butterfly' with *Stenotaphrum secundatum* 'Variegatum' or *Alternanthera* 'Gold Thread'.

OVERWINTERING. Cool and bright. Cut back in late fall to promote winter bloom.

PROPAGATING. Cuttings.

COMMON PEST PROBLEMS. Aphids. (See Specific Pests and Diseases, page 64.)

Aristolochia
Dutchman's pipe

HARDINESS VARIES, BUT THOSE LISTED BELOW ARE HARDY TO AT LEAST 30°F

This large group includes shrubs and woody vines that occur in diverse parts of the world. Nearly all have curiously shaped and colored flowers, many of which have an unpleasant odor. Some of the most interesting tender species originate in South America. Most species are summer blooming and prefer partial shade.

SPECIES AND CULTIVARS. *Aristolochia gigantea* is a Brazilian species with large, heart-shaped leaves and dramatic, six-inch maroon flowers that are veined with cream. *A. brasiliensis* has even larger blossoms — 10 inches across — which are mottled in cream and an earthy shade of red. The center of each fragrant flower is outlined with black and has a yellow center. *A. grandiflora,* the "pelican flower," is a Central American species with eight-inch-wide flowers of deep maroon/black and cream. Inflated pouches form the center of each flower, and the pouches themselves boast a red center as well. These extraordinary flowers also trail distinctive foot-long streamers.

DESIGN IDEAS. Aristolochias are so dramatic in their appearance that it is best to pot them up by themselves.

OVERWINTERING. Warm, moist, and light (not quite bright). Best above 60°F. Prune back to increase the plant's manageability before moving it indoors.

PROPAGATING. Cuttings.

COMMON PEST PROBLEMS. None.

Aristolochia gigantea

Artemisia 'Powis Castle'

Artemisia
Artemisia, wormwood

HARDY TO AT LEAST 0°F

Although many artemisias are perfectly hardy in Zone 5, we have grown a few that weren't. Their fine qualities justify consideration as tender perennials.

SPECIES AND CULTIVARS. *Artemisia* 'Powis Castle', with its finely cut silver foliage, is such an attractive plant that for years we've kept a stock plant in the greenhouse. It quickly assumes it's full 30- by 48-inch stature when planted outdoors. Frequent pruning promotes the most attractive growth, and can be used to shape the plant.

DESIGN IDEAS. You really can't go wrong with silver. Mix artemisias with pastel-colored flowers, like those of anisodontea or diascia. Combine with plants that have dark-colored foliage, like *Ricinus communis* 'Pasadena Red'; another great combination is wormwood's silver leaves with flowers that are in the electrically hot range of color, such as *Dahlia* 'Bednall Beauty' or *Salvia involucrata* 'Mulberry Jam'.

OVERWINTERING. Cool and bright. Drought tolerant, artemisias require a minimum of moisture.

PROPAGATING. Cuttings.

COMMON PEST PROBLEMS. Aphids. (See Specific Pests and Diseases, page 64.)

Arundo donax
Giant reed

HARDY TO AT LEAST 15°F

These tropical and subtropical grasses are big ones. Because of their rhizomatous habit, perhaps we should be grateful that they do not survive more northern winters out of doors.

SPECIES AND CULTIVARS. The green-leaved *Arundo donax* makes quite a statement with its two-foot leaves and 18-foot height. We are particularly fond of the nine-foot *A. d.* 'Variegata', whose massive, white-striped leaves have provided a dramatic backdrop for many combinations of plants in our display gardens. *A. d.* 'Macrophylla' has mauve-tinted stems, and *A. d.* var. *versicolor* boasts glaucous leaves that are larger than those of the species, measuring close to four feet in length.

DESIGN IDEAS. In the garden, giant reed is a stellar choice for large spaces, especially where a divider or high wall would be welcome. Our favorite planting is at the Rhode Island garden Green Animals, where a splendid clump of plain green arundo survives the winter outdoors, making a memorable backdrop for a much smaller wooden bench. *Arundo donax* is generally too large in scale for containers, but other species of this grass are suitable to be grown in pots.

OVERWINTERING. Cool and bright. You definitely want to keep these dormant until the weather is relatively warm. Cut back plants to eight-inch stumps before bringing them in for the winter.

PROPAGATING. Division; propagate species from seed.

COMMON PEST PROBLEMS. None.

Arundo donax 'Variegata'

Asclepias
Butterfly weed

HARDINESS VARIES; THOSE LISTED BELOW ARE HARDY TO AT LEAST 20°F

Some butterfly weeds are perfectly hardy — *Asclepias incarnata* and *A. tuberosa,* both grown as hardy perennials in Zone 5, are actually fine up to Zone 3. But we have also found some of the more tender species to be valuable in both containers and the garden. Asclepias seem to attract numerous dedicated butterfly pollinators.

SPECIES AND CULTIVARS. *Asclepias curassavica,* also known as blood flower, is a South American species with deep maroon flower clusters that add a dramatic note to the lepidopterous landscape. It is a favored food plant for monarch butterflies, as is the African *A. fruticosa,* which is perhaps most notable for its curious spiny, inflated four-inch silver-green seedpods. One of our favorites, *A. perennis,* has delicate ruby-colored stems with soft pink buds that open continually to creamy flower clusters. Most asclepias bloom in midsummer.

DESIGN IDEAS. Because they're so drought tolerant and tough, asclepias are tremendously useful for mixed containers. *Asclepias perennis* is particularly lovely in combination with the glaucous foliage of *Canna iridiflora* or the dark leaves of *Colocasia* 'Black Magic'.

OVERWINTERING. Cool and bright. Prune hard before moving indoors.

PROPAGATING. Cuttings. If plants set seed in the previous season, however, this is also a good way to grow more of them.

COMMON PEST PROBLEMS. Watch out for brightly colored aphids in the garden! Fortunately, their appearance is generally late in the summer, and they do not pose a serious threat.

Asclepias perennis

Astelia chathamica

Astelia chathamica
Astelia

HARDY TO AT LEAST 25°F

New Zealand natives, these sedgelike plants are members of the lily family. They prefer wet, peaty soils.

SPECIES AND CULTIVARS. 'Silver Spear' has handsome silver leaves but insignificant, pale green flowers. It tolerates partial shade.

DESIGN IDEAS. We have enjoyed 'Silver Spear' in containers, where its swordlike leaves create fine contrast against darker leaves such as those of 'Arabian Knights' coleus and *Ophiopogon planiscapus* 'Nigrescens'. In the garden, astelia makes an excellent companion for *Setaria palmifolia* and the darker-leaved begonias.

OVERWINTERING. Cool and bright.

PROPAGATING. Division.

COMMON PEST PROBLEMS. None.

Azorina vidalii
Azorina

HARDY TO AT LEAST 35°F

Also known as *Campanula vidalii,* this dwarf evergreen shrub is at home on the sea cliffs of the Azores, predisposing it to a preference for excellent drainage. When growing there, or anywhere outdoors, the bell-shaped flowers bloom pink, but when grown indoors, they are white. The plants bloom late winter through early summer.

DESIGN IDEAS. We like to grow this as a specimen in its own pot.
OVERWINTERING. Cool and bright; do not overwater. Azorinas dislike humid conditions.
PROPAGATING. Seed.
COMMON PEST PROBLEMS. None.

Azorina vidalii

Ballota pseudodictamnus

Ballota
Ballota

HARDY TO AT LEAST 25°F

Shrubby, drought-tolerant Mediterranean plants, these make good container specimens in non-Mediterranean climates, too; each provides a unique and distinctive textural interest.

SPECIES AND CULTIVARS. *Ballota pseudodictamnus* has outstanding woolly rounded leaves of silver-green with small greenish white flowers. 'All Hallows Green' is a handsome, finely textured plant with gray-green leaves.
DESIGN IDEAS. Plants with foliage this attractive are always useful, especially in the shades these come in, like pale chartreuse and gray. Combine *Ballota pseudodictamnus* with the bright pink flowers of *Pelargonium ionidiflorum.* Also try B. 'All Hallows Green' with *Anagallis monelli* 'African Sunset'. Most unlike the others is *B. nigra* 'Variegata', which has thin green leaves splashed with cream, making an attractive foil for partners with darkly colored flowers or leaves, such as those of *Alternanthera* 'Purple Knight'.
OVERWINTERING. Cool and bright.
PROPAGATING. Cuttings.
COMMON PEST PROBLEMS. None.

Begonia 'Caravan'

Begonia 'Marmaduke'

Begonia
Begonia

HARDY TO AT LEAST 45°F

An outstanding group of plants for growing in containers as well as in the garden, begonias originate in tropical and subtropical regions of the Americas. Many make excellent houseplants, even for those who normally eschew indoor gardening.

SPECIES AND CULTIVARS. Fibrous and rhizomatous begonias have the reputation for being the easiest types to grow, although we have also found many species begonias to be quite durable and rewarding. It's difficult for us to list just a few. 'Selph's Mahogany' has splendid, big russet and olive leaves. The Logee's introduction 'Northern Lights' has substantial, swirled apple green leaves veined in rust. *Begonia acetosa*, a Brazilian species, boasts hairy copper/green leaves with wine reverse and contrasting white flowers.

DESIGN IDEAS. Although there is really no reason that you can't use them in combinations, we tend to prefer begonias planted by themselves. If you do plant these with companions, just make sure to choose other shade-loving plants that can also tolerate the well-drained conditions most begonias like. It is a good idea to prune back begonia stems when they become scraggly and have sparse leaves. At most times of year, this will result in a flourish of new growth.

OVERWINTERING. Either cool and bright or warm and sunny; begonias are an adaptable group of plants.

PROPAGATING. Leaf or stem cuttings.

COMMON PEST PROBLEMS. None.

Bessera elegans
Bessera, coral drops

HARDY TO AT LEAST 35°F

A member of the lily family, bessera is native to southern Mexico. The performance of these little corms has enchanted the many visitors who have seen them in our August garden. In what seems like no time at all, they proceed from bare pot to tidy tufts of grasslike foliage, and then to splendid nodding umbels of coral-scarlet, a supreme late-summer treat.

DESIGN IDEAS. Coral drops are best planted in containers by themselves, but can be delightful planted into the ground in a rock garden setting, where they will enjoy the well-drained, sunny conditons.

OVERWINTERING. Either in the pot and placed in a dark place or simply inside a paper bag.

PROPAGATING. From the many cormlets the mother plant produces.

COMMON PEST PROBLEMS. None.

Bessera elegans

Billardiera longiflora

Billardiera longiflora
Billardiera 🪴

HARDY TO AT LEAST 25°F

In its Tasmanian home, billardiera climbs delicately in damp forests and near running water, its twisting stems clothed in leathery, linear, deep green leaves. Appearing in late summer through fall, the waxy, cream to greenish yellow tubular flowers are purple tipped and become oval, grape-sized purple fruit that are quite lovely.

DESIGN IDEAS. This is an ideal candidate for narrow spaces with height; try trellising billardiera in the back of a fairly narrow container with *Ipomoea batatas* 'Blackie' in the foreground.
OVERWINTERING. Cool and bright. Prune to make the plant more manageable before moving it indoors.
PROPAGATING. Cuttings.
COMMON PEST PROBLEMS. None.

Bouvardia
Bouvardia 🪴

HARDY TO AT LEAST 35°F

Although they are hardy shrubs in the warmer regions of North and South America, to which they are native, bouvardia are more frequently seen in florists' buckets than they are in gardens farther north. Their showy flowers are just as wonderful an addition to gardens and conservatories as they are to bouquets.

SPECIES AND CULTIVARS. *Bouvardia ternifolia,* has handsome dark green foliage and continuous bright orange-red flowers, and *B. longiflora* has tubular white flowers that emit an intoxicating sweet scent reminiscent of jasmine or citrus. Some bouvardias are fall or winter bloomers, although this can depend on their storage and growing conditions. *B. terniflora* and *B. longiflora,* however, bloom through the summer, making them the most useful species for gardeners.
DESIGN IDEAS. As it grows, bouvardia has a tendency to become leggy at its base (ruthless hard pruning when the plant is young will encourage the most desirable habit). You may want to situate something trailing, but fairly substantial, like *Helichrysum petiolare,* there. Depending on the shape of your plant, other silver trailers will work equally well.
OVERWINTERING. Cool and bright.
PROPAGATING. Root cuttings.
COMMON PEST PROBLEMS. None.

Bouvardia terniflora

Brachyglottis monroi

Brachyglottis
Brachyglottis

HARDY TO AT LEAST 25°F

This fairly sizable group of plants indigenous to New Zealand includes shrubs, vines, and herbaceous perennials. Most have daisylike flowers in late summer. Brachyglottis likes full sun and good air circulation, but otherwise is not fussy.

SPECIES AND CULTIVARS. *Brachyglottis monroi* has felty, oval-shaped silver leaves, making it valuable both in the garden and for outdoor containers — as well as quite handsome when it's moved inside for the winter. Occasional light pruning will keep this plant attractive.
DESIGN IDEAS. The foliage color and form of *Brachyglottis monroi* make it highly useful in combinations. Try it with the dark leaves of *Phormium tenax* 'Atropurpureum' or *Eucomis* 'Sparkling Burgundy.'
OVERWINTERING. Cool and bright.
PROPAGATING. Cuttings.
COMMON PEST PROBLEMS. None.

Brugmansia
Angel's trumpet, brugmansia

HARDY TO AT LEAST 35°F

Forming small trees or shrubs in their native South America, brugmansias are certainly the flashiest members of the nightshade family (Solanaceae). Grown in containers as tender perennials farther north, their buds may not unfurl until late summer, but from then until heavy frost, their intoxicating perfume will fill the air.

SPECIES AND CULTIVARS. The classic cultivar 'Charles Grimaldi' bears a profusion of extremely fragrant salmon flowers. 'Peaches and Cream' is a Logee's introduction that juxtaposes large, fragrant, soft tangerine bells against elegant cream variegated gray-green foliage. The pale peach— to yellow-flowered 'Inca Sun' is a recent hybrid from Iowa that blooms much more continuously than previous selections. 'Cypress Gardens' begins blooming at a young age, with an abundance of pendulous white night-fragrant flowers that fade with age to pale salmon.
DESIGN IDEAS. Brugmansias are such large plants that the only combination you might be tempted to try is carpeting the pot surface beneath the plant. In this case, you will probably want to consider the flower color before making a choice. Low-growing sedums, dichondra, trailing begonias like *B. fagifolia* and *B. glabra,* and even some fuchsias, like *F. procumbens* 'Variegata', are all possibilities.

Brugmansia cultivar

OVERWINTERING. Brugmansias should be stored in their pots for the winter in cool and bright conditions. Prune to maintain a manageable plant.
PROPAGATING. Cuttings taken before flower-bud initiation.
COMMON PEST PROBLEMS. Whitefly. (See Specific Pests and Diseases, page 64.)

Buddleia marrubifolia

Buddleia
Buddleia, butterfly bush 🍂

HARDINESS VARIES; THOSE LISTED BELOW ARE HARDY TO AT LEAST 15°F

Although selections of *Buddleia davidii* can be hardy in Zone 5, few other species are. We have never allowed this to limit our selection of buddleias, however. They make fine additions to both the indoor and outdoor landscape, and butterflies don't seem to discriminate on the basis of hardiness.

SPECIES AND CULTIVARS. *Buddleia fallowiana* var. *alba,* from Burma, has densely felted leaves and fragrant white flowers with orange eyes; *B. marrubifolia* has woolly silver foliage with brilliantly colored balls of orange florets.
DESIGN IDEAS. We like to plant this as a specimen in its own container.
OVERWINTERING. Cool and bright conditions will keep most buddleias blooming all winter long. Prune as desired to shape.
PROPAGATING. Cuttings.
COMMON PEST PROBLEMS. None.

Calocephalus brownii
Calocephalus, cushion bush 🍂

HARDY TO AT LEAST 35°F

This intriguing plant grows into a small shrub in its Australian home. Forming an intricate structure of fine silver twigs, it inspires curiosity as well as admiration.

DESIGN IDEAS. Silver is endlessly useful in containers, and this plant's unique texture makes it even more so. Possible combinations abound — for maximum contrast, try it with *Euphorbia fulgens* 'Purple Selection' or *Carex comans*. Planting it with *Acaena* 'Blue Haze' and *Echeveria* 'Topsy Turvy' results in an outstanding monochromatic composition.
OVERWINTERING. Cool and bright.
PROPAGATING. Cuttings.
COMMON PEST PROBLEMS. None.

Calocephalus brownii

Canna
Canna

HARDY TO AT LEAST 25˚F

Native to South and Central America, cannas were seized upon by Victorian gardeners with such enthusiasm and then so overused by them in their bedding schemes that the plants' subsequent popularity has been limited by this association for nearly a century. Now that gardeners have once again allowed themselves to enjoy these flamboyant plants, there are numerous cultivars to choose from. Cannas bloom from mid- to late summer until frost.

SPECIES AND CULTIVARS. 'Panache', with its subtle cream and rosy salmon flowers, usually surprises those who claim not to like cannas. The giant selection 'Intrigue' sports bright orange flowers amid huge purple-maroon leaves and is definitely not for the shy border. The handsome, glaucous leaves of the Peruvian *Canna iridiflora* are a fine complement to its deep rose flowers. *C.* 'Striata', with its jazzy yellow-striated leaves and bright orange flowers, makes an excellent container subject by itself.

Canna 'Striata'

Canna iridiflora

DESIGN IDEAS. Cannas are great planted in the garden in full sun, and as vertical statements go, a single canna in a pot can be sufficient. But if your containers are large, and you'd like to combine other plants with them, the sky's the limit. Consider something that has big contrasting leaves like 'Japanese Giant' coleus or *Dahlia* 'Bednall Beauty', or a plant that will keep happily busy at the canna's feet, like *Cuphea cyanea*.

OVERWINTERING. Dark, cool, and moist — though make sure rhizomes stay above freezing. Dig up rhizomes before frost hits, and store in a tightly closed plastic trash bag or ice chest (see page 55).

PROPAGATING. It's easy to propagate these productive plants. Simply separate the rhizomes according to size and the number of containers you want to fill. Keep in mind that even a fairly small rhizome will provide quite a show.

COMMON PEST PROBLEMS. None.

Capsicum
Capsicum, pepper

HARDY TO AT LEAST 25°F

It's hard to imagine what world cuisine was like before the introduction of pepper from the New World. Most of the plants listed below are those with highly ornamental qualities that happen to bear edible hot fruit.

SPECIES AND CULTIVARS. 'Bellingrath Gardens Purple' has small, satiny, deep purple-black leaves, variegated in their juvenile stage with swirls of purple, green, and cream. Its purple flowers become small fiery peppers, first greenish purple in cast, then purple-orange, and finally red. 'Numex Twilight' is grown primarily for its colorful fruit, which begin purple, then ripen to yellow, orange, and then red. 'Black Pearl' is another fine cultivar with near-black fruits.

DESIGN IDEAS. These are useful in mixed border plantings, although they're also well adapted to container culture, where a single plant would be effective on its own.

OVERWINTERING. Cool and bright. You can continue harvesting peppers through the winter, too. Sometimes an older plant will benefit from hard pruning.

PROPAGATING. From seed or cuttings.

COMMON PEST PROBLEMS. Aphids. (See Specific Pests and Diseases, page 64.)

Capsicum 'Numex Twilight'

Carex 'Orange Green'

Carex
Carex, sedge

HARDINESS VARIES; THOSE LISTED BELOW ARE HARDY TO AT LEAST 5°F

Lack of hardiness need not prevent you from growing these tender species, many of which originate in New Zealand. They require little fuss, and with their grasslike leaves, they add wonderful character and texture to container combinations.

SPECIES AND CULTIVARS. We enjoy the bronze and purple blades of *Carex comans*, and also the Ginny Hunt introduction *C.* 'Orange Green', with its fountain of slender, spring green leaves initially touched with rusty orange, becoming increasingly orange into the fall.

DESIGN IDEAS. Carex leaves offer such wonderful texture and color that they make natural combination elements. Try juxtaposing *Carex comans* with haloragis or *Leptinella* 'Platt's Black'. *Carex* 'Orange Green' mingles well with *Cuphea* 'Black Ash'.

OVERWINTERING. Cool and bright. Do not cut back. Simply remove old foliage by pulling out individual blades.

PROPAGATING. Division or from seed.

COMMON PEST PROBLEMS. None.

Ceanothus 'El Dorado'

Ceanothus
California lilac, ceanothus 🌿

HARDY TO AT LEAST 25°F

With the exception of *Ceanothus americanus* (Zone 4) and *C. fendleri* (Zone 5), most ceanothus cultivars are related to species originally from California and New Mexico. They are grown outdoors there as they are in much of southern Europe, but must be brought indoors anywhere colder. In such climates, these small- to medium-size shrubs are well worth growing in containers for their summertime ethereal flower panicles in shades of blue.

SPECIES AND CULTIVARS. 'El Dorado' has chartreuse leaves variously marked by mid-zone areas of deeper green. Another good container candidate, the small-statured 'Wheeler Canyon', features narrow flower clusters, pink in bud, that open to a fine blue.
DESIGN IDEAS. Like many larger shrubby tender perennials, California lilac is probably best planted alone in a container.
OVERWINTERING. Cool and bright.
PROPAGATING. Cuttings.
COMMON PEST PROBLEMS. None.

Centaurea
Knapweed, star thistle 🌿

HARDINESS VARIES; THOSE LISTED BELOW ARE HARDY TO AT LEAST 5°F

There are numerous *Centaurea* species that are hardy to Zone 5 or 6. Some of the most interesting ones from a foliar perspective do, however, require dry conditions in winter in order to survive. Overwintered in containers, where you can monitor their humidity, they will be available for stunning container combinations in the warmer months.

SPECIES AND CULTIVARS. *Centaurea cineraria* 'Colchester White' has elegantly divided, felted white leaves, and is a fine candidate for containers in blazing sun. Also worthwhile is the southern European species *C. rutifolia,* with its sizable and delightfully fuzzy silver leaves.
DESIGN IDEAS. Their silver leaves make centaurea valuable for both containers and borders in hot sun. Try situating *Centaurea rutifolia* with *Salvia guaranitica* or *S. involucrata* 'Bethellii'. *Centaurea* 'Colchester White' consorts well with *Capsicum* 'Bellingrath Gardens' or *Dahlia* 'Bednall Beauty'. You may want to trim spent flowers; otherwise just prune to encourage a more compact shape.
OVERWINTERING. Cool and bright. Centaureas thrive in dry winter conditions.
PROPAGATING. Cuttings.
COMMON PEST PROBLEMS. None.

Centaurea cineraria

Ceratostigma willmottianum

Ceratostigma wilmottianum
Ceratostigma, Chinese plumbago 🔳

HARDY TO AT LEAST 15°F

Native to western China and Tibet, this plant has the sky blue flowers we generally associate with the genus or, for that matter, with anything called "plumbago." In this case, they are splendidly set off by cranberry-colored bracts and deep emerald-green leaves flushed with russet overtones.

DESIGN IDEAS. If your container is large enough, you can accommodate other plants along with your Chinese plumbago — although it is plenty entertaining on its own. Perhaps the best approach is to pair it with something low-growing, like *Dichondra argentea*.
OVERWINTERING. Cool and bright. Given these conditions, ceratostigma will bloom happily most of the winter.
PROPAGATING. Cuttings.
COMMON PEST PROBLEMS. Aphids sometimes like this plant. (See Specific Pests and Diseases, page 64.)

Cestrum
Cestrum, jessamine 🔳

HARDY TO AT LEAST 35°F

This genus from the nightshade family (Solanaceae) includes many wonderful tropical and subtropical species from South America. Most are evergreen shrubs in their native habitat, and have funnel-shaped flowers. The fragrant flowers of some species made them prized Victorian conservatory plants.

SPECIES AND CULTIVARS. *Cestrum nocturnum*, also known as night jessamine (because of the intoxicating perfume of its night-opening flowers). is worth trying, as long as you don't keep it in a small space — its scent is powerful! *C. elegans* 'Smithii', a selection of the Mexican species, has perhaps the prettiest clear pink flowers, and although the flowers are scentless, the plant blooms all year.
DESIGN IDEAS. These large plants work well in the back of big containers, mingled with companions of lower stature and contrasting foliage. *Cestrum elegans* 'Smithii' is lovely with dichondra. Try combining *C. nocturnum* with *Ipomoea batatas* 'Blackie'.
OVERWINTERING. Cool and bright. Cestrum has a tendency to get a bit rangy — don't hesitate to prune fairly hard to shape the plant in the fall, but avoid removing the flower buds.
PROPAGATING. Cultivars are best propagated from cuttings, but the species may be propagated from seed.
COMMON PEST PROBLEMS. None.

Cestrum elegans 'Smithii'

🟩 Sunny & Warm, page 44   🔳 Cool & Bright, page 50   🔳 Dark & Damp, page 54   🔳 Dark & Dry, page 56

Chondropetalum tectorum
Restio

HARDY TO AT LEAST 20°F

This South African member of the restio family (Restionaceae) has handsome, wiry, deep green stems banded by dark brown stripes and topped with small green flowers that turn into rich chocolate-colored seeds. It is highly drought resistant, preferring sandy soils and heat.

DESIGN IDEAS. Although it can be moved into well-drained soils for the summer, *Chondropetalum tectorum* is most striking when potted solo in a well-chosen container.

OVERWINTERING. Cool, bright, and dry. Do not prune — simply remove old leaves by pulling them off the plant.

PROPAGATING. Seeds or division. Because chondropetalum occurs in fire communities in its native South African habitat, germination of the seed requires exposure to smoke.

COMMON PEST PROBLEMS. None.

Chondropetalum tectorum

Cissus discolor

Cissus discolor
Grape ivy

HARDY 45°F

Comprising a large group that includes shrubs, herbs, and vines, these generally have small, greenish-white flowers and are grown largely for their foliage. *Cissus* species tend to come from tropical locales, including Africa, the Amazon, and Australia.

SPECIES AND CULTIVARS. *Cissus discolor,* the rex begonia vine, has elongated, heart-shaped leaves with a puckered surface that is punctuated with metallic spots.

DESIGN IDEAS. The recumbent habit of *Cissus discolor* makes it a perfect candidate for hanging baskets or for the foreground of a mixed container, where it can trail over the edge. It is particularly handsome in combination with contrasting, simpler foliage such as that of *Phormium tenax* 'Atropurpureum' or colocasia. Cissus can also be trained vertically at the back of a container. Prune to shape as desired.

OVERWINTERING. Warm and sunny.

PROPAGATING. Cuttings.

COMMON PEST PROBLEMS. None.

Citrus
Citrus

HARDINESS VARIES; THOSE LISTED BELOW ARE HARDY TO AT LEAST 25°F

Sixteen small evergreen tree and shrub species comprise this group. They're distinguished by spines in their leaf axils; waxy, fragrant flowers, usually white; and, in most cases, fruits that we would recognize as those of citrus. They originate in Southeast Asia, and in some species, the Pacific islands. Seventeenth-century Italians discovered that citrus make ideal container plants for cool, bright spaces — although due to differences in size, some are more suitable than others.

SPECIES AND CULTIVARS. *Citrus auriantiifolia* 'Key Lime' has oval leaves and the famously aromatic small fruit we now associate with Florida; it is well suited to container culture. A specimen of *C. limon* 'Ponderosa', also known as the American wonder lemon, has been established in one of Logee's greenhouses, in Danielson, Connecticut, for many decades. Loaded with intoxicating flowers and ponderously large fruit — sometimes weighing as much as five pounds each — this "lemon" is one we always make sure to visit when we're at Logee's. Despite the fruit size, the plant itself can be kept to manageable dimensions, and we have found it particularly useful for the freezing of copious amounts of grated rind for baking projects. *C. limon* 'Variegata Pink' has colorfully variegated foliage as well as pink-fleshed fruit. *C.* × *meyeri,* or the Meyer lemon, is described as "the hardiest and most compact lemon," and has long been one of our favorites. The fruit has exceptionally thin skin and can be consumed in its entirety; we are fond of a fresh relish made with entire Meyer lemons that makes a delightful accompaniment to seafood.

DESIGN IDEAS. Like 17th-century Italians, we prefer to pot these up each to its own container.

OVERWINTERING. Cool and bright.

PROPAGATING. Cuttings.

COMMON PEST PROBLEMS. Scale. (See Specific Pests and Diseases, page 64.)

Citrus auriantiifolia 'Key Lime'

Citrus × *meyeri*

Colocasia cultivar

Colocasia
Colocasia, elephant's ear, taro 🌿 🌱

HARDY TO AT LEAST 45°F

Grown for hundreds of years in much of tropical Asia as a food crop, colocasias appreciate both heat and humidity. Thus, they seem perfectly happy growing in the "dog days" of even a New England summer.

SPECIES AND CULTIVARS. *Colocasia esculenta* 'Black Magic', with its dramatic deep purple-black elephant's-ear foliage, brings a decidedly tropical air to our garden, particularly when the languor of a July breeze lifts a leaf to expose its dusky underside. *C. esculenta* 'Illustris' has distinctive, nearly black leaves with contrasting bright green veins.

DESIGN IDEAS. In recent years, colocasias have become a popular element in container combinations; they can also be dramatic, and will grow larger, in the ground. Some of our favorite combinations with colocasia have involved smaller, more finely textured plants that also provide a contrast in color — coleus (*Solenostemon*), banana (*Musa*), and sweet potato vine (*Ipomoea batatas*) are some good ones to consider. Of course, colocasias are also satisfying as single specimens in containers.

OVERWINTERING. Either warm and sunny or dormant and cool in a plastic trash bag or ice chest (see page 55).

PROPAGATING. Offsets from the tubers.

COMMON PEST PROBLEMS. Aphids. (See Specific Pests and Diseases, page 64.)

Convolvulus
Bindweed 🌱

MOST SPECIES HARDY TO AT LEAST 45°F

Resembling morning glories, especially in their dainty, cup-shaped flowers, these mostly Mediterranean plants make excellent container subjects and often bloom during the winter.

SPECIES AND CULTIVARS. *Convolvulus cneorum* is an elegant plant, with its smooth, silver foliage and white flowers. Sporting flowers of true blue, *C. sabatius* has a charming trailing habit. Occasional deadheading and pruning to shape the plant should be all that is required — but don't remove the flower buds.

DESIGN IDEAS. These are lovely as single specimens in containers, but you can also combine them with other plants. Try *C. sabatius* with *Helichrysum* 'Moe's Gold' or *Brachyglottis monroi*.

OVERWINTERING. Cool and bright. It's critical to keep these plants dry; let them dry out well between waterings.

PROPAGATING. Cuttings

COMMON PEST PROBLEMS. None.

Convolvulus cneorum

Coprosma × kirkii 'Variegata'

Coprosma
Coprosma

HARDY TO AT LEAST 45°F

Coprosma species originate in the Pacific islands, from Hawaii to Java, as well as in Australia and New Zealand. In those places they grow into evergreen shrubs, even trees.

SPECIES AND CULTIVARS. *Coprosma* 'Beatson's Gold' is a stunning, elegant plant with small emerald leaflets, each one blazed with a lime center, creating the impression en masse that this plant is glowing from within. *C. × kirkii* 'Variegata' has tiny ovoid leaves outlined in cream tinged with pink. These cultivars are fairly slow growing — an occasional trim is all that they require to maintain a pleasing form.
DESIGN IDEAS. These lend structure to mixed containers, but because their appearance is somewhat busy, it's best to combine coprosma with plants that have just one color or contrasting, broad leaves. 'Beatson's Gold' could be paired with *Ipomoea batatas* 'Blackie'.
OVERWINTERING. Cool and bright.
PROPAGATING. Cuttings.
COMMON PEST PROBLEMS. None.

Cordyline
Cabbage tree

HARDY TO AT LEAST 45°F

One of the hardiest of palmlike trees, *Cordyline australis* grows to truly arboreal dimensions in its native New Zealand. Its pyramidal white flower panicles are fragrant, and are reputed to appear fall to winter, although we have not had the good fortune to see them. *C. terminalis* originated in Southeast Asia. In the Hawaiian Islands, it is called *ti* and has a reputation for bringing good luck.

SPECIES AND CULTIVARS. *Cordyline australis* 'Torbay Red' is a striking maroon-leafed form. *C. australis* 'Alberti' has leaves of dull green that are edged and striped with cream. *C. terminalis* 'Baby Doll' is a dwarf plant with maroon leaves edged in pink. The cultivar 'Kiwi' has green leaves that are simaltaneously chartreuse, cream, and yellow, all traced in fine red lines.
DESIGN IDEAS. *Cordyline australis* is an excellent plant to use for upright, linear effects, inviting combination with a trailer, like *Begonia* 'Withlacoochee', helichrysum, or *Hedera helix*. Pair 'Baby Doll' with *Ipomoea batatas* 'Ace of Spades' and *Dichondra argentea*.
OVERWINTERING. Cool and bright.
PROPAGATING. Seed or cuttings.
COMMON PEST PROBLEMS. None.

Cordyline australis

Sunny & Warm, page 44   Cool & Bright, page 50   Dark & Damp, page 54   Dark & Dry, page 56

Cosmos atrosanguineus

Cosmos atrosanguineus
Chocolate cosmos

HARDY TO AT LEAST 25°F

This tuberous plant is native to Mexico, but is now rarely found in the wild. Its common name may be traced to the chocolate-colored flowers, as well as their characteristic scent, which resembles either chocolate or vanilla depending on both the hour and the nose encountering it.

DESIGN IDEAS. Because of its special dormancy requirements, it's best to plant chocolate cosmos by itself in a pot.
OVERWINTERING. Unearth the tubers after frost has affected the tops. Store in slightly moist peat moss, as you would dahlias. Alternatively, leave in the pot over the winter and do not water.
PROPAGATING. The tubers will produce offsets or you can take cuttings early in spring.
COMMON PEST PROBLEMS. None.

Cotyledon
Cotyledon

HARDY TO AT LEAST 45°F

Most of these are native to South Africa; the remainder originate in other parts of the African continent. All are shrubby plants, with thick, fleshy leaves and nodding, bell-shaped flowers. There is some variation in their bloom times, but the majority blossom in summer.

SPECIES AND CULTIVARS. *Cotyledon ladismithensis*, also known as bear paws plant, has fleshy, toothed oval leaves that are, in fact, fairly furry. Its nodding flowers are tubular and reddish brown, with up to 10 on each flower stalk.
C. macrantha is a low, succulent shrub with green leaves edged in red. Clusters of nodding, green-tipped red flowers appear on three-foot stems above the leaves. *C. undulata* 'Powdered Sugar' is a handsome selection of a low shrub-forming species, with leaves that are ruffled and appear coated in a white powder, earning it the common name silver crown.
DESIGN IDEAS. We find it is best either to pot these up alone or combine with other succulent plants that share their cultural requirements.
OVERWINTERING. Cool and bright. Water sparingly.
PROPAGATING. Cuttings taken from nonflowering plants.
COMMON PEST PROBLEMS. None.

Cotyledon undulata 'Powdered Sugar'

Crassula perforata

Crassula
Crassula 📋 🔲

HARDY TO AT LEAST 35°F

The most familiar member of this very large (more than 300 different species are known), entirely South African genus is probably the jade plant (*Crassula ovata*), which grows into a small tree, topping seven feet in its native habitat. But there is an enormous variety of leaf shape and plant form among the crassulas, and they are generally quite easy to grow. All have small flowers grouped in clusters, and many are winter blooming.

SPECIES AND CULTIVARS. *Crassula arborescens* forms a small tree with thick succulent, red-edged silver leaves and starry white flowers that turn pink with age. *C. perforata* grows pairs of rounded leaves that appear to be pierced through their centers, earning it the common name string of buttons. Its flowers have yellow petals. *C. teres,* also known as the rattlesnake crassula, has tightly overlapped green leaves and very fragrant white flowers.

DESIGN IDEAS. We find it is best either to pot these up alone or combine with other succulent plants that share their cultural requirements.

OVERWINTERING. Cool and bright or at room temperature in your living space.

PROPAGATING. Cuttings. Choose young growth and stick into a well-drained mix. Crassulas require remarkably little water, and fragments that drop into the soil beneath an established plant will often root on their own.

COMMON PEST PROBLEMS. None.

Crocosmia
Crocosmia, montbretia 🔲

HARDY TO 10°F

Members of the iris family, crocosmias are native to South Africa. Their swordlike foliage and colorful flowers make them valuable garden and container specimens. In addition, their flowers have a long vase life when cut. Because the corms spread easily, crocosmias have become an invasive problem in some warm-climate gardens.

SPECIES AND CULTIVARS. Although hybridizing has resulted in some selections with improved hardiness, (the brilliant red-flowered 'Lucifer' is rated as hardy to Zone 5, and wintered over outdoors in our garden for many years) most should be stored in protected

Crocosmia 'Solfatare'

conditions in colder climates. We are particularly fond of *Crocosmia × crocosmiflora* 'Solfatare', with its luscious apricot, yellow flowers, complemented by dusky bronze foliage. Also quite lovely is 'Lady Hamilton' with large, soft orange-yellow flowers that feature an apricot center and small splashes of maroon.

DESIGN IDEAS. Though there's no reason not to combine them with other plants, we prefer to pot up crocosmias as solo specimens, both for design reasons and to make overwintering easier. Of course, they're also quite lovely planted en masse in the border. And if you're unsure about hardiness, you could always try leaving a few in the ground, well-mulched, over the winter. Just remember that like many South African bulbs, their growing season requirements are full baking sun, and excellent drainage.

OVERWINTERING. Dark and dry.

PROPAGATION. Propagate by planting new cormlets or from seed.

PESTS. None.

Cuphea cyanea

Cuphea
Cigar plant

HARDY TO AT LEAST 25°F

This huge, largely South American genus is packed with plants that thrive in hot and dry conditions. Genuine workhorses in the sunny garden, they are exceptionally dependable container subjects, too.

SPECIES AND CULTIVARS. *Cuphea cyanea* is a captivating species, with its canary yellow and bright pink, nonstop flowers. But we're susceptible to the understated elegance of *C.* 'Black Ash' as well. *C. miniata* var. *llavea* 'Georgia Scarlet' has remarkably large flowers of saturated scarlet. In our experience, most cupheas begin blooming in winter, and then bloom continuously from early summer through frost.

DESIGN IDEAS. Cupheas are stellar performers, either in containers by themselves, in combinations with a wide variety of other heat- and drought-tolerant candidates, and in the ground. We have enjoyed them with large-leaved companions, such as colocasia, datura, and musa, and suggest that in making combinations, you look for unifying color elements that the individual plants share.

OVERWINTERING. Cool and bright. Prune back plants by half at the end of the summer.

PROPAGATING. Cuttings.

COMMON PEST PROBLEMS. Aphids. (See Specific Pests and Diseases, page 64.)

Curcuma petiolata 'Emperor'
Queen lily

HARDY TO AT LEAST 45°F

This Malaysian member of the ginger family (Zingiberaceae) boasts regal and tropical-looking leaves elegantly edged in cream. These are enhanced in late summer by cone-shaped, pale pink flowers.

DESIGN IDEAS. Like many other large-leaved tropicals, curcuma grows well in considerable shade and also associates nicely with plants that have smaller leaves and finer texture. Try the smaller coleus, sweet potato vine (*Ipomoea batatas*), and, if your container is a nice large one, *Stenotaphrum secundatum* 'Variegatum'.
OVERWINTERING. Store the plant dormant in the container in a dark, cool place and water sparingly.
PROPAGATING. Division.
PEST PROBLEMS. None.

Curcuma petiolata 'Emperor'

Dahlia
Dahlia

HARDY TO AT LEAST 25°F

Dahlias originated in Mexico and Guatemala, where they were first observed by the Spanish conquistadors in the mid-16th century. Species dahlias have been bred beyond recognition to produce the numerous cultivars with which we are now most familiar. We enjoy the original species the most, along with a few hybrids that retain some of their original forthright charm.

SPECIES AND CULTIVARS. *Dahlia coccinea,* with deep flame-red flowers, can grow to nine feet in its native habitat, but is usually a less monumental plant elsewhere. One of our favorites is *Dahlia* 'Moonfire', a maroon-leaved plant with flowers that have pale yellow to apricot petals surrounding a deep burnt-orange center. Also worth growing is *D.* 'Bednall Beauty', with its deep burgundy foliage and bright red flowers. Dahlias bloom from early summer to frost.
DESIGN IDEAS. You can't go wrong planting most dahlias singly in containers or situating them in borders as if they were hardy perennials (just don't forget to dig them up after the first frost). We've also composed lovely pots with 'Moonfire' and a variety of phormiums. And the dark foliage of 'Bednall Beauty' suggests combination with many plants; try *Artemisia* 'Powis Castle' or *Dichondra argentea* for maximum contrast.
OVERWINTERING. Dig up tubers and store in damp peat moss for the winter. Alternatively, if they were growing in a container, leave them in the pot and place in the dark. Keep the soil slightly damp.
PROPAGATING. Collection and division of tubers.
COMMON PEST PROBLEMS. None.

Dahlia 'Amber Queen'

Dahlia 'Bednall Beauty'

Datura
Thorn apple

HARDINESS VARIES; THOSE LISTED BELOW ARE HARDY TO AT LEAST 30°F

These robust plants have large and dramatic, generally fragrant flowers. Many of the species have been used since ancient times for medicinal and religious purposes and are highly poisonous. Children should be warned of their danger; even pets may be at risk if they ingest parts of the plant.

SPECIES AND CULTIVARS. *Datura inoxia* subsp. *inoxia,* also known as angel's trumpet, has fragrant upward-facing flowers that are either white or violet tinted. This native of the Pacific Northwest and Mexico can grow into a bushy three-foot-high plant. *D. metel* has ethereal, trumpet-shaped white blooms that emit a lovely fragrance in the evening, and *D. metel* 'Double Purple' produces ruffled, double, bright purple seven-inch trumpets that are also quite fragrant. *D. metel* 'Belle Blanche' has notably gray-green foliage in combination with upward-facing, cream-colored blooms. Daturas bloom from July to frost.

DESIGN IDEAS. The drama of one datura in bloom is sufficient for the creation of a successful container by itself, but these plants can also be combined, particularly in large containers, with a variety of smaller-flowered, perhaps also smaller-leaved, companions. Try *Datura metel* with *Ipomoea batatas* 'Ace of Spades', or *D. metel* 'Double Purple' with *Petunia* 'Fantasy White'.

OVERWINTERING. Cool and bright. Daturas do tend to grow a bit rangy; feel free to prune back to a desirable shape and size.

PROPAGATING. Seeds.

COMMON PEST PROBLEMS. None.

Datura inoxia

Dianella caerulea
Flax lily

HARDY TO AT LEAST 35°F

Originating in New South Wales, this species sports irislike foliage and a multitude of small, true-blue flowers with bright cadmium yellow anthers. These are succeeded by electric violet, olive-sized berries. Plants generally bloom in late winter to spring.

SPECIES AND CULTIVARS. *Dianella caerulea* 'Variegata' adds variegated leaves to the high level of drama provided by the species.

DESIGN IDEAS. These plants are so entertaining on their own that we just plant them that way.

OVERWINTERING. Cool and bright. Avoid pruning just before bloom.

PROPAGATING. Division.

COMMON PEST PROBLEMS. None.

Dianella caerulea 'Variegata'

Diascia
Twinspur

HARDY TO AT LEAST 25°F

Native to South Africa, these make great contributions to sunny gardens and especially to containers, for which their trailing habits are particularly well suited.

SPECIES AND CULTIVARS. We have never grown a diascia we didn't like. Its flowers are predominantly in shades of pink and coral. Hybrids include 'Ruby Fields', with lovely rich pink flowers; the weaving apricot-flowered 'Blackthorn Apricot'; soft peach-flowered 'Hector Harrison'; and 'Joyce's Choice', with salmon flowers that fade to pale pink. In Zone 5, diascias bloom in winter to early summer, but in cooler climates they may bloom through the summer.
DESIGN IDEAS. Although they also do well situated in gardens, the trailing habits and lovely flower shades of these plants suggest myriad container possibilities. Try 'Wendy' with *Centaurea rutifolia* or 'Blackthorn Apricot' with *Brachyglottis monroi*.
OVERWINTERING. Cool and bright. Prune hard in late summer, and repeat as necessary.
PROPAGATING. Cuttings, although the species grows easily from seed.
COMMON PEST PROBLEMS. Aphids. (See Specific Pests and Diseases, page 64.)

Diascia barberae 'Ruby Fields'

Dichondra argentea

Dichondra argentea
Dichondra

HARDY TO AT LEAST 45°F

This native of East Asia is used as a lawn in some dry (and warm) climates. In colder climates, though, it is most often seen in containers, out of which its delicate tendrils spill and cascade most winningly.

SPECIES AND CULTIVARS. A selection called *D. argentea* (sometimes sold as *Dichondra micrantha* 'Argentea') has truly silver leaves. The cultivar 'Silver Falls' is also widely available.
DESIGN IDEAS. In our most successful planting of dichondra as a ground cover, we juxtaposed it with red-leaved rice (*Oryza sativa* 'Red Dragon'). In containers, the possibilities are endless. For maximum contrast, combine it with dark-colored leaves, like those of *Phormium tenax* 'Atropurpurea' and *Dahlia* 'Bednall Beauty'. For a subtler effect, try it with diascias or underplant shrubby specimens in containers.
OVERWINTERING. Cool and bright.
PROPAGATING. Sow fresh seed in the fall. Dichondra can also be grown from cuttings, although plants will take some time to develop.
COMMON PEST PROBLEMS. None.

Dicliptera suberecta

Dicliptera suberecta
Dicliptera, jacobinia, justicia 🌿

HARDY TO AT LEAST 45°F

Related to acanthus and originating in Uruguay, this handsome plant with velvet gray, oval leaves and brightly coral-colored, tubular flowers is a guaranteed hummingbird magnet. Dicliptera has been a fairly continuous bloomer for us.

DESIGN IDEAS. Dicliptera is in itself a wonderful combination of color and texture and might be sufficiently entertaining all alone. But if you want to combine it with other plants, consider the fuzzy purple leaves of *Tripogandra* species or the large dark leaves of one of the many colocasias.

OVERWINTERING. Cool and bright. Prune as desired to maintain a compact shape.

PROPAGATING. Cuttings.

COMMON PEST PROBLEMS. None.

Duranta
Sky flower, pigeon berry 🌿

HARDY TO AT LEAST 25°F

This member of the verbena family (Verbenaceae) is an evergreen shrub in its native South American setting, and makes a fine container subject elsewhere.

SPECIES AND CULTIVARS. The completely yellow new foliage of *Duranta repens* 'Aurea' turns somewhat greener with age, and forms a vigorous trailing plant. *D. repens* 'Golden Edge' has jagged, golden leaves with variable central zones of green. *D. erecta* 'Alba' is a free-flowering plant, with arching racemes of fragrant blossoms that bloom over a long period. Most durantas bloom in spring and early summer.

Duranta repens 'Golden Edge'

DESIGN IDEAS. The yellow-leaved forms of *Duranta repens* make excellent foreground plants in mixed containers; try 'Aurea' with the brighter phormiums, such as 'Maori Chief' and 'Maori Sunrise'. Pair 'Golden Edge' with larger green leaves, like those of cannas or bananas (*Musa*). The arching habit of *D. erecta* 'Alba' makes it a great candidate for a hanging basket.

OVERWINTERING. Cool and bright. Prune as desired to maintain a compact shape.

PROPAGATING. Cuttings.

COMMON PEST PROBLEMS. None.

Echeveria 'Topsy Turvy'

Echeveria
Echeveria

HARDY TO AT LEAST 25°F

This largely Mexican genus of succulents forms distinctive rosettes. In their original habitats, echeverias cling to steep, dry mountainsides and are consequently accustomed to excellent drainage.

SPECIES AND CULTIVARS. *Echeveria agavoides* has substantial, thick, pointed leaves with exceptionally smooth surfaces. The wavy, pale blue leaves of *E.* 'Blue Curls' form a five-inch rosette. *E. fimbriata* is composed of large green leaves with subtly fringed edges that blush ruddy shades in the sun. Always attracting attention, *E.* 'Topsy Turvy' has glaucous, white-dusted leaves that appear folded upon themselves.

DESIGN IDEAS. We find it best to either pot these up alone or combine with other succulent plants that have similar cultural requirements.

OVERWINTERING. In your living space, as long as there is adequate light; otherwise, cool and bright.

PROPAGATING. Division of offsets.

COMMON PEST PROBLEMS. None.

Ephedra
Joint fir, Mormon tea

HARDINESS VARIES; THOSE LISTED BELOW ARE HARDY TO AT LEAST 5°F

Members of this group of shrubs and climbers share the jointed appearance of horsetails, the more familiar North American plants of the genus *Equisetum*. Fascinatingly, these plants photosynthesize mostly through their shallowly ridged stems, nearly dispensing with the need for leaves — although for brief periods, tiny scalelike leaves may appear at the nodes.

SPECIES AND CULTIVARS. *Ephedra rupestris,* from Costa Rica, forms cute bushlets that develop into dense, one-foot-by-three-foot mounds of blue-green stems and coral fruit. *E. tweediana*, from Argentina, is a climbing shrub with pendulous, deep green branches. *E. viridis* is native to the southwestern United States, and its bright green branches add a textural presence to the landscape.

DESIGN IDEAS. We pot up ephedra by itself.

OVERWINTERING. Cool and bright. Most ephedras like dry conditions; *Ephedra tweediana* is an exception.

PROPAGATING. Seeds or by layering in spring.

COMMON PEST PROBLEMS. None.

Ephedra viridis

Erodium
Storksbill, heronsbill ⚄

HARDINESS VARIES; THOSE LISTED BELOW ARE HARDY TO AT LEAST 5°F

These members of the geranium family (Geraniaceae) originate in various temperate parts of the world, although chiefly in the Mediterranean region.

SPECIES AND CULTIVARS. *Erodium pelargoniiflorum,* a Greek species, has fragrant foliage and one-inch-wide white flowers. *E. reichardii* 'Album' is a mat-forming perennial in Mallorca and Corsica, where its myriad small, pink veined white flowers must be quite a sight. Erodiums are spring bloomers.

DESIGN IDEAS. Erodiums associate well both visually and culturally with many succulent plants like agaves, echeverias, crassulas, and tender sedums.

OVERWINTERING. Cool and bright. Water sparingly.

PROPAGATING. Cuttings.

COMMON PEST PROBLEMS. None.

Erodium reichardii 'Album'

Erysimum pulchellum 'Variegatum'

Erysimum
Wallflower ⚄

HARDY TO AT LEAST 5°F

Although many wallflowers are biennial, there are a few perennial species. These can be worth storing for the winter in climates where they might not survive outdoors.

SPECIES AND CULTIVARS. *Erysimum pulchellum* 'Variegatum' is a compact plant with handsome cream and gray-green variegated foliage. It has lavender-colored flowers in the spring. Although *E. cheiri* is frequently cultivated as a biennial, it is actually a perennial. Nothing else quite matches its glowing, yellow-orange flowers in early spring.

DESIGN IDEAS. Because its handsome foliage remains even after the bloom period is past, *Erysimum pulchellum* 'Variegatum' is a valuable addition in the partially shaded garden, as well as in containers that are not in full sun. In either setting, try combining it with the contrasting foliage of *Tradescantia* 'Purple Queen' or the larger leaves of *Begonia* 'Hocking Bravura'.

OVERWINTERING. Cool and bright. Trim off spent flowers, and prune to maintain a compact shape.

PROPAGATING. Cuttings.

COMMON PEST PROBLEMS. None.

Eucomis
Pineapple lily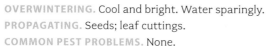

HARDY TO AT LEAST 25 °F

Native to Natal and the Transvaal region of South Africa, these summer-growing members of the hyacinth family have handsome, swordlike foliage, the undersides of which are frequently spotted in burgundy. The distinctive, cylindrical flower scapes are studded with star-shaped florets, giving rise to the common name. Eucomis blooms in midsummer.

SPECIES AND CULTIVARS. *Eucomis bicolor* is smaller than many of the other species, with purple-flecked stems and wavy, pale green leaves; its flowers are pale green also. *E. humilis* has unusually broad, deep green leaves and lovely, purple-centered white flowers. *E. comosa* 'Sparkling Burgundy' is a Tony Avent introduction that boasts rich purple leaves and flowers resembling miniature purple pineapples.

DESIGN IDEAS. One of our most successful plantings of pineapple lily in the ground comprised *Eucomis comosa* 'Sparkling Burgundy', *Melianthus major,* and 'Purple Duckfoot' coleus. In containers, try surrounding 'Sparkling Burgundy' with *Dichondra argentea* or *Ipomoea batatas* 'Margarita'. Other possibilities to consider are coleus varieties with an appropriate shade of purple in their leaves, dark-leaved begonias, and *Cissus discolor*.

OVERWINTERING. Cool and bright. Water sparingly.

PROPAGATING. Seeds; leaf cuttings.

COMMON PEST PROBLEMS. None.

Eucomis cultivar

Euphorbia cotinifolia

Euphorbia
Crown of thorns, spurge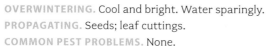

HARDINESS VARIES; THOSE LISTED BELOW ARE HARDY TO AT LEAST 45 °F

The 2,000 annual, biennial, and perennial species of this genus originate in virtually all the corners of the world. Many are succulent, and most have a milky sap (which can be a skin irritant for some people). They are an extremely tough group of plants.

SPECIES AND CULTIVARS. *Euphorbia cotinifolia* is an outstanding shrubby species, originally from Mexico, with oval leaves that change from luminous russet to shades of purple and maroon over time. *E. fulgens* 'Purple Leaf' is a dramatic selection of another Mexican species. Its green-leaved form is prized by florists for the striking orange flowers, which are particularly long-lasting when cut. Its willowy and slender deep maroon leaves, brushed with olive, are an equally good reason to grow it. *E.* 'Flame Leaf' is a self-sower that makes a fantastic container specimen, with its slender, ovoid maroon leaves edged in khaki. *E. milii,* also known as crown of thorns, is native to Madagascar, where it reaches nearly six feet in height. Selections of this charmingly thorny plant have been made for less gigantic proportions; our favorite smaller selection is *Euphorbia milii* 'Dead Milkmen'. Another entertaining member of this family is 'Thai Giant', a vigorous seed-grown hybrid strain that blooms in a delightful color range, including shades of salmon and pink.

OVERWINTERING. Cool and bright. Prune as desired to encourage the shape you want.
PROPAGATING. Cuttings, and seeds (when propagating species).
COMMON PEST PROBLEMS. None.

Euphorbia milii 'Thai Giant'

Evolvulus pilosus

Evolvulus pilosus
Evolvulus 🌿

HARDY TO AT LEAST 15°F

A subshrub native from South Dakota and Montana to Arizona, this member of the convolvulus family tolerates dry conditions, covering itself in a multitude of white-centered blue flowers that are reminiscent of morning glories. Evolvulus blooms in winter, spring, and early summer.

SPECIES AND CULTIVARS. 'Blue Daze', which is similar to the species, is a fine selection.
DESIGN IDEAS. Both the gray leaves and bright blue and white flowers of *Evolvulus pilosus* make it useful in mixed containers when combined with upright, silver-leaved plants like *Brachyglottis monroi* or juxtaposed with other drought-tolerant candidates, such as *Aloe ferox* or many of the agaves.
OVERWINTERING. Cool and bright.
PROPAGATING. Cuttings.
COMMON PEST PROBLEMS. None.

Felicia amelloides
Kingfisher daisy, blue marguerite 🗹

HARDY TO AT LEAST 45°F

Originating in Africa and Arabia, blue marguerites make excellent candidates for conservatories and other sunny windows in winter, where they can be counted on to bloom incessantly.

SPECIES AND CULTIVARS. The cultivar 'Astrid Thomas' has especially full flowers of intense Wedgwood blue on a plant that is both compact and floriferous. 'Variegata' contributes handsome cream and dark green foliage as well as the standard blue daisies.

DESIGN IDEAS. The startling blue color of blue marguerite flowers suggests silver companions; *Helichrysum petiolare*, *Plecostachys serpyllifolia,* and *Dichondra argentea* would all be lovely. The cream splotches in the leaves of *Felicia amelloides* 'Variegata', however, create an element of busyness that might be better complemented by *Begonia fagifolia* or possibly by an upright plant, such as *Buddleia fallowiana* var. *alba*.

OVERWINTERING. Cool and bright.

PROPAGATING. Cuttings.

COMMON PEST PROBLEMS. None.

Felicia amelloides 'Variegata'

Ficus carica 'Brown Turkey'

Ficus carica
Common fig 🗹

HARDY TO AT LEAST 5°F

Originating in the region of present-day Turkey and Afghanistan, the edible fig has been cultivated since Neolithic times. In the 16th century, figs were introduced to both England and China. European selections found their way eventually to locations as distant as Japan, the West Indies, and Australia. Figs make beautiful small trees, growing 10 to 30 feet high with trunks rarely more than seven inches in diameter. There are many cultivars — differentiated largely on the basis of fruit characteristics. If you enjoy eating figs and live in a climate where they can't grow and fruit outdoors, it's well worth your efforts to overwinter a fig tree or two.

Ficus carica

Ficus carica 'Celeste'

SPECIES AND CULTIVARS. *Ficus carica* 'Brown Turkey' is certainly the best-known cultivar among North American gardeners, and its fruits are considered to be of good quality. It is both prolific and reliable, and was awarded the Royal Horticultural Society's Award of Garden Merit. *F. c.* 'Marseillaise' produces white (actually pale green) fruits that ripen over a long season. The outer skin of the fruit of the Italian variety, *F. c.* 'Black Ischia', is blushed with a deep-blue bloom, revealing violet-red pulp within. With its glossy, shallowly lobed leaves, it makes a particularly ornamental tree, and bears heavily as well.

DESIGN IDEAS. Because of their size and special requirements, when fig trees are grown as tender perennial plants, situate them in pots by themselves.

OVERWINTERING. In borderline climates in Europe, it became common practice to plant figs against south-facing walls that not only protected them from winter winds, but also retained heat during the growing season. Success with this method has been recorded as far north as Columbus, Ohio, where an urban gardener made use of a south-facing brick wall and wrapped the tree with leaf-filled paper bags for the winter. And there is always the classic outdoor pit, favored by many Italian-American émigrés of the last century. This method involves digging a one-foot-deep trench in a well-drained area. The trench should be long enough to accommodate the length of the fig tree. Set the pot or root-ball in the trench and lay the entire tree on its side. Then fill in the trench with about six inches of soil and top with another six inches of a fairly porous mulch material, such as leaves.

Figs can also be overwintered indoors, either as a dormant plant left in the pot and stored in a basement or garage or as a houseplant in a cool and bright space. To overwinter using the first method, allow the plant to lose its leaves in fall before bringing the container indoors. For the second method, bring the plant indoors well before the first frost. You'll want to prune your fig when it becomes too large for your space. Otherwise, just remove old leaves.

PROPAGATING. Layering is the favored method, although cuttings can also be taken from mature wood. To layer, select 8- to 12-inch shoots and bury them so that only a few nodes are above the soil surface. Hardwood cuttings can also be taken after the tree has lost its leaves — preferably no later than the end of December. With either method, developing sufficient roots on fig cuttings is not a quick process — they may become established by the end of the following year.

COMMON PEST PROBLEMS. Scale. See page 69 for suggestions on how to cope with an infestation.

Fuchsia
Fuchsia, lady's eardrops

MOST HARDY TO AT LEAST 45°F

Shrubby, semi-climbing plants native to South America, New Zealand, and the West Indies, fuchsias there can assume the form of small trees. Because their origins are tropical, they are especially well suited to warmer greenhouse and conservatory conditions. We have enjoyed growing species fuchsias, as well as the many lovely hybrids.

SPECIES AND CULTIVARS. The magnificent Peruvian *Fuchsia boliviana,* with its soft downy foliage and pendant, six-inch red flowers, was cultivated by the Incas. *F. magellanica* 'Aurea' has golden foliage that would brighten the shadiest corner, although it will also grow in a sunny window for the winter. *F.* 'Oriental Lace' is a charming, fine-textured plant with small, bright pink flowers appearing all summer and fall. The upright *F.* 'Gartenmeister Bonstedt' is a deservedly popular container subject, its bronze leaves contrasting handsomely with showy clusters of drooping brick red to orange flowers.

Fuchsia 'Gartenmeister Bonstedt'

DESIGN IDEAS. Fuchsias are among the most spectacular of tender perennials, and their showiness is particularly valuable given their tolerance for shade. Whether planted in the ground or in containers, they affiliate nicely with other shade-loving plants, including many hardy perennials like hostas, wild gingers (*Asarum*), and hellebores (*Helleborus*). Among the tender possibilities are begonias and impatiens. Fuchsias also look great in pots by themselves, and can be easily trained into standards, as is often done in the United Kingdom.
OVERWINTERING. Cool and bright. Because fuchsias need more water than do many other plants, we recommend that you store them individually. Be careful not to let them dry out completely, but don't allow them to become waterlogged, either. They may have difficulty if planted in containers that are too large. Generally speaking, pruning fuchsias is a good idea. If plants become lanky, cut them back hard. Of course, any trimming will probably result in the loss of some flower buds, but the plant will also respond with greater vigor.
PROPAGATING. Cuttings taken in late winter or early spring.
COMMON PEST PROBLEMS. Botrytis is fond of fuchsia, and the paler-flowered forms seem to be most susceptible. In the winter months, many fuchsias are also prone to rust, which can be discouraged by the removal and disposal of infected leaves. Aphids and whiteflies can also pose a problem. (See Specific Pests and Diseases, page 64.)

Fuchsia magellanica 'Aurea'

Sunny & Warm, page 44   Cool & Bright, page 50   Dark & Damp, page 54   Dark & Dry, page 56

Gardenia
Gardenia 🌿

HARDY TO AT LEAST 25°F

This evergreen shrub or tree (to 36 feet) is a native of southeast China and southern Japan. *Gardenia jasminoides* 'Veitchiana' is the double-flowered, most fragrant form. *G. jasminoides* 'Variegata' is a vigorous cultivar that has cream-splashed leaves and double white flowers. *G.* 'Belmont' boasts attractive flowers that are reminiscent of roses and emits an intoxicating perfume. In our experience, gardenias bloom in winter and early spring, with sporadic summer bloom. Like citrus, gardenias require humid conditions in winter, as well as shade from hot sun throughout the year.

DESIGN IDEAS. Although there is no reason you can't combine other plants with your gardenia, this is one we prefer to plant in its own pot.
OVERWINTERING. Cool and bright. The humidity supplied by a greenhouse or conservatory environment is best. If you lack these special conditions, mist frequently and keep the humidity as high as you can. A humidifier may help considerably. If your plant is getting rangy, prune it back hard.
PROPAGATING. Cuttings.
COMMON PEST PROBLEMS. Red spider mites. Keeping the soil dry in winter, and feeding regularly during warmer weather may help prevent infestations. (See Specific Pests and Diseases, page 64.)

Gardenia jasminoides 'Variegata'

Gazania 'Talent'

Gazania
Treasure flower 🌿

HARDY TO AT LEAST 45°F

South Africa is the origin of many *Gazania* species, which explains this plant's reputation for drought tolerance. Few members of the daisy family (Compositae) can bloom as tirelessly in window boxes and other containers throughout long, hot dry seasons.

SPECIES AND CULTIVARS. The cultivar 'Christopher Lloyd' sports petals of rose-pink surrounding a black-rimmed, bright green center. The 'Talent' series features handsome silver foliage with gaily colored flowers.
DESIGN IDEAS. Whether in the garden or featured in containers, gazanias are outstanding plants for dry, sunny conditions. Plantings of a single color are effective by themselves, but you might also try a medley of *Gazania* 'Talent Orange' with *Carex* 'Orange Green' or *G.* 'Christopher Lloyd' with *Calocephalus brownii* and *Ipomoea batatas* 'Blackie'.
OVERWINTERING. Cool and bright.
PROPAGATING. Seeds; some cultivars can be propagated only by cuttings, best taken early in the season.
COMMON PEST PROBLEMS. In the garden, rabbits are fond of both gazania foliage and buds.

Geranium
Cranesbill

HARDINESS VARIES; THOSE LISTED BELOW ARE HARDY TO AT LEAST 20°F

This large group originates in a variety of temperate to cold regions, and includes many species we grow as hardy perennials. But depending on where you garden, species from milder areas, such as Greece, Turkey, Madeira, and the Canary Islands, may require winter protection.

SPECIES AND CULTIVARS. *Geranium incanum,* with its scented, finely dissected leaves on trailing stems and small but striking magenta flowers, is a distinctive South African species well suited to pot culture. *G. maderense,* considered by many to be the most spectacular of all geranium species, originates in the foggy mountain regions of Madeira. This monocarpic species (any plant that flowers and produces fruit only once during its life cycle, after which it dies) will bloom in its second season when grown in an ample container.

DESIGN IDEAS. Grow as a specimen in its own container.

OVERWINTERING. Cool and bright.

PROPAGATING. Collect and sow seed when ripe, or take cuttings early in the season.

COMMON PEST PROBLEMS. None.

Geranium maderense

Gladiolus callianthus 'Murielae'

Gladiolus
Gladiolus

MOST SPECIES ARE HARDY TO AT LEAST 30°F

Over 150 gladiolus species originate in South Africa alone, but North American gardeners are most familiar with the cultivated hybrids resulting from crosses made between only five or six of them.

SPECIES AND CULTIVARS. *G. callianthus* is a native of Ethiopia, and was until recently known as *Acidanthera bicolor.* Its scarlet-eyed, graceful white blooms are fragrant and held on shorter stems than many gladiolus. They make a delicate display when planted in drifts among perennials and shrubs. *G. dalenii* has five-foot-tall stems and brilliant orange flowers.

DESIGN IDEAS. Some gladiolus flower spikes can appear awkward in mixed borders, and are easily blown over if not staked. Both from a visual and a cultural standpoint, it may be best to situate them in the vegetable garden, where they can be planted in long rows and easily cultivated, staked, and eventually harvested. In any case, make sure to locate them in full sun and well-drained soil. Glads do not thrive in heavy soils, and the blooms will be negatively affected by less than optimal sunlight. Plant once danger of frost has passed, and for continuous summer bloom, continue planting every two weeks.

OVERWINTERING. Wait for early frosts to kill foliage in the fall, then cut the stems a few inches above the corms. Dig them up, shake off soil, and sort by cultivar. Allow corms to cure in an airy, warm space for about three weeks. Then separate the older, spent corms that bloomed this season from the smaller new corms, discarding the old ones. Store corms in well-ventilated, dark, dry, and cool conditions.

PROPAGATING. The very smallest corms, known as "cormels," may be saved and grown on in subsequent seasons.

COMMON PEST PROBLEMS. Glads are susceptible to a number of pest and disease problems. To minimize these, discard any mushy or unsound corms. Thrips are a major pest issue. Storage temperatures between 35 and 40°F may reduce the chances of thrip damage. As an added precaution, the corms can be dipped briefly in 160°F water, then dried thoroughly before storage. Practice crop rotation when planting them out, choosing a different location each season. If foliage appears streaked or stunted, they may be infected by a virus, and should be discarded.

Gunnera manicata
Giant rhubarb, gunnera 🌿 🌼

HARDY TO AT LEAST 25°F

Gunnera originates in southern Brazil and Colombia, and is guaranteed to become a focal point outdoors wherever you plant it. Under favorable conditions, this massive plant can reach dimensions that are six feet by six feet across and nearly as high. Its huge, heavily corrugated green leaves have the texture of sandpaper and are covered with prickles. With winter protection, either indoors or out (see below), it may produce large, bottlebrush-like flowers in its second season.

DESIGN IDEAS. Best in a large pot by itself.

OVERWINTERING. A controversial question. Some gardeners have successfully overwintered *Gunnera manicata* in the ground in Zone 5, but this requires fairly elaborate coverings — including electric lightbulbs and insulation to keep the plant crown warm, not to mention the cooperation of Mother Nature. For most gardeners in colder climates, growing it in a pot, which is brought inside during the winter, is probably the most reliable approach. If temperatures are sufficiently cold — around 35°F — store gunnera in the dark. Otherwise, keep your gunnera in cool and bright conditions.

Gunnera manicata pictured with *Agapanthus africanus*

PROPAGATING. Seeds.

COMMON PEST PROBLEMS. No insect pests or diseases have dared to bother our gunneras, but persistent wind can cause damage to the leaves, especially when a plant first moves outdoors. For this reason, make sure to maintain adequate moisture for your plant, especially during such transitions, and choose a moving day that isn't terribly windy. Alternatively, create a protective structure or shield to help your gunnera adjust to the move.

Gynura aurantiaca

Gynura aurantiaca
Velvet plant 📙

HARDY TO AT LEAST 40°F

This vigorous vine originates in Java, where it is winter blooming. Under cultivation in cooler climes, its malodorous orange daisies are most proliferous in summer.

DESIGN IDEAS. The strikingly fuzzy, purple leaves and stems of *Gynura aurantiaca* 'Purple Passion' suggest numerous combinations. Try it with the silver of *Helichrysum petiolare,* which will cascade downward in a full-sun container, while 'Purple Passion' goes up. Or pair it with a contrasting coleus, such as *Solenostemon* 'Swinging Linda', for a combination with pizzazz in partial shade. Frequent pruning of the plant keeps the color of new growth most intensely purple.

OVERWINTERING. Warm and bright.

PROPAGATING. Cuttings.

COMMON PEST PROBLEMS. None.

Haloragis erecta 'Wellington Bronze'
Haloragis 📗

HARDY TO AT LEAST 45°F

Although *Haloragis erecta* 'Wellington Bronze' originates in New Zealand, this distinctive, bronze-leaved plant comes from the same family as gunnera. Grown entirely for its attractive leaves, which provide contrast for a wide variety of other plants, its flowers are not particularly notable.

DESIGN IDEAS. This handsome foliar accent has worked well for us in containers, especially when paired with other plants in a rusty earth-colored range, like *Carex* 'Orange Green' and *Acalypha* 'Kilauea', as well as in fine combinations with most phormiums.

OVERWINTERING. Cool and bright. Occasional pruning will keep this plant more compact.

PROPAGATING. Cuttings or seeds.

COMMON PEST PROBLEMS. None.

Haloragis erecta 'Wellington Bronze'

Hamelia patens
Firebush, hamelia 🦋

HARDY TO AT LEAST 45°F

Forming a small tree or shrub in its tropical South American home, *Hamelia patens* has green-bronze leaves. Its tubular scarlet flowers appear in midsummer to early fall, and these are followed by purple berries in the fall. It is an excellent nectar source for butterflies, and is also frequented by hummingbirds. This slow-growing shrub can easily be kept within dimensions that are suitable for moving indoors — it reaches two feet by two feet after two years.

DESIGN IDEAS. Hamelia is best grown in its own container.
OVERWINTERING. Cool and bright. This plant likes regular watering. Frequent pruning may be necessary to keep it happy in a pot.
PROPAGATING. Cuttings.
COMMON PEST PROBLEMS. None.

Hamelia patens

Haworthia truncata × maughanii

Haworthia
Haworthia 🌿 🦋

HARDY TO AT LEAST 35°F

There are more than 70 species of this stemless, succulent, evergreen perennial, and all of them originate in Africa. In addition to being striking container plants in the summer garden, they make exceptional and undemanding houseplants, tolerating a range of light conditions from full sun to fairly limited.

SPECIES AND CULTIVARS. *Haworthia comptoniana* is a handsome though slow-growing species, with plump leaves and attractive markings. *H. truncata × maughanii* is a hybrid of two of the choicest and most distinctive haworthia species. The result has stubby deep green leaves, streaked at the tips, and is reminiscent of chunky fingers and toes engaged in a very slow elongation.
DESIGN IDEAS. We prefer to grow this in a pot by itself, although you can combine it with other succulent plants in a larger container.
OVERWINTERING. In your living space, but if light conditions are not adequate, cool and bright is also fine.
PROPAGATING. Division of offset rosettes.
COMMON PEST PROBLEMS. None.

Hebe
Hebe

HARDY TO AT LEAST 25°F

The genus comprises 75 different species — all evergreen shrubs in their native Australia and New Zealand. Where they might not winter outdoors, hebes make fantastic conservatory subjects. It's easy to see why they were named for the Greek goddess Hebe, personification of youth and immortality.

SPECIES AND CULTIVARS. The cultivar 'Amy' is particularly handsome, with glossy, oval, purple-veined leaves of deep olive-green fanning out tidily from purple-bronze stems. Its fat purple flower spikes are flecked with pale yellow pollen, causing them to appear sparkling and jewel-like. 'Pascal' has linear leaves, which are wine-red when young, then mature to blue-green. *Hebe pimeleoides* 'Quicksilver' has finely textured, pointy, diminutive, leaves that appear green washed with silver — quite lovely with the pale violet flowers. The hebes we've grown bloom in midsummer, but their foliage alone is sufficiently ornamental to earn a place in the garden or container.

DESIGN IDEAS. We grow hebes in their own containers, but there is no reason they can't be combined with other plants. Try 'Amy' with *Acaena* 'Blue Haze' or 'Quicksilver' with *Ophiopogon planiscapus* 'Nigrescens'.

OVERWINTERING. Cool and bright.

PROPAGATING. The cultivars should be propagated by cuttings.

COMMON PEST PROBLEMS. Aphids. (See Specific Pests and Diseases, page 64.)

Hebe 'Amy'

Helichrysum petiolare 'Variegatum'

Helichrysum
Everlasting flower

HARDINESS VARIES; THOSE LISTED BELOW ARE HARDY TO AT LEAST 25°F

Of the more than 500 species of *Helichrysum*, most originate in either South Africa or Australia. Inherently drought tolerant, they're very well suited to container culture.

SPECIES AND CULTIVARS. *Helichrysum confertum* has unusually wide, pleated leaves that form an attractive gray-green cushion. The ever-popular *H. petiolare* grows into a surprisingly large, trailing, gray-leaved plant that is also available in a variety of foliar variations, including *H. p.* 'Limelight', which has pale yellow leaves, and *H. p.* 'Variegatum', which has handsome cream and dark green variegated leaves. *H. retortum* is a trailing plant with small silver leaves, and its fall- to winter-blooming white flowers are tipped by spots of maroon. From the mountains of South Africa, *H. argyrophyllum* 'Moe's Gold' makes a great container subject with its satiny, crisp silver leaves.

DESIGN IDEAS. All helichrysums are well suited to container culture. Choosing one for a particular pot is simply a matter of scale and texture — which silver is the right one? 'Moe's Gold' is perfect for hanging containers as well as the perimeters of those on the ground. Try it with the rich pink flowers of *Pentas* 'Cranberry Punch'. The cultivar 'Limelight' is stunning paired with blue or purple flowers, like those of *Petunia* 'Azure Pearls'.

OVERWINTERING. Cool and bright. Allow soil to dry out thoroughly between waterings. Cut back helichrysums when they start looking ragged.

PROPAGATING. Cuttings.

COMMON PEST PROBLEMS. In our climate, late June to early July is when certain lepidoptera larvae begin inflicting their damage on helichrysum foliage. An application or two of *Bacillus thuringensis* (Bt) and removal of the affected leaves will usually take care of the problem.

Helichrysum petiolare 'Limelight'

Heliotropium arborescens 'Iowa'

Heliotropium arborescens
Cherry pie, heliotrope 🌿

HARDY TO AT LEAST 33°F

This Peruvian native has white flowers that turn purple with age, but the numerous selections made by admiring Victorians isolated plants with deeper color, as well as those that remain perpetually white. Among these cultivars, there is also a variety of scents — some more vanilla, others more like baby powder. Planted outdoors, heliotrope performs best in partial shade with good moisture.

SPECIES AND CULTIVARS. 'Alba' has white flowers with a fresh vanilla scent. The cultivar 'Iowa' has the deepest violet flowers we've seen, with a wonderful, complex perfume. 'Haskell's Form' features an upright habit, well suited to topiary, an art that was practiced to perfection by late nurseryman Allen Haskell. Its flowers are a soft shade of lavender and emit the unmistakable and intense fragrance of baby powder. In our experience, heliotrope is a continuous bloomer.

DESIGN IDEAS. Our heliotropes grown in partial shade in the ground have thrived. If you plant them in containers, choose fairly large ones, position them away from hot sun and harsh winds, and water them regularly. Because purple-flowered heliotropes associate well with silver, try planting them with *Helichrysum petiolare,* which tolerates quite a bit of shade. Or for a really stunning window box, combine 'Iowa' with *Plumbago auriculata* 'Powder Blue' and *Dichondra argentea.*

OVERWINTERING. Cool and bright. Heliotrope's growth will slow considerably in cool temperatures, but it will continue to bloom. You may want to prune back straggly growth.

PROPAGATING. Cuttings.

COMMON PEST PROBLEMS. Aphids seem to find these as sweet as humans do. (See Specific Pests and Diseases, page 64.)

Hibiscus
Chinese hibiscus, mallow

MOST HARDY TO AT LEAST 45°F

This large genus comprises shrubs and trees in the subtropical and tropical regions in which most but not all species originate. We are not discussing here the species indigenous to more-temperate zones.

SPECIES AND CULTIVARS. *Hibiscus rosa-sinensis,* also known as Chinese hibiscus, is the familiar tropical hibiscus, which can form hedges in tropical climates. Although it has a confused history, this plant seems to have first been available to English gardeners as early as 1731, when Philip Miller, the curator of the Chelsea Physic Garden of London, introduced several cultivars, including a double-flowered one. *H. acetosella* 'Red Shield' is an East African species grown mainly for its handsome, deep crimson foliage and stems.

DESIGN IDEAS. The dark maroon leaves and stems of 'Red Shield' are a dramatic foil for silver foliage, like that of *Calocephalus brownii* or of any of the helichrysums.

OVERWINTERING. *Hibiscus rosa-sinensis* prefers warm, sunny conditions; *H. acetosella* can tolerate much cooler temperatures.

PROPAGATING. Cuttings.

PESTS PROBLEMS. Aphids, whitefly. (See Specific Pests and Diseases, page 64.)

Hibiscus acetosella 'Red Shield'

Impatiens 'Variegated Peach'

Impatiens balfourii

Impatiens
Busy Lizzie, impatiens, jumping Jack 🌿

HARDY TO AT LEAST 45°F

We have found both the species and the hybrids created by Victorians so much more interesting than the ubiquitous modern ones that carpet most suburban shade. Although jewelweed (*Impatiens capensis*) is native to North America, the majority of impatiens species originate in China, India, and Africa, and grow easily in warm, moist conditions.

SPECIES AND CULTIVARS. *Impatiens balfourii,* a western Himalayan native with delicate pink and white flowers, thrives in all but deep shade. *I. zombensis,* from the wet cliffs and streams of Mozambique, forms a bushy plant, with delicate leaves and small rose-pink flowers. *I. walleriana* 'Variegated Peach' sports double salmon flowers that stand out against its white and green foliage, and is a nonstop bloomer in both partial shade outdoors and east- or west-facing windowsills inside. *I. w.* 'Cherry Lemonade' is a recent Doug Lohman selection that pairs shocking pink flowers with chartreuse foliage, and is not for the slavishly tasteful.

DESIGN IDEAS. Impatiens are most familiar to us as shade ground covers, but the species and older cultivars include plant habits that are suited to a wider variety of applications. *Impatiens balfourii, I. cristata,* and *I. glandulifera* are best grown in the ground, where they tend to self-sow for future seasons — in the case of *I. glandulifera,* perhaps a little too exuberantly. *I. zombensis* is a wonderful container subject, and would grow happily as well as pleasingly in combination with *Ophiopogon planiscapus* 'Nigrescens'. The harmonious sunset hues of *I.* 'Papaya' (Seashell Series) suggest a combination with *Oxalis vulcanicola* 'Copper Glow', which has foliage in a similar color range.

OVERWINTERING. Warm and moderately sunny.

PROPAGATING. Species *Impatiens* are easily grown from seed, which you must have quick reflexes to collect — they're not called jumping Jacks for nothing! The cultivars, many of them preserved since their Victorian introductions, are easily multiplied by cuttings.

COMMON PEST PROBLEMS. Aphids love impatiens indoors. (See Specific Pests and Diseases, page 64.)

Iochroma grandiflorum

Iochroma
Iochroma 🗓

HARDY TO AT LEAST 35°F

This group of shrubs and small trees in the nightshade family (Solanaceae) originates in tropical America, where they often grow in open woodlands. This seems to predispose them to a certain amount of shade, but in cooler climates, they will also grow in full sun. In either location, their flowers create an impressive spectacle from midsummer to frost.

SPECIES AND CULTIVARS. Considered one of the showiest species, with its rich violet flowers, *I. grandiflorum* is a native of Ecuador and Peru. *Iochroma australe* is an elegant, semievergreen Argentinian native with pendant purple flowers.

DESIGN IDEAS. A great container subject, iochroma's deep purple flowers are a stunning sight with almost anything silver, but the filigreed foliage of *Artemisia* 'Powis Castle' is a perfect height to cover iochroma's often long legs.

OVERWINTERING. Cool and bright. Prune hard to soften the plant's naturally lanky habit.

PROPAGATING. Cuttings.

COMMON PEST PROBLEMS. None.

Ipomoea
Moonflower, morning glory, sweet potato vine 🗓 🗓

HARDINESS VARIES, BUT FEW ARE HARDY BEYOND 5°F

This large and varied genus ranges from edible (and ornamental) sweet potatoes to the traditional 'Heavenly Blue' morning glory. Most, but not all, have funnel-shaped flowers and twining stems. All are attractive to hummingbirds. A number of species are from Mexico; the rest seem to have originated in pan-tropical regions.

SPECIES AND CULTIVARS. *Ipomoea alba*, or moonflower, is a tropical, night-blooming species that enjoyed great popularity at the turn of the 20th century, particularly in the South. Its magnificent, six-inch, heavily scented white blooms unfurl at dusk and remain open into the morning (especially on cloudy days). *I. batatas*, the edible sweet potato, is now available in some highly ornamental forms, including types with purple or bronze leaves, like *I. b.* 'Blackie' and the 'Caroline' series. Equally useful is the chartreuse-leaved form, *I. b.* 'Margarita.' *I. b.* 'Pink Frost,'

Ipomoea × *imperialis* 'Chocolate'

Ipomoea batatas 'Margarita'

Ipomoea batatas 'Blackie'

though a less vigorous grower than the others, offers elegantly variegated foliage. In recent years, these plants have become a common sight, due to their enormous versatility and toughness under a variety of conditions. They all like heat, and should not be put outdoors until the weather is reliably warm. The tropical *I. indica* (also known as *I. acuminata*), or the blue dawn flower, has blooms in a remarkable shade of saturated blue.

The *I. tricolor* selections made by Japanese collectors have provided the rest of the world with a remarkable variety of morning glory flowers. They range from pale blue to deep red with white centers, rims, or splotches; the shape and size of the blossoms also vary tremendously. *I.* × *sloteri,* a cross between *I. hederifolia* and *I. quamoclit,* was raised by Mr. L. Sloter in 1910. The culmination of 11 years of work, it produced a single seedling. The resultant cardinal climber, as it's called, has abundant, small bright red trumpets and deeply cut dark green foliage and is an elegant, vigorous addition to vertical spaces.

DESIGN IDEAS. There are few summer sights more enjoyable than that of morning glories, trained onto a trellis, in full bloom. But they are also quite lovely in other circumstances, including trained onto tepees and other forms in borders, as well as planted in containers and trained onto relatively small armatures. The various cultivars of *Ipomoea batatas* tend to be trailing plants, and these are useful foliar accents for conditions of hot sun and partial shade, both in containers and in the ground.

OVERWINTERING. When keeping any vining or twining plant in a temporary confined space, it is desirable to limit its growth. For this reason, keep ipomoeas in as cool an environment as possible to discourage winter growth. They do best on the dry side. Alternatively, cut back the vines and store the tubers in dark, somewhat damp conditions.

PROPAGATING. Some types, such as *Ipomoea indica,* can be propagated only by cuttings; others start as tubers — *I. batatas,* for example. These are also delicious to eat, so make sure you save a few to plant in your summer containers. All of the *I. tricolor* cultivars are easily started from seed.

COMMON PEST PROBLEMS. The only insect to bother our ipomoeas is a distinctive one — the sweet potato leaf beetle. This beetle has a rectangular, iridescent body, and generally arrives as soon as plants are set outside in the spring. It punctures the foliage with multiple holes, but doesn't seem to hurt the plants seriously. Indoors under cool temperatures, red spider mites may also be a problem. (See Specific Pests and Diseases, page 64.)

Iresine herbstii
Bloodleaf

HARDY TO AT LEAST 35°F

Native to Brazil, where it forms a shrubby perennial, the waxy, variously colored leaves of this member of the amaranthus family made it a Victorian favorite.

SPECIES AND CULTIVARS. The cultivar 'California' is a delightful, vigorous selection with large brown-black leaves interspersed with pink veins and held on very pink stems. 'Aureoreticulata' sports green leaves with lemon veins on a magenta-stemmed plant.

DESIGN IDEAS. Bloodleaf is satisfying either in the ground or in a container by itself. You can also coordinate it with plants that pick up on the particular coloring of the cultivar in question. For example, try 'California' with *Alternanthera* 'Red Thread' or *Ipomoea batatas* 'Blackie'. Pair 'Aureoreticulata' with *Alternanthera bettzichiana* 'True Yellow' or *Ipomoea batatas* 'Margarita'.

OVERWINTERING. Cool and bright.

PROPAGATING. Cuttings.

COMMON PEST PROBLEMS. None.

Iresine herbstii 'California'

Jasminum polyanthum

Jasminum
Jasmine, jessamine

THE SPECIES AND CULTIVARS LISTED BELOW ARE HARDY TO AT LEAST 30°F

This genus includes 200 shrubs and woody climbers from almost every temperate part of the globe. Most are grown for the pungent, sweet perfume of their small yellow or white flowers.

SPECIES AND CULTIVARS. *Jasminum polyanthum* bears numerous highly fragrant white flowers that open in midwinter when grown on a sunny windowsill. *J. officinale* 'Fiona Sunrise', with its striking golden leaves, is a valuable foliage plant apart from the allure of its fragrant white blooms. *J. sambac*, or Arabian jasmine, most likely originated in India, where it is still prized for its sweetly fragrant, small, waxy white flowers. This vigorous twiner blooms continuously; don't remove too many flower buds when you prune.

DESIGN IDEAS. Best in its own container; some are adapted to hanging baskets.

OVERWINTERING. Cool and bright.

PROPAGATING. Cuttings.

COMMON PEST PROBLEMS. Whiteflies. (See Specific Pests and Diseases, page 64.)

Juanulloa mexicana
Juanulloa 🌿

HARDY TO AT LEAST 25°F

This epiphyte (a plant that grows above ground level and uses other plants for support, generally in an effort to reach better light conditions) originates in southern Mexico and northern Peru, where it grows in rain forests and blooms in summer. The waxy, tubular flowers, which are the color of a ripe mango, look edible, although to our knowledge they are not. When siting juanulloa in the summer garden, make sure to provide some shade. Prune to shape as desired, but keep in mind that this is a slow-grower.

DESIGN IDEAS. Juanulloa creates a striking and colorful accent in the shade garden, where it might be happy blooming alongside *Begonia* 'Selph's Mahogany' or perhaps *B.* 'Boomer'. In containers, the smaller and deeper flowers of *B. sutherlandii* should blend nicely with those of juanulloa — as would the dark leaves of *B.* 'Othello' or *Begonia* 'Hocking Bravura'.

OVERWINTERING. Warm and moderately sunny — keep in mind that indoor sun in winter does not have the same intensity as outdoor sun. Thus, even though *Juanulloa mexicana* prefers shade in summer, even a southern exposure will not be excessively sunny for its winter storage.

PROPAGATING. Cuttings.

COMMON PEST PROBLEMS. None.

Juanulloa mexicana

Juncus 'Afro'

Juncus
Rush 🌿

HARDINESS VARIES; THOSE LISTED BELOW ARE HARDY TO AT LEAST 15°F

Although there are also plenty of hardy rushes, we have found that the tender ones add a textural dimension to a variety of container plantings. They originate in most parts of the world, with the exception of the tropics. Although a few are wetland species, the ones listed below thrive in well-drained container gardens.

SPECIES AND CULTIVARS. The firmly upright clumps of *Juncus pallidus* add wonderful texture and form to the garden. With its spiraling, deep-green stems, *J. inflexus* 'Afro' grows as happily in aquatic conditions as it does in drier, soil-based containers. *J.* 'Silver Spears' is an atypical rush that faces hot, dry conditions with equanimity. It sports stiff, needlelike, silvery green leaves.

DESIGN IDEAS. 'Silver Spears' can pair with a wide variety of succulent plants, and would be particularly handsome with the contrasting foliage of *Aeonium* 'Zwartkop' or *Aloe ferox.* In an aquatic planting, 'Afro' forms a handsome medley with the fine-leaved appearance of duckweed (*Spirodela polyrrhiza*).
OVERWINTERING. Cool, bright, and dry.
PROPAGATING. Divide; in the case of the species, start from seed.
COMMON PEST PROBLEMS. None.

Kalanchoe
Kalanchoe

HARDINESS VARIES; THOSE LISTED BELOW ARE HARDY TO AT LEAST 35°F

Originating mostly in various parts of Africa, the species of this diverse genus share succulent foliage that is well adapted for drought tolerance. They are wonderfully suited to arid indoor container culture, making them low-maintenance plants to overwinter.

SPECIES AND CULTIVARS. *Kalanchoe pumila*, native to Madagascar, is ideally suited to homes where watering is an infrequent activity. It is happiest in a sunny window, where at the most dreary point of winter, an abundance of pink flowers will open against the backdrop of its chalky, gray-green, scallop-edged leaves. *K. tomentosa,* also known as pussy ears, is another species from Madagascar, with fuzzy, silver-gray leaves of variable shapes that are edged in chocolate-brown. Infrequently augmented in late winter to early spring by small chartreuse flowers, it seems to be a cross between a plant and a cat. *K. uniflora* is a seasonally spectacular species, ideally suited to hanging baskets, from which a multitude of coral blossoms will cascade during the bitterest months of winter. Prune plants after bloom and to shape.
DESIGN IDEAS. *Kalanchoe pumila* is perfect for hanging baskets, although it would be great in any container, either by itself or in a medley with other succulents. The latter arrangement will work for most kalanchoe.
OVERWINTERING. Cool or room temperature with sun.
PROPAGATING. Cuttings.
COMMON PEST PROBLEMS. None.

Kalanchoe pumila

Kleinia
Peppermint stick

HARDY TO AT LEAST 45°F

These are mostly succulent members of the composite family, and tend to come from either Africa or southern India and Sri Lanka. Tolerant of dry conditions and often dramatic in appearance, they make excellent houseplants.

SPECIES AND CULTIVARS. *Kleinia amaniensis* has four-inch, ovoid, dusty green leaves edged with a fine purple line, and its flowers are purple and orange.
DESIGN IDEAS. Combine kleinia with other succulent, drought-resistant plants.
OVERWINTERING. Sunny, warm, and dry.
PROPAGATING. Cuttings; seeds.
COMMON PEST PROBLEMS. None.

Kleinia amaniensis

Kniphofia uvaria 'Border Ballet'

Kniphofia
Kniphofia, red hot poker

HARDINESS VARIES; THOSE LISTED BELOW ARE HARDY TO AT LEAST 5°F

Although it seems that British gardeners can grow these anywhere they please, most North American gardeners are better off bringing them indoors for the winter. This may be due to their requirement for dry winter conditions. Kniphofias make fantastic accents in the garden, and handsome container subjects too.

SPECIES AND CULTIVARS. The South African species *Kniphofia typhoides* is a tall, slender plant that grows there in marshy places. It has dramatically chocolate-colored, honey-scented flowers that are popular with bees. Other kniphofias we have enjoyed are *K. baurii,* which sports lovely chartreuse blooms, and hybrids like 'Border Ballet', blooming in a range of colors between cream and orange. Kniphofias generally bloom from mid- to late summer.
DESIGN IDEAS. We love kniphofias in the garden, where their hot-colored flowers and exotic foliage lend variety and interest to the border. Planted in large containers, most kniphofias also make handsome single specimens. Or combine 'Border Ballet' with contrasting leaf shapes that are in a similar color range, like that of 'Kingwood Critter' coleus or *Oxalis vulcanicola* 'Copper Glow'.
OVERWINTERING. Cool, bright, and dry.
PROPAGATING. Species are grown easily from seed, the hybrids should be propagated from divisions.
COMMON PEST PROBLEMS. None.

Lantana
Lantana, shrub verbena 🦋

HARDY TO AT LEAST 45°F

Lantana has become a ubiquitous addition to the hanging basket in this country, but it's a shame that this exuberant bloomer's use is limited in this fashion. It thrives in hot weather, growing vigorously and offering many brightly colored possibilities for gardens as well as for containers. Throughout much of the tropics, lantana's tendency to colonize areas of disturbed soil has led to its rampant proliferation. All parts of the plant are poisonous, but the flowers of lantana are highly attractive to pollinating butterflies.

SPECIES AND CULTIVARS. *Lantana montevidensis* 'Silver Mound' has simple cream flowers with lemon centers, an elegant combination against the rich green foliage. *L. m.* 'Samantha' has creamy yellow flowers and glossy leaves that are swirled with yellow.

DESIGN IDEAS. As long as you stick with candidates that love the heat, lantana pairs well with whatever happens to blend with its flower color. Try coordinating the shades of lantana blooms with *Ipomoea batatas* and various coleus cultivars for a sophisticated, tropical effect.

OVERWINTERING. Sunny and warm or dormant in the pot (see page 58).

PROPAGATING. Cuttings taken early in the season before bud initiation.

COMMON PEST PROBLEMS. Aphids and whiteflies both love lantanas. (See Specific Pests and Diseases, page 64.)

Lantana camara 'Greg Grant'

Lavandula 'Goodwin Creek Grey'

Lavandula
Lavender 🌱

HARDINESS VARIES; THOSE LISTED BELOW ARE HARDY TO AT LEAST 15°F

Despite the hardier varieties of this Mediterranean shrub, there remain some that — either due to their finicky response to winter cold or because they don't withstand wet winter conditions (reliable snow cover is sometimes a factor) — simply must be grown as tender perennials. In some climates, this may be the *only* way to grow lavender successfully. Many North American gardeners seem to engage in a remarkable amount of denial about their ability to grow this plant outdoors.

SPECIES AND CULTIVARS. Forming compact shrublets that are exceptionally attractive in bloom, *Lavandula stoechas* 'Lutske's Dwarf' is a dwarf form of Spanish lavender. *L.* 'Goodwin Creek Grey' is the result of a cross between *L. lanata* and *L. × heterophylla,* and has large, tooth-edged leaves that resemble those of *L. dentata.* Its soft lavender-blue flowers appear continuously through winter. Although *L. angustifolia* is one of the hardier lavenders, many gardeners have difficulty getting it to overwinter outside, and must therefore bring it indoors. The cultivar 'Old English' has fine, silvery foliage and lavender flowers that impart a definite colognelike fragrance. The distinction of having the longest leaves of any *L. angustifolia* cultivar belongs to 'Graves'. It also boasts abundant deep violet flowers held within paler purple calyxes, and is excellent for drying.

DESIGN IDEAS. Where conditions are mild, lavender is commonly situated in the garden — often planted as a hedge. In harsher climates, it is handsome located in a pot by itself; training it as a topiary is another option. Shearing back plants after bloom will keep lavender plants compact and attractive.

OVERWINTERING. Cool and bright.

PROPAGATING. Cuttings.

COMMON PEST PROBLEMS. None.

Lavandula stoechas

Leonotis leonurus

Leonotis
Lion's ear, lion's mane 🦁

HARDY TO AT LEAST 25°F

This relatively large family (30 species) of fragrant plants includes many South African species. Leonotis flowers consist of velvet-textured, tubular florets arranged in distinctive whorls, and make a memorable appearance for human eyes as well as those of hummingbirds and butterflies, which are attracted in large numbers for nectar.

SPECIES AND CULTIVARS. *Leonotis menthifolia* is a compact species (two to three feet tall) that makes an ideal container subject. Its handsome, scallop-edged leaves complement dusty orange whorls; this plant was much remarked upon in our gardens. *L. ocymifolia* (also called *L. leonurus*) is, at six feet, a considerably larger plant — an upright subshrub — with velvet red flowers. This species is better suited to planting out in the garden.

OVERWINTERING. Cool and bright.

PROPAGATING. Cuttings or seed, but take care when collecting the seeds: because the whorls are prickly, and contact with the plant can cause allergic dermatitis in some individuals, wear gloves when collecting.

COMMON PEST PROBLEMS. None.

Leptinella
Brass buttons

HARDINESS VARIES; THOSE LISTED BELOW ARE HARDY TO AT LEAST 10°F

Species of this genus, a member of the daisy family (Compositae), occur in both South Africa and New Zealand. They are characterized by stiff, petal-free, (generally) yellow flowers and also by their ability to thrive in dry, unpromising locations.

SPECIES AND CULTIVARS. 'Platt's Black', with delicate filigreed leaves the shade of weathered bronze, is a useful carpeting plant for containers and also in gardens.

DESIGN IDEAS. The texture and color of 'Platt's Black' just beg for the plant to be placed in proximity with succulents and sedges. Try *Carex comans, C.* 'Orange Green', phormiums, and *Calocephalus brownii*.

OVERWINTERING. Cool and bright.

PROPAGATING. Division in winter.

COMMON PEST PROBLEMS. Aphids. (See Specific Pests and Diseases, page 64.)

Leptinella squalida 'Platt's Black'

Lonicera
Honeysuckle

HARDINESS VARIES; THOSE LISTED BELOW ARE HARDY TO AT LEAST −5°F

This is another genus of plants that we tend to grow mainly as hardy perennials — but there are some very attractive ones that do not winter over when temperatures fall below 20°F or so. These make fine container subjects, however.

SPECIES AND CULTIVARS. *Lonicera nitida* 'Lemon Beauty' is a slow-growing, shrubby plant with symmetrically arranged, very linear leaves. Each leaf has a green center and is edged in pale yellow to cream. Native to northwestern Mexico, *L. pilosa* bears stunning clusters of tubular orange flowers in spring to early summer; these are quite elegant juxtaposed against its glaucous leaves.

DESIGN IDEAS. *Lonicera nitida* 'Lemon Beauty' is a great candidate for containers, especially in combination with leaves that provide both proportional and color contrast, like those of most cannas, colocasias, and phormiums.

OVERWINTERING. Cool and bright. Prune freely; loniceras can be fairly vigorous.

PROPAGATING. Cuttings.

COMMON PEST PROBLEMS. None.

Lonicera nitida 'Lemon Beauty'

Loropetalum chinense f. *rubrum*
Loropetalum

HARDY TO AT LEAST 20°F

This is the red-flowered form of a plant native to the dry open woods of Assam, southern Japan, and the warmer regions of China. With its shiny evergreen foliage and slender-petaled carmine flowers, it makes an exceptionally attractive subject for container culture, putting on its show of blooms in spring.

DESIGN IDEAS. This is best planted alone in a container.
OVERWINTERING. Cool and bright.
PROPAGATING. Cuttings.
COMMON PEST PROBLEMS. None.

Loropetalum chinense f. rubrum

Lotus berthelotii

Lotus
Parrot's beak

HARDY TO AT LEAST 35°F

Species of lotus occur in nearly all regions of the world, from the Mediterranean to Africa and Australia — even in parts of the western United States. Many of the most ornamental and frequently grown ones, however, are indigenous to Tenerife, where they have become quite rare in the wild, with a few others that grow on Madeira and the Canary and Cape Verde Islands. These subshrubs have a cascading habit, and are adapted to the growing conditions on cliffs along the coast. It remains a mystery that their flowers appear to be adapted for pollination by birds, despite the unlikelihood of bird pollinators ever reaching them in this setting. These lotuses all thrive in dry, sunny conditions.

SPECIES AND CULTIVARS. *Lotus berthelotii* has trailing stems of delicate silver foliage, punctuated by clawlike, bright vermilion flowers in winter and spring, making it a delightful component of mixed containers. *L.* 'Gold Flash' has similar but more finely textured foliage, and is another fantastic ingredient for mixed containers. The flowers of *L. jacobaeus* are a deep brown, and the leaves are green, not silver.
DESIGN IDEAS. Lotuses seem invented for containers, from which their lacey silver foliage spills most obligingly. They combine excellently with arctotis in the 'Harlequin' series (such as 'Flame' and 'Mahogany'), *Anagallis monelli* 'Orange', *Asclepias curassavica,* and *Carex* 'Orange Green', among many others.
OVERWINTERING. Cool and bright — in a greenhouse, our plants generally bloomed in mid-winter, an exhilarating and cheery sight. To avoid eliminating blooms, do not prune back before overwintering.
PROPAGATING. Cuttings.
COMMON PEST PROBLEMS. None.

Lupinus albifrons
Silver lupine

HARDY TO AT LEAST 25°F

We first saw this stupendous shrubby California native at Wave Hill in Bronx, New York. In its native habitat — predominantly rocky and sandy locations along the California coast — it forms a rounded shrub. Its extremely silver, soft leaves make this plant a delightful element in the garden and even more so in containers. For years, we have grown it for the foliage alone, but when it blooms — generally a late-winter event in the greenhouse — the flowers spikes are a spectacular violet-blue, and well worth the wait.

DESIGN IDEAS. Superb alone in a container, although it can also be combined with other drought-tolerant plants.
OVERWINTERING. Cool and bright. Allow soil to dry out very well between waterings. Do not prune if you want winter blooms.
PROPAGATING. Cuttings taken early in winter, before bud initiation.
COMMON PEST PROBLEMS. None.

Lupinus albifrons

Malvastrum lateritium

Malvastrum lateritium
Malvastrum

HARDY TO AT LEAST 25°F

This sub-shrubby plant from Uruguay has maplelike foliage, an elegantly trailing habit, and lovely, pale apricot flowers that resemble those of miniature hibiscus. Malvastrum makes a nice container subject, as it continues to bloom for much of the winter when set in a cool, sunny window.

DESIGN IDEAS. The luscious apricot shade of these flowers calls out for silver companions. Try it with *Artemisia* 'Powis Castle' or any helichrysum.
OVERWINTERING. Cool and bright. The habit of malvastrum is open and somewhat rangy — prune lightly to shape, but watch out for those flower buds!
PROPAGATING. Cuttings.
COMMON PEST PROBLEMS. Aphids seem to find most malvaceous plants delicious. (See Specific Pests and Diseases, page 64.)

Malvaviscus arboreus
var. *drumondii*

Malvaviscus arboreus
Wax mallow ⚡

HARDY TO AT LEAST 35°F

This native of Florida, Texas, and Mexico south to Peru and Brazil is frequently described as having "flowers that never open." They are amusing in their own way, suggesting, along their shrubby branches, small, pendant, red hibiscus blooms that will all, at some moment very soon, unfurl simultaneously. They never do. Malvaviscus blooms continuously all summer.

SPECIES AND CULTIVARS. Over the years, we have enjoyed the cultivar 'Fiesta', a particularly floriferous, bright red-flowered selection with variegated foliage.
DESIGN IDEAS. The bright red flowers of 'Fiesta' are set off spectacularly by contrasting foliage like that of *Ipomoea batatas* 'Blackie' or of *Lotus berthelotii*.
OVERWINTERING. Cool and bright; keep on the dry side.
PROPAGATING. Cuttings.
COMMON PEST PROBLEMS. None.

Mandevilla
Chilean jasmine, mandevilla ⚡

HARDY TO AT LEAST 45°F

These twining climbers tend to have funnel-shaped flowers, and many sport shiny green leaves. All the species are native to South America, originating variously in Brazil, Ecuador, Bolivia, and Argentina. With the exception of *Mandevilla laxa,* the attractive flowers have no scent. As far as we know, all mandevillas are summer bloomers.

SPECIES AND CULTIVARS. *Mandevilla × amabilis* 'Alice du Pont' is the best known cultivar, with rich, bright pink flowers and attractive shiny foliage. We especially enjoy *Mandevilla laxa* — also known as Chilean jasmine (although this vine is actually a native of Argentinia and Bolivia). Its white flowers, smaller than those of most mandevillas, are spectacularly fragrant, having a scent very like that of jasmine.
DESIGN IDEAS. Unless your container is really large, allow the mandevilla to have one all to itself.
OVERWINTERING. Cool and bright; cool temperatures minimize insect infestations. Prune as necessary to keep the plant manageable.
PROPAGATING. Cultivars by cuttings; species by seed, although it may be a year or so before they bloom.
COMMON PEST PROBLEMS. Aphids, whiteflies. (See Specific Pests and Diseases, page 64.)

Mandevilla × amabilis 'Alice du Pont'

Manihot esculenta 'Variegata'

Manihot
Cassava, manioc, tapioca 🌿 🏚

HARDY TO AT LEAST 45°F

This member of the Euphorbia family comprises 98 trees, shrubs, and herbs, and, like other euphorbias, has a milky latex sap. The source of the starchy foodstuff for which these plants are most commonly known is generally located in the roots and root nodules.

SPECIES AND CULTIVARS. *Manihot esculenta* 'Variegata' is too pretty for pudding, with its deeply lobed leaves concentrically banded in tropical yellow, orange, and red. It thrives in hot, humid conditions.
DESIGN IDEAS. 'Variegata' provides such a riot of color on its own that the best plants to combine with it from a visual perspective are the simplest; try *Dahlia* 'Bednall Beauty' or *Eucomis bicolor* 'Alba'.
OVERWINTERING. Warm and sunny. If not kept warm enough, manihot may go dormant, but it will revive with increased light and warmth in spring. Keep it on the dry side all winter. You can let it go dormant and set it in a cooler, darker spot, like the basement, but in this case, make sure it doesn't ever dry out completely. Do not prune.
PROPAGATING. Cuttings.
COMMON PEST PROBLEMS. None.

Manettia
Firecracker vine, manettia 🏚

HARDY TO AT LEAST 45°F

The most familiar member of this large family of vines from the tropical Americas is known as the firecracker vine. All manettias have funnel-shaped flowers, and most of them are twining plants, blooming from midsummer until frost.

SPECIES AND CULTIVARS. *Manettia cordifolia* has flowers of vivid red to deep orange fading to yellow and can climb up to six feet. The flowers of *M. luteorubra,* or the Brazilian firecracker, are bright red, tubular blooms tipped with yellow. This species can extend to 12 feet.
DESIGN IDEAS. The bright primary colors of manettia flowers bring their own fiesta to containers and trellises, so their best companions may be restrained ones. Try yellow-leaved coleus cultivars or *Ipomoea batatas* 'Margarita' and the red-flowered *Dahlia* 'Bednall Beauty', with its deep burgundy foliage.
OVERWINTERING. Cool and bright. This vigorous plant may benefit from a pruning now and then.
PROPAGATING. Easy to grow from seed.
COMMON PEST PROBLEMS. None.

Manettia luteorubra

Marrubium
Horehound, marrubium

HARDINESS VARIES; THOSE LISTED BELOW ARE HARDY TO AT LEAST 35˚F

Sun-loving aromatic plants that thrive in hot, dry conditions, marrubiums are well suited to pot culture. Most originate in temperate Eurasia. Some species may be hardier than 35˚F, but they must be wintered in relatively dry conditions to survive.

SPECIES AND CULTIVARS. Originating in Greece and Albania, *Marrubium cylleneum* has reflexed, furry chartreuse leaves and a fairly bushy habit. *M. rotundifolium* has round, woolly gray-green leaves rimmed with pale cream, lending an air of luminescence to this trailing plant and its white flowers. The Balkan species *M. incanum* has handsome white tomentose (fuzzy) leaves.

DESIGN IDEAS. The lovely grays of marrubium foliage lend themselves to myriad uses in bright, dry locations. Planted in the ground, they are natural candidates to front a sunny border, and when used in containers, they suggest countless medleys. Pinks, purples, and blues are all even more outstanding when placed next to silver and gray. Just make sure that the other plants don't overwhelm and take over — marrubiums will suffer when crowded out and shaded by their companions.

OVERWINTERING. Cool and bright. Water sparingly.

PROPAGATING. Cuttings; given time, most species will grow from seed.

COMMON PEST PROBLEMS. None.

Marrubium rotundifolium

Melianthus major

Melianthus
Honey flower, peanut butter plant

HARDY TO AT LEAST 35˚F

Melianthus major is by far the most commonly cultivated, but all six species originated in South Africa and subsequently naturalized in parts of India. Evergreen in milder climates, the jagged-edged, glaucous leaves of melianthus present an exceptionally elegant appearance. Interpretations of its fragrance are highly subjective. The *Royal Horticultural Society Index of Garden Plants* describes it as "foetid," which is probably an accurate description of how the British regard the smell of peanut butter. In our experience, melianthus doesn't smell *that* bad. The infrequent but intriguing appearance of its nectar-laden, dark purple to brownish red blooms suggests the origin of one of its common names, honey flower.

SPECIES AND CULTIVARS. Highly desirable selections are 'Antonow's Blue', with sharply serrated leaves that are a breathtaking shade of iridescent blue, and the Roger Raiche introduction 'Purple Haze', which has the appearance of being awash in purple light, especially in its saturated purple stems.

DESIGN IDEAS. The glaucous leaves of melianthus are stunning in a simple terra-cotta pot, and we've combined it to happy effect in the ground with plants whose leaves are full of saturated color such as 'Inky Pink' coleus or *Iresine* 'California'. The addition of something darkly contrasting — such as 'Purple Duckfoot' coleus or *Ipomoea* 'Ace of Spades' — unifies the composition

OVERWINTERING. Cool and bright. Prune back hard in the fall.

PROPAGATING. Species are easily grown from seed. The cultivars are trickier, and must be vegetatively propagated.

COMMON PEST PROBLEMS. None that we know of, although situating the plants in a location that is too windy or too sunny can result in damaged foliage. Placement in semi-shade is best in most North American gardens.

Michelia figo
Banana shrub

HARDY TO AT LEAST 25°F

This evergreen Chinese member of the magnolia family has lustrous green foliage and fascinating ivory flowers with petals that are tinged and edged in purple. Its common name refers to the sweet and extraordinary banana-like fragrance of these flowers. Although we enjoy it the most in the winter, *Michelia figo* blooms year-round.

DESIGN IDEAS. We plant *Michelia figo* in its own pot.

OVERWINTERING. Cool and bright.

PROPAGATING. Cuttings.

COMMON PEST PROBLEMS. None.

Michelia figo

Mirabilis
Four-o'-clock, marvel of Peru

HARDY TO AT LEAST 25°F

Although these are commonly grown as annuals from seed, their tuberous roots can cause mirabilis to behave as a perennial in many situations, including in our own Zone 5b garden. Thus, although you may not have to give special effort to keep them in your garden, they do, in fact, fit the definition of a tender perennial. They are also terrific fun to grow. Four-o'-clocks became favorites in European gardens soon after the conquistadores first saw them; they are among the Mexican plants first described and pictured in a Spanish manuscript that dates to 1552.

Mirabilis jalapa 'Limelight'

Mirabilis cultivar

SPECIES AND CULTIVARS. As one of the common names implies, the best-known species, *Mirabilis jalapa,* originated in Peru. Its fragrant flowers, which open in the late afternoon, vary from purple through white, with possibilities in the crimson, apricot, and yellow shades, often with more than one color occurring in each flower, sometimes in striped or mottled patterns. Another marvelous selection is 'Limelight', which adds pretty, chartreuse foliage, with some occasional green variegation, to the zingy bright pink flowers of *M. jalapa*. Quite different but charming in its own right, *M. longiflora* has white flowers and a more recumbent and relaxed habit, and is nocturnally fragrant. All of these have overwintered in the ground for us when they were situated against a foundation or patio stones. Four-o'-clocks bloom from midsummer to frost.

DESIGN IDEAS. Four-o'-clocks are versatile in their light requirements; we have grown them in conditions ranging from blazing hot sun to considerable shade. The bright colors of their flowers lend themselves to cheery tropical combinations — try *Mirabilis jalapa* with *Calibrachoa* 'Cabaret Apricot' or 'Cherry Pink' and *Pennisetum setaceum* 'Rubrum'. The lovely chartreuse foliage of *M. jalapa* 'Limelight' is a fine foil for green-leaved four-o'-clocks, as well as for *Talinum* 'Kingwood Gold', which blooms in a similar fuchsia color range but with contrasting habit and flower shape. 'Limelight' would also be handsome with the chocolate shades of *Ipomoea batatas* 'Ace of Spades' and one of the many phormiums.

OVERWINTERING. If you can count on having *Mirabilis* survive outdoors, this is the best way. We suggest, however, that you save seed annually just in case — it's easy and fun to collect. Overwintering the dormant plant in a pot is also fairly straightforward — just put it in a dark basement and don't water. In the spring, move it to a lighter location and water sparingly until you see some growth.

PROPAGATING. Growing these from seed is quick and efficient.

COMMON PEST PROBLEMS. None.

Monopsis
Gold lobelia, monopsis 🟦

HARDY TO AT LEAST 25°F

These wispy, almost grasslike perennials are natives of South Africa, where they grow in damp areas and are known as wild violets. Members of the campanula family (Campanulaceae), they have flowers reminiscent of those of lobelia, and most are deep purple. Monopsis bloom from winter to early spring.

SPECIES AND CULTIVARS. *Monopsis lutea* is a charming species, with small, bright yellow flowers. *M. unidentata* 'Bronze Beauty' has needlelike green foliage and bright yellow flowers with deep purple centers. The deep purple flowers of *M. unidentata* 'Royal Flush' have even darker centers.

DESIGN IDEAS. Monopsis grow happily in full sun and well-drained soil, and are wonderful in mixed containers, where their low, trailing habits are quite valuable. Use 'Royal Flush' in baskets and window boxes with *Helichrysum* 'Moe's Gold' and *Plumbago auriculata* 'Blue Powder'. *M. lutea* will mingle well with *Salvia thymoides* and *Tradescantia* 'Purple Queen'.

OVERWINTERING. Cool and bright. Note that this plant likes moisture.

PROPAGATING. Seed.

COMMON PEST PROBLEMS. None.

Monopsis unidentata 'Bronze Beauty'

Musa morelii

Musa
Banana, plantain 🟩

HARDINESS VARIES; THOSE LISTED BELOW ARE HARDY TO AT LEAST 40°F

This genus is familiar to us, in large part, because of the now ubiquitous edible banana, a descendant of *Musa × paradisiaca*. Perhaps no other plant's fruit and leaf so embody that which we picture when we say the word *tropical*. In recent years, introductions of *M. basjoo* (the Japanese banana) have been touted as possessing superior cold-hardiness, but bananas remain essentially tropical plants, with tropical requirements. You will astound and impress visitors if you have one growing in the middle of your perennial garden. Ours, which was visible from the road, continually inspired the question, "Is that hardy?"

SPECIES AND CULTIVARS. We've never grown a banana we didn't enjoy. In addition to *Musa basjoo,* there is the gorgeous *M. zebrina,* with leaves mottled by elegant wine-red variegation. The cream-streaked *M.* 'Ae Ae', once available only to Hawaiian royalty, grew happily in our gardens, producing, in typical monocarpic fashion, not only several pups, but fruit as well. *M. velutina* has lovely, three-foot-long leaves that are deep green above and reveal red midribs on their reverse. If this species from northeast India were to fruit in your garden, the bananas would be fuzzy and pink.

DESIGN IDEAS. Although it's possible to grow one in a large container, from a logistical as well as a cultural standpoint, bananas are best planted in the ground. Because of their dimensions, they become top heavy, and containers will easily blow over in a strong wind.

OVERWINTERING. Warm and sunny; winter temperatures should not go below 40°F. Many gardeners also have success overwintering dormant bananas in a dark basement; if using this method, be sure to keep the soil dry.

PROPAGATING. Division of pups. Because bananas are monocarpic, the parent plant dies after one full season. In cold climates, this may take more than one calendar year, but in our experience, once a banana has bloomed, the parent plant will not survive long.

COMMON PEST PROBLEMS. None.

Mussaenda erythrophylla

Mussaenda
Mussaenda

HARDY TO AT LEAST 45°F

Although the majority of these shrubby, sometimes twining species originate in tropical Asia, a few come from Africa. Their blooms consist of starry, loose-panicled flowers, often distinguished by a single enlarged sepal that resembles a brightly colored leaf. Mussaendas are dramatic plants, and well suited to winter life in the conservatory or a warm, sunny room.

SPECIES AND CULTIVARS. *Mussaenda frondosa,* a native of Indochina and Malaysia, has delightful star-shaped florets of saffron yellow. Its large white sepals, resembling the bracts of poinsettias, wave enticingly like flags for pollinators in the summer breeze. The West African species *M. erythrophylla* has red sepals with hairy pink flowers.

DESIGN IDEAS. We have planted mussaenda by itself in a pot, but it would also be wonderful situated in the garden.

OVERWINTERING. Warm and sunny. Prune to shape when necessary.

PROPAGATING. Cuttings.

COMMON PEST PROBLEMS. None.

Myoporum
Boobyalla, false sandalwood

HARDY TO AT LEAST 35°F

Most are native to Australia and New Zealand, and range from trees to heathlike ground-covering plants. They all bear ovoid fruits.

SPECIES AND CULTIVARS. *Myoporum parvifolium* is a small, ground-covering shrub in its native habitat, with shiny, linear green leaves in clusters along trailing stems. Its white flowers are honey-scented, and appear spring to summer. In our experience, myoporums grow slowly and densely, and therefore do not require much pruning.
DESIGN IDEAS. Myoporum makes a fine trailing element in a mixed container — try planting it with succulents.
OVERWINTERING. Cool and bright.
PROPAGATING. Cuttings.
COMMON PEST PROBLEMS. None.

Myoporum parvifolium

Neoregelia vandorme

Neoregelia
Neoregelia

HARDY TO AT LEAST 45°F

These South American members of the bromeliad family (Bromeliaceae) grow in funnel-shaped rosettes. Neoregelia's stiff leaf edges tend to be spiny and toothed, and their inflorescences are usually hidden inside the rosette's center.

SPECIES AND CULTIVARS. *Neoregelia carolinae* is a Brazilian species with glossy leaves that form a pronounced central zone of bright red in the middle of the rosette. The cultivar 'Flandria' retains this red center, with cream margins along the leaf edges. Another selection, 'Marechalii', has plain green leaves. They all have dense, pale blue flowers, and grow well outdoors in partial shade.
DESIGN IDEAS. The dramatically tropical appearance of neoregelias make them equally fun to situate in a shady spot in the ground or in containers along a shady porch for the summer. We pot them singly, although multiples of these containers grouped together can look distinctive. They'll also grow well in hanging baskets or in containers.
OVERWINTERING. These are easy to keep as houseplants, and they're reasonably happy without a large amount of sunshine. Neoregelias are especially appreciative of visits to the shower. Particularly in dry indoor heat, it's a good idea to keep the plant's central funnel filled with water. Removal of old leaves is a good idea now and then, but otherwise, no pruning is necessary.
PROPAGATING. Division of offsets.
COMMON PEST PROBLEMS. None.

Nepeta
Catmint, nepeta

HARDINESS VARIES; THOSE LISTED BELOW ARE HARDY TO AT LEAST 5°F

We are so accustomed to growing hardier species of these in the garden that we may neglect those from other climates. Due to their innately Mediterranean preference for well-drained, sunny conditions, the following seem to make superior container plants.

SPECIES AND CULTIVARS. *Nepeta phylloclamys* is a charmer, with its tidy, rounded yet triangular leaves of felty gray and lilac-pink flowers. *N. tuberosa* is an upright species that grows in Spain, Portugal, and Sicily. Its unusually large, fuzzy, gray-green foliage is complemented by substantial spikes of lavender blossom. Nepetas are midsummer bloomers, and may be encouraged to rebloom if they are cut back after the first flush of flowers.

DESIGN IDEAS. Just like their hardy counterparts, tender nepetas provide invaluable foliar interest when planted in the garden, particularly when situated alongside foliage that is visually contrasting. *Nepeta tuberosa* is especially valuable when used in this manner, combining nicely with orange- and yellow-flowered perennials. *N. phylloclamys* is an excellent container candidate, charming by itself, or perhaps paired with contrasting, larger leaves like those of *Euphorbia cotinifolia* or *Salvia buchananii*.

OVERWINTERING. Cool and bright. Keep them on the dry side. Cut back hard in the fall and keep an eye on how it continues to grow through the winter; additional haircuts may be necessary.

PROPAGATING. Cuttings.

COMMON PEST PROBLEMS. None.

Nepeta tuberosa

Nerium oleander 'Variegatum'

Nerium oleander
Oleander, rose bay

HARDY TO AT LEAST 35°F

Taking the form of a small shrub or tree in the mostly Mediterranean region that runs from southern Spain to Syria and Jordan, oleander is also found in Turkey and Iran, and even grows in the Himalayas at heights of up to 5,000 feet. In all these places, it usually grows near or in streams or other watery locations. Despite the plant's drought-tolerance once it is established, oleander requires ample water when grown in containers, particularly during the summer. All parts of the plant are highly toxic.

SPECIES AND CULTIVARS. The cultivar 'Mademoiselle Dubois' has elegant pale yellow, sometimes semi-double flowers. The single apricot blossoms of 'Tito Poggi' are particularly lovely. 'Variegatum' has creamy white-edged leaves and double rich pink blooms. The strongly talcum-scented double flowers of the vintage variety 'Peach Blossom' are a soft shade of pink. Nerium can bloom from spring to frost.

DESIGN IDEAS. Oleander makes a spectacular container subject, and is best situated in its own pot.

OVERWINTERING. Cool and bright.

PROPAGATING. Cuttings.

COMMON PEST PROBLEMS. None.

Nicotiana
Flowering tobacco, tobacco

HARDINESS VARIES; THOSE LISTED BELOW ARE HARDY TO AT LEAST 25°F

Nicotiana × *hybrida* 'Domino Salmon Pink'

The Royal Horticultural Society Index of Garden Plants defines the 65 species of *Nicotiana* as "mostly clammy aromatic, annual or perennial herbs and shrubs." Some come from Namibia, but most nicotiana species originate in North and South America, although a few are indigenous to Australia and the South Pacific. *Nicotiana tabacum,* or common tobacco, was used ceremonially by Native American cultures, but once introduced to Europeans, its role in human societies became a dramatically different one, as it quickly assumed the status of a major agricultural crop. In growing various species ourselves, we've noted with interest that even *N. tabacum* is quite an ornamental plant. When we consider the length of nicotiana bloom, the variety of flower type and color, the fragrance of most non-hybridized forms, the versatility of a plant that thrives in both full sun and considerable shade, with anywhere from little to abundant moisture, and then the fact that many nicotiana generously self-sow, it seems apparent that this is a plant that should be in every garden. Although ornamental tobacco is generally grown as an annual in our climate, the only way to ensure the maintenance of a selected form from one year to another is to overwinter that plant and then propagate it from stem or root cuttings. All nicotiana flowers attract hummingbirds, and most bloom from midsummer to fall.

SPECIES AND CULTIVARS. *Nicotiana alata,* the jasmine tobacco of Brazil, has sweetly scented, trumpet-shaped white flowers. Equally fragrant are the lime green flowers of *N. a.* 'Lime Green'. *N. mutabilis* is an especially entertaining species that was collected by Fred Meyer in Brazil. Its small, nodding flowers begin white, then age to pale pink and finally rose-pink, creating an enchanting assemblage of different shades at any one moment. *N.* 'Stonecrop Mauve' has remarkable large, rich mauve- to cocoa-colored flowers. With delicate drooping white flowers that have their own distinctively sweet fragrance, *N. suaveolens* is our favorite Australian species. *N. sylvestris,* or woodland tobacco, is an Argentinian perennial with large, bold basal leaves and clusters of highly fragrant, drooping white tubular flowers that attract hummingbird moths.

Nicotiana mutabilis

DESIGN IDEAS. Nicotianas are useful both in the ground and in containers. Set them on a patio or near the porch, where you will catch the scent of their fragrance in the evening. Although they grow well in full sunlight, their ability to tolerate partial sun makes them particularly versatile in plantings. And the range of their flower color makes nicotianas especially valuable in combinations with other plants. Try salmon, pink, and red-flowered tobaccos in juxtapostion with silver leaves, like those of *Plectranthus argentatus* or *Dichondra argentea*. Combine *Nicotiana* 'Stonecrop Mauve' with *Helichrysum petiolare*. *N. alata* 'Lime Green' and *Nicotiana langsdorfii* are great in a range of possibilities — with the blue flowers of salvias (try them with *Salvia patens* or *S. guaranitica*) and with other flowers in shades of pink and white.

OVERWINTERING. Cool and bright. Nicotianas are probably easiest to overwinter when they are kept cut back, but you may not be able to resist having a blooming stem or two.

PROPAGATING. Species grow easily from seed; the best way to guarantee the preservation of any nicotiana selection, however, is to take root cuttings.

COMMON PEST PROBLEMS. You would think that a plant as poisonous as tobacco wouldn't be bothered by anything. But the same pests that like other plants in the nightshade family (Solanaceae) will also be interested in this one. The worst pests in our neighborhood, where we are surrounded by potato farms, are Colorado potato beetles. An application or two of *Bacillus thuringensis* (Bt) should address this problem. Whiteflies may also pose a problem.

Ocimum americanum
African basil

HARDY TO AT LEAST 45°F

Although most gardeners are familiar with the annual sweet basil (*Ocimum basilicum*), those craving a basil that can be harvested year-round indoors would do well to acquaint themselves with the perennial types. As the common name implies, this plant originates in tropical Africa.

SPECIES AND CULTIVARS. *Ocimum* 'Aussie Sweetie' is a fine, vertically oriented cultivar eminently suitable for herbal hedging (see below) as well as the occasional tasty leaf for a winter salad. Its upright nature also makes it appropriate for containers.

DESIGN IDEAS. This African basil forms a nice little pillar-shaped tree that is handsome featured alone in a pot. But we've also put groups of them in the ground for the summer, where they can grow into an herbal hedge. The vertical orientation of *Ocimum americanum* suggests combinations with recumbent companions, such as *Origanum* 'Kent Beauty' or *Dichondra* 'Emerald Falls'. If you'd like to plant an edible container, pair it with 'Zaatar' oregano and 'Green Forest' parsley.

OVERWINTERING. Bright, but not too cool. Storage between 50 and 65°F is best; warmer temperatures will encourage the growth of aphid populations. Water sparingly. Frequent pruning for culinary use and for shaping is an excellent idea.

PROPAGATING. Cuttings.

COMMON PEST PROBLEMS. If this plant is kept too wet or does not receive adequate sunlight, botrytis, mildew, and damping-off are all possibilities.

Ocimum 'Aussie Sweetie'

Ophiopogon planiscapus 'Nigrescens'

Ophiopogon planiscapus
Mondo grass, ophiopogon

HARDY TO AT LEAST 0°F

This often stoloniferous relative of the familiar lily-of-the-valley can be a hardy perennial depending upon your location — it has been for us. We include this Japanese and Chinese native because ophiopogon's texture and color make it such a splendid container subject, and also because, in locations where its winter hardiness is questionable, keeping it indoors for the winter is a good way to hedge your bets.

SPECIES AND CULTIVARS. 'Nigrescens' is our favorite cultivar, with its truly black leaf blades and equally black berries. It thrives in heat, especially late-day western sun, although it tolerates moisture and some shade. The dramatic color of its leaves contrasts nicely with a wide variety of other plants.

DESIGN IDEAS. Mondo grass is great in containers all by itself, but you can also put it to excellent use in container medleys. Plant 'Nigrescens' with *Leptinella* 'Platt's Black' and *Calocephalus brownii*. In an equally elegant and very simple composition, accompany it with *Acaena* 'Blue Haze'.

OVERWINTERING. Cool and bright.

PROPAGATING. Division.

COMMON PEST PROBLEMS. None.

Origanum
Marjoram, oregano 🗂

HARDINESS VARIES; THOSE LISTED BELOW ARE HARDY TO AT LEAST 5°F

These Mediterannean plants grow, for the most part, where winters are mild and dry and summers are hot. Their inability to survive outdoors in your region may have as much to do with the moisture of your winter as it does with the cold. They are valuable not only for ornamental purposes, but occasionally for culinary ones as well.

SPECIES AND CULTIVARS. The cultivar 'Kent Beauty', with its lovely trailing habit, round, silver-veined leaves, and large salmon-tinged bracts, makes an outstanding container subject, especially well suited to window boxes. 'Silver Anniversary' is another pretty one, with small green leaves bordered in cream. It grows vigorously, and is also quite flavorful.

DESIGN IDEAS. The tender oreganos are probably best kept in containers, where you can monitor their water supply. Because their exuberant growth habit can lead to crowding with other plants, consider their companions carefully. They might coexist happily with the smaller sages, such as *Salvia officinalis* 'Compacta' or *S. officinalis* 'Purpurascens'.

OVERWINTERING. Cool and bright; keep dry. Cut back hard before bringing inside; may need additional haircuts throughout the winter.

PROPAGATING. Cuttings.

COMMON PEST PROBLEMS. None.

Origanum 'Kent Beauty'

Orthrosanthus chimboracensis
Orthrosanthus

HARDY TO AT LEAST 35°F

This showy Mexican plant resembles a giant blue-eyed grass (*Sisyrinchium*) with large, rich blue flowers in summer. It thrives in hot and dry conditions.

DESIGN IDEAS. Orthrosanthus is probably best grown in a container by itself; if you plant it in the ground, make sure there is adequate drainage.
OVERWINTERING. Cool and bright. Cut back flower stems and remove older foliage.
PROPAGATING. Seed.
COMMON PEST PROBLEMS. None.

Orthrosanthus chimboracensis

Osmanthus fragrans
Sweet olive

HARDY TO AT LEAST 35°F

Although it grows into a small tree in its native habitat, sweet olive, with its origins in the Himalayas, China, and Japan, is ideally suited to pot culture in a greenhouse or other sunny spot indoors. Although the appearance of neither flower nor foliage will grab your attention, the overwhelmingly lovely fragrance of the small, creamy flowers most certainly will; it blooms in fall and winter.

DESIGN IDEAS. As it grows into a fairly large shrub, sweet olive is best planted in a container by itself. In three years, it might measure three feet high by two feet wide.
OVERWINTERING. Cool and bright. Any pruning is best done after bloom, in the spring.
PROPAGATING. Cuttings.
COMMON PEST PROBLEMS. None.

Osmanthus fragrans

Osteospermum 'Sunny Side Up'

Osteospermum
Osteospermum 🗂

HARDY TO AT LEAST 35°F

Including shrubs as well as herbaceous perennials, this family of composites from Africa and the Arabian peninsula has received considerable attention from hybridizers in recent years. Most of the species and hybrids are drought tolerant and boast showy flowers, attributes that make them great plants to have in the garden as well as in winter containers.

SPECIES AND CULTIVARS. *Osteospermum* 'Sunny Side Up', with its butter yellow petals and dazzling purple-blue eyes, sells itself on sight. *O.* 'Silver Sparkler' has cream-edged leaves that set off each stunning white daisy with a blue petal reverse and an electric blue center. This plant blooms in spring and fall, but the foliage is eye-catching all year. One of a British hybrid series, 'Cannington Katrina' boasts unusually large, rich purple flowers in abundance throughout the summer.

DESIGN IDEAS. Osteospermums are perfect candidates for container planting; try 'Sunny Side Up' with *Tradescantia* 'Purple Queen' or 'Cannington Katrina' with *Helichrysum petiolare*.

OVERWINTERING. Cool and bright. As osteospermums bloom during the winter, refrain from pruning except for removal of spent blooms.

PROPAGATING. Species can be grown easily from seed. The hybrids should be propagated by cuttings.

COMMON PEST PROBLEMS. If osteospermums experience stressful conditions, aphids may find them attractive. (See Specific Pests and Diseases, page 64.)

Oxalis
Oxalis, shamrock 🗂

HARDINESS VARIES; THOSE LISTED BELOW ARE HARDY TO AT LEAST 30°F

Comprising a very large family — some 800 annual and perennial members — oxalis originate in many parts of the world, but with centers of diversity in South Africa and South America. Grown chiefly for the fascinating variations of their foliage, oxalis have been gaining fans in recent years.

SPECIES AND CULTIVARS. An entertaining Peruvian species, *Oxalis herrerae* has thick trunks and succulent, needlelike leaves; its flowers are bright yellow. *O. regnelli* 'Atropurpurea' has deep burgundy leaves, each marked by a fuchsia chevron, and these are strikingly juxtaposed with drooping pale pink flowers that reveal a lavender interior. *O. vulcanicola* 'Copper Glow' is a remarkable foliage plant, with delicate chartreuse-to-golden yellow leaves edged and

Oxalis regnelli 'Atropurpurea'

blushed with coppery pink to salmon. This exceptional container subject also has yellow flowers, and will tolerate conditions ranging from considerable shade to full sun.

DESIGN IDEAS. The dark leaf color of many oxalis makes them a great choice for mixed containers that need an element of contrast. In general, combine them with other drought-tolerant candidates, and make sure that they aren't crowded out by their companions. *Oxalis vulcanicola* 'Copper Glow' is better adapted for combination containers than most other oxalis; this herbaceous plant will consort with almost anything. Interesting combinations will result from mixing with plants that present a similar color range — many of the phormiums, and impatiens, particularly 'Papaya' (in the Seashell Series), come to mind.

OVERWINTERING. Cool and bright. Dormant types will require little active care. Those that continue to grow through the winter may benefit from a light shearing at some point.

PROPAGATING. This depends on the type. *Oxalis* species that have a dormant period are best propagated by repotting the corms. Other types can remain in containers and continue to grow even in the winter, given cool and relatively bright conditions. Propagate these species from cuttings.

COMMON PEST PROBLEMS. None.

Pachyphytum
Pachyphytum 🔲

HARDY TO AT LEAST 35° F

This Mexican genus contains attractive species, many of which form rosettes of congested leaves and have cup-shaped flowers. The Greek origin of their name is quite descriptive — it means "thick leaves." Because of their remarkable drought tolerance, they overwinter indoors with little maintenance.

SPECIES AND CULTIVARS. *Pachyphytum oviferum* forms nice rosettes of plump, powdered white leaves. The nubbly thick leaves of purplish gray distinguish *P. bracteosum*. *P.* 'Garnet Fudge' forms a tidy rosette of tear-shaped, violet-colored leaves.

DESIGN IDEAS. As with many succulents, we plant pachyphytum in its own container, but you could certainly combine it with other succulents.

OVERWINTERING. In your living space, at room temperature.

PROPAGATING. Leaf cuttings.

COMMON PEST PROBLEMS. None.

Pachyphytum bracteosum

🔲 Sunny & Warm, page 44   🔲 Cool & Bright, page 50   🔲 Dark & Damp, page 54   🔲 Dark & Dry, page 56

Parahebe
Digger's speedwell

HARDY TO AT LEAST 25°F

A genus that largely comprises trailing subshrubs, these are native to New Zealand, New Guinea, and Australia, and are closely related to the hebes. Their handsome foliage and attractive forms make them ideal greenhouse subjects. Many parahebes are summer blooming.

SPECIES AND CULTIVARS. *Parahebe perfoliata,* or digger's speedwell, has lovely, matte gray-green leaves perforated by slender stems. Its flowers are held in racemes that measure up to eight inches long and are a fine shade of blue-violet. A low-growing species with nearly succulent leaves, *P. lyalli* forms a low mound about 12 inches across, with small pale lavender flowers. *P.* 'Snowcap' is a charming, compact shrublet with delicate purple branches and glossy, dark green leaves as well as spires of airy white blossoms.

DESIGN IDEAS. Most parahebes are probably best planted in containers by themselves, although they can also be put in the ground for the summer.

OVERWINTERING. Cool and bright.

PROPAGATING. Cuttings, seed.

COMMON PEST PROBLEMS. None.

Parahebe 'Snowcap'

Passiflora 'Amethyst'

Passiflora
Passionflower

HARDINESS VARIES; THOSE LISTED BELOW ARE HARDY TO AT LEAST 45°F

This genus comprises nearly 450 vines and scandent (climbing) shrubs, with species originating in diverse parts of the world, though the majority are tropical (hardy to 45°F). The "passion" of the common name refers not to human passion, but to that of Christ, whose trials were brought to the minds of medieval botanists by the curiously shaped flowers. Many passionflowers bear edible fruit.

SPECIES AND CULTIVARS. *Passiflora apetala* sports handsome, bat-winged foliage and small, jewel-like bright green flowers, which are followed by inedible black fruits. Recently introduced by John MacDougal, who discovered it growing in Honduras, *P. citrina* is continuously covered by exquisite star-shaped lemon-yellow flowers when grown in full sun, and is a magnet for fritillary butterflies. *P. coccinea,* also known as red granadilla, has oblong leaves and bright scarlet flowers. When these are pollinated, they eventually become edible green fruits. With its petite stature and multitude of charming small deep pink flowers, the Ecuadoran *P. sanguinolenta* is an ideal subject for container culture. Passionflowers generally bloom from early summer on.

DESIGN IDEAS. Most passionflowers are well suited to container culture and are particularly handsome when grown in hanging baskets or trained onto trellises. Because of their exuberant twining habits, they are best given their own container and freedom to roam. We have seen *Passiflora citrina* trained into an attractive standard.

OVERWINTERING. Cool and bright. Passionflowers require good drainage and thrive on frequent feeding. Because they're vigorous growers, regular pruning will keep them looking their best.

PROPAGATING. Many of the species can be grown from seed, although this may be challenging. Collect fresh seed and soak it before sowing. Most passionflowers are easily rooted from tip cuttings taken in early spring.

COMMON PEST PROBLEMS. Whiteflies and spider mites may find these attractive. (See Specific Pests and Diseases, page 64.)

Pelargonium
Geranium

HARDY TO AT LEAST 45°F

The majority of these originate in South Africa, although their cultivation in gardens and subsequent hybridization have made them truly cosmopolitan. Like so many plants from this region, they are rugged and tough, as well as beautiful, and this has ensured their widespread popularity.

SPECIES AND CULTIVARS. Over the years, we have collected so many geraniums that it is difficult to mention just a few. 'Black Tartan' is a dwarf plant with deep green leaves that mature to black and sports double flowers of brilliant scarlet. Named for the famous glass house Prince Albert commissioned for the 1851 Great Exposition, 'Crystal Palace Gem' has large, clear yellow leaves splashed with green and is further electrified by bright orange-red flowers. *Pelargonium ionidiflorum* has dainty flowers of shocking pink and glossy green leaves — it will add pizzazz to window boxes. With large, fuzzy leaves redolent of mint, *P.* 'Peppermint' is our favorite scented geranium. *P. sidoides* is a choice species, boasting gray felty leaves edged in exquisite scallops, with infrequent small flowers of deep burgundy. Golden fan-shaped leaves with maroon centers and bright chartreuse venation and edging distinguish *P.* 'Vancouver Centennial'. This compact and mounding plant, with its bright orange-red flowers, is superb in containers.

Pelargonium 'Crystal Palace Gem'

Pelargonium 'Vancouver Centennial'

DESIGN IDEAS. Pelargoniums are perfect for containers, where their drainage requirements are easily met. The container need not be large, but make sure the pelargoniums are not overly crowded by other plants. *Pelargonium ionidiflorum* would be lovely with large silver plants such as *Brachyglottis monroi* or *Plectranthus argentatus*. Similarly, pair 'Black Tartan' simply and elegantly with *Dichondra argentea*. 'Peppermint' is an ideal subject for hanging baskets.

OVERWINTERING. Cool and bright. Water sparingly; remember that the South African winter is a dry one. Keep dead leaves picked off, and trim spent flower clusters as needed.

PROPAGATING. Cuttings.

COMMON PEST PROBLEMS. During the winter months, geraniums may be troubled by rust; discourage this problem by removing and disposing of infected leaves. Botrytis, which can also be a seasonal issue, will be similarly discouraged by the removal of spent blossoms and the prevalence of good air circulation.

Pennisetum setaceum 'Rubrum'
Red fountain grass ▥

HARDY TO AT LEAST 25°F

A maroon-leaved member of the fountain grass genus, *Pennisetum setaceum* 'Rubrum' has hardier, green-leaved forms. Its striking foliage and silvery flower plumes make it a valuable container and landscape element, even if it requires special winter care.

OVERWINTERING. Dark and damp. Cut back after frost and either dig out of the ground and pot up or move its container indoors. Leave in the pot or bag it up. Move it to a cool area, either dark or light. The plant should go dormant and not require further attention.

PROPAGATING. Division in spring.

COMMON PEST PROBLEMS. None.

Pennisetum setaceum 'Rubrum'

Pentas
Pentas, star cluster

HARDY TO AT LEAST 20°F

Native from the Middle East to the bush of East Africa, pentas are frequently featured in garden plantings throughout the tropics. These plants have an appetite for hot weather.

SPECIES AND CULTIVARS. The cultivar 'Tu-Tone' has distinctive bicolor flowers of rose and paler pink. The jazzy 'Stars and Stripes' juxtaposes green and chartreuse foliage with bright red flowers, creating an effect that, like patriotism, comes across as either dazzling or embarrassing, depending on your point of view. We have also grown some excellent single-color selections, including the white-flowered 'Silver Star' and 'Cranberry Punch'.

DESIGN IDEAS. The tireless bloom and heat resistance of pentas make them ideal elements in containers. Try 'Tu-Tone' with *Brachyglottis monroi* and *Plectranthus naiadensis* — or 'Silver Star' with *Ipomoea batatas* 'Ace of Spades' and *Haloragis erecta* 'Wellington Bronze'.

OVERWINTERING. Although pentas bloom and grow best in warm conditions, they will store well in a cool, bright location where they will become dormant.

PROPAGATING. Cultivars must be propagated by cuttings.

COMMON PEST PROBLEMS. Aphids, whiteflies. (See Specific Pests and Diseases, page 64.)

Pentas 'Stars and Stripes'

Phormium
Flax lily, New Zealand flax

HARDY TO AT LEAST 35°F

Our first sight of phormiums was in an Irish garden, a setting in which they attain dramatic proportions because of the mild, moist island weather. We returned from our Irish sojourn with six different cultivars, and haven't stopped growing phormiums since, despite the fact that in New England, we have to bring them indoors each winter. Even under these less-than-ideal circumstances, they can attain considerable size over time, and quite a few of our specimens have bloomed, attracting enthusiastic catbirds to drink the nectar of their curious flowers.

Phormium 'Maori Sunrise'

SPECIES AND CULTIVARS. We have enjoyed every phormium we have grown, but we do have a few favorites. *Phormium tenax* 'Atropurpureum', with its huge maroon leaves, creates a dramatic accent wherever it is situated. *P. colensoi* 'Maori Chief' is a midsize selection for those wary of larger phormiums. Its leaves are striped with pink, red, and tan. 'Maori Sunrise' is even smaller, with slender apricot- and pink-edged bronze leaves. Wonderful new selections continue to be introduced each year from hybridzers in New Zealand. The new smaller cultivars are easier to keep over the winter.

DESIGN IDEAS. When they reach a mature size, there's usually not much room left in the pot for anything else, but while they're smaller, phormiums are great fun to combine with all sorts of other plants. With their pink and yellow striations, all the Maori variations combine wonderfully with companions like *Oxalis vulcanis* 'Copper Glow', many coleus cultivars, and dark reddish or brown leaves such as those of *Haloragis erecta* 'Wellington Bronze' or *Carex comans*. The deep tones of *Phormium tenax* 'Atropurpureum' create fantastic contrast, especially with silvers like *Plectranthus argentatus* and *Dichondra argentatus*.

OVERWINTERING. Although they benefit from a considerable amount of water when in active growth, we have found that the key to the successful overwintering of phormiums is to keep them dry in cool and bright conditions. Wet and cool conditions can stress them, predisposing them to winter demise. Phormiums should not be pruned; merely remove old leaves as needed.

PROPAGATING. Species may be grown from seed, especially if your plant flowers and sets seed. The cultivars are generally produced by division. Newly divided plants will take some time to recover.

COMMON PEST PROBLEMS. Most problems we have encountered with phormiums stem from overwatering, not pests.

Phormium 'Sundowner'

Phormium 'Yellow Wave'

Phygelius
Cape fuchsia, phygelius

HARDY TO AT LEAST 25°F

From South Africa, where they form evergreen shrubs, these charming plants have pendant, tubular flowers that are as intriguing to hummingbirds as they are to humans. In North American gardens they seem to benefit from a little shade.

SPECIES AND CULTIVARS. 'African Queen' is a particularly floriferous selection, with multitudes of yellow-throated, pale red flowers beginning in early summer. The blooms of 'Sensation' are a magnetic shade of fuchsia, with flared rims of red, attracting attention in both the greenhouse and the garden. In addition to its rich red flowers, 'Sunshine' features chartreuse foliage. A remarkably long-blooming selection, 'Tommy Knockers' has large, creamy apricot flowers that reveal yellow-striped throats. 'Yellow Trumpets' is arrayed in lovely lemon-yellow blooms.

DESIGN IDEAS. Phygelius are well adapted to either container or garden culture, though they are happiest with a little shade. Try 'Tommy Knockers' with *Phormium* 'Maori Sunrise' and *Ipomoea batatas* 'Ace of Spades'. Or try 'African Queen' with *Helichrysum petiolare* 'Limelight' and *Pentas* 'Stars and Stripes'.

OVERWINTERING. Cool and bright. Cut plants back hard in the fall and repeat as needed.

PROPAGATING. Cuttings.

COMMON PEST PROBLEMS. None.

Phygelius 'Yellow Trumpets'

Phygelius 'Tommy Knockers'

Plectranthus argentatus

Plectranthus amboinicus

Plectranthus
Plectranthus 🌿

HARDY TO AT LEAST 35°F

This marvelous group includes many that, like Swedish ivy, are well known as houseplants. The majority of plectranthus originate in South Africa. Although grown mainly for their foliage, often they possess lovely flowers. We have found them to be valuable and trouble-free plants, excellent in containers, as well as planted out in the ground. They will tolerate some shade.

SPECIES AND CULTIVARS. *Plectranthus amboinicus* — variously known as Spanish thyme, Cuban oregano, or Mexican mint — has fragrant leaves that have been selected for their attractive color variations, including the sport 'Ochre Flame', which has scallop-edged leaves of chartreuse and lime, and 'Variegated', with leaves that are bright yellow and lime. *P. argentatus* is an outstanding species, with its fuzzy silver leaves and infrequent white and pale blue flowers. It makes a superb — if large — container plant, and is majestic in the garden. *P. fruticosus* 'James' has ruffled, bright green leaves with burgundy reverse and stems. Although they are tiny, this plant's prolific blue-mauve flowers are very showy. *P. madagascariensis,* or variegated mintleaf, has trailing stems with cheery cream and bright green variegation decorating its rounded leaves, and sports white flowers; it is well suited for hanging containers. *P. naiadensis,* with its fuzzy heart-shaped leaves of lime green, is a personal favorite. Its dusty maroon flower spikes are bejeweled with silver buds that open to icy white flowers — these are etched by delicate mauve lines. Bees also find it attractive. *P. oertendahlii* has white flowers as well as cupped and furry, highly textural dark olive leaves lined in white, which appear deep purple on their reverse. This trailing plectranthus is happiest in considerable shade.

DESIGN IDEAS. Plectranthus are trouble-free plants in the ground and in containers, offering a wide variety of foliage types and plant habits. Most of them are best in full sun, although *Plectranthus oertendahlii* thrives in the shade. Try it with *Colocasia esculenta* 'Illustris' and begonia cultivars. *P. argentatus* provides a spectacular silver presence, handsome with *Capsicum annuum* 'Black Pearl' and *Angelonia* 'Serena Rose'. The fuzzy lime green leaves of *P. naiadensis* mix elegantly with many begonia cultivars.

OVERWINTERING. Cool and bright. Prune to shape as desired.

PROPAGATING. Species may be grown from seed. Cultivars are best grown from cuttings.

COMMON PEST PROBLEMS. None.

Plumbago auriculata 'Powder Blue'

Plumbago
Leadwort

HARDY TO AT LEAST 20°F

A popular mainstay of Victorian conservatories, the phloxlike flowers of *Plumbago auriculata* still provide an unbeatable show through the winter in a cool, sunny window. This shrubby plant from South Africa is both heat and drought tolerant, and its powder blue flowers have earned it a special place in the heart of many a gardener. Plumbago blooms almost continuously. If for some reason it's exposed to the minimum hardiness temperature, it should resprout from old wood.

SPECIES AND CULTIVARS. *Plumbago auriculata* 'Powder Blue' is a recent selection of the Cape leadwort that combines exceptional vigor with flowers of a startling shade of creamy ice blue. Although *P. auriculata* is much more widely grown than any other species, the genus does include others of merit. *P. indica* is a trailing Indian species with long flower spikes that range from pink to scarlet and purple. The Peruvian *P. caerulea* has rich purple and deep blue flowers on arching stems.

DESIGN IDEAS. Stunning window boxes are the result when you plant *Plumbago auriculata* 'Powder Blue' with *Heliotropium arborescens* 'Iowa' and *Dichondra argentea*.

OVERWINTERING. Cool and bright. Prune to shape in the fall.

PROPAGATING. Species may be grown from seed. Cultivars should be grown from cuttings.

COMMON PEST PROBLEMS. Both spider mites and whiteflies adore plumbago; be vigilant. (See Specific Pests and Diseases, page 64.)

Polianthes tuberosa
Tuberose

HARDY TO AT LEAST 35°F

The tuberose is what is known as a cultigen — that is, a plant cultivated by humans for so long that we have lost any trace of its origins in nature. Its cultivation dates back to at least pre-Columbian Mexico, and its very fragrant, waxy white flowers have been prized by a long succession of human noses. Tuberose is a member of the agave family (Agavaceae), and was particularly popular in Victorian conservatories, where the moment when it released its sweet evening fragrance was much anticipated. Tuberose blooms in late summer.

DESIGN IDEAS. We prefer to pot these up by themselves.

OVERWINTERING. Cool and bright.

PROPAGATING. The bulbs form offsets that are easily divided.

COMMON PEST PROBLEMS. None.

Polianthes tuberosa

Punica granatum
Pomegranate

HARDY TO AT LEAST 35°F

Originating in the region between northeastern Turkey and the western Himalayas, the pomegranate is widely naturalized throughout the Mediterranean. This shrubby small tree grows readily where summers are hot and dry and winters are mild. For those of us who lack those essential conditions, there are dwarf cultivars that do nicely in containers.

SPECIES AND CULTIVARS. *Punica granatum* var. *nana* forms an intricately branched little tree and bears deep red flowers in its first year from seed. In their scale, both the flowers and the fruits are perfectly suited to life in a fairly small pot. *P. granatum* 'Chico' is also dwarf, with double flowers of brilliant orange. They are both mid- to late-summer bloomers.

DESIGN IDEAS. We prefer to pot pomegranates by themselves.

OVERWINTERING. Cool and bright. Prune to shape as desired.

PROPAGATING. Species are easily grown from seed, and cultivars should be propagated from cuttings.

COMMON PEST PROBLEMS. None.

Punica granatum var. *nana*

Puya species

Puya
Puya

HARDY TO AT LEAST 35°F

There are more than 100 species of puya, all native to the Andean region, where they thrive at an altitude higher than any other bromeliad. They have adapted to this environment with surprising degrees of both drought and cold tolerance. Their relatively slow rate of growth discourages commercial growers from selling them, so it may be necessary to start them yourself from seed.

SPECIES AND CULTIVARS. *Puya coerulea* is a Chilean species, perhaps the hardiest member of the pineapple family, with rosettes of serrated gray leaves and spikes of exotic blue-green flowers. Noted plantsman Graham Stuart Thomas said that it's "worth the cost and effort to grow this rare plant." Many puyas are spring bloomers.

DESIGN IDEAS. Like many succulents, these are great in a container by themselves, but you can combine them with other plants that thrive under similar conditions.

OVERWINTERING. Think of the Andes: cool and bright. Puya should not be pruned.

PROPAGATING. Generally by seeds.

COMMON PEST PROBLEMS. None.

Rhodochiton atrosanguineus
Purple bell vine, rhodochiton 🌿 🪴

HARDY TO AT LEAST 25°F

This charming Mexican vine is sometimes grown as an annual, but there are advantages to holding on to it as a tender perennial — namely, a much larger, more mature plant in the subsequent season. Rhodochiton's pendant, bell-shaped fuchsia and purple flowers are arranged along the stems in graduated sequence, and will appear in mid- to late summer.

DESIGN IDEAS. Because it is not a particularly large or vigorous vine, rhodochiton is well suited to container culture and will remain relatively easy to control. And — unusual for tender vines — it prefers shade.
OVERWINTERING. Cool and bright. It can also be placed in warmer and sunny conditions, but then it will stay in active growth. In either case, prune back fairly hard to reduce the size of the plant.
PROPAGATING. Seeds.
COMMON PEST PROBLEMS. None.

Rhodochiton atrosanguineus

Rosa chinensis 'Mutabilis'

Rosa chinensis
China rose 🌿

HARDINESS VARIES; THOSE LISTED BELOW ARE HARDY TO AT LEAST 5°F

The inclusion of this familiar genus is bound to raise a few eyebrows, so we should explain that the roses meant here are indeed tender ones, not just the same finicky hybrid teas that we've been told should thrive outdoors but don't under most actual circumstances. These roses are, in fact, the early ancestors of those same hybrid teas. Introduced to European gardeners in the mid- to late 1700s, this rose had a much older history, and is identifiable in Chinese paintings of the 10th century. It still grows in China today, where, along with other forms of *Rosa chinensis,* it is referred to as a "monthly" rose, because of its perpetual bloom schedule. Most of these roses are dwarf ones, and were probably selected over many centuries by Chinese gardeners for both their compact size and their recurrent bloom. As a group, *Rosa chinensis* are fascinating to grow as living pieces of the historical record; they are also quite lovely in their own right. Their delicate single flowers provide olfactory as well as visual delight.

SPECIES AND CULTIVARS. *Rosa chinensis* 'Mutabilis' has leaves that are tinged copper or purple when young, but it is the everchanging, fragrant single flowers that earn it this name. Beginning as yellow, the flowers transform into coppery salmon, eventually turning deep pink. The cultivar 'Single Pink China' is another lovely old variety that still grows in Chinese gardens — and may be a sport of 'Parson's Pink'. It has graceful single flowers that fade from deep rose to pale pink with age.

DESIGN IDEAS. We plant these roses by themselves in their own containers; they make superb conservatory plants.

OVERWINTERING. Cool and bright. When they are happy, these will bloom through the winter. Prune to shape as needed.

PROPAGATING. Cuttings.

COMMON PEST PROBLEMS. Aphids and powdery mildew. (See Specific Pests and Diseases, page 64.)

Rosmarinus officinalis
Rosemary

HARDY TO AT LEAST −5°F

Texans and Italians can enjoy seven-foot-tall hedges of rosemary, but the rest of us must be content with smaller specimens in containers. There is no justice, but under the right conditions, rosemary can make a successful indoor subject. As a hedge, it must simply be a more modest one that you enjoy only in summer.

SPECIES AND CULTIVARS. These are just some of our favorites; new selections appear all the time. *Rosmarinus officinalis* 'Huntington Carpet' is an especially handsome strain, both flavorful and fragrant, with lustrous deep green foliage and a lengthy season of lavender-blue bloom in cool, sunny winter conditions. 'Lockwood de Forest' is a good form of prostrate rosemary, and 'Golden Rain' has attractive green leaves streaked with yellow.

OVERWINTERING. Cool and bright — the cooler and brighter, the better. Prune to shape.

PROPAGATING. Cuttings.

COMMON PEST PROBLEMS. Aphids. Powdery mildew is often a serious problem when overwintering rosemary indoors. The best preventives are good air circulation and cool growing conditions — temperatures between 30 and 40°F are ideal. It is also important not to overwater. (See Specific Pests and Diseases, page 64.)

Rosmarinus officinalis var. *prostratus*

Ruellia brittoniana

Ruellia
Christmas pride, monkey plant, ruellia ▣

HARDINESS VARIES FROM -25 TO 30°F

There are 150 species of herbs and shrubs in this genus originating in tropical America, Africa, Asia, and even temperate North America. We have found them to be excellent container and garden plants. We do not, however, advise growing any ruellia where it is hardy: it can be invasive in some regions.

SPECIES AND CULTIVARS. *Ruellia brittoniana,* the so-called Mexican petunia, with its bright lavender flowers and bronze foliage, is a showy, long-blooming plant that we have enjoyed. Don't grow this plant where it is hardy — *R. brittoniana* is currently classified as a category-one invasive species by the Florida Exotic Pest Plant Council. Apparently, when it has access to moisture and can freely overwinter, it has a tendency to invade wetlands. *R. elegans* is a Brazilian native with intense bright red flowers on a low, spreading plant. It may seed in warmer climates, but blooms throughout the winter when brought indoors.

DESIGN IDEAS. Planted out in the garden, the showy *R. brittoniana* quickly becomes a focal point. Its saturated purple flowers and dark foliage stand out with bright red companions, such as *Salvia microphylla* 'Red Velvet'. In containers, it mixes well with plants that have silver leaves, such as *Dichondra argentea* and *Brachyglottis monroi*.

OVERWINTERING. Cool and bright. Do not be afraid to prune hard in the fall and when necessary thereafter.

PROPAGATING. Cuttings root rapidly. Species can be grown from seed.

COMMON PEST PROBLEMS. None.

Saccharum officinarum var. *violaceum*
Purple sugarcane ▣

HARDY TO AT LEAST 35°F

Also sold as 'Pele's Smoke', this form of edible sugarcane has both purple stems and leaves. We really enjoy this flamboyant member of the grass family.

DESIGN IDEAS. *Saccharum officinarum* var. *violaceum* makes a stunning statement in containers, but can also be planted in the ground for the summer, where it will add a tropical dimension to the garden. This sugarcane combines wonderfully with many coleus cultivars, begonias, and plectranthus, and grows well in both sun and partial shade.

OVERWINTERING. Warm and bright, above 50°F. Should not require pruning through the winter at these temperatures.

PROPAGATING. Take cuttings from new side shoots in the spring.

COMMON PEST PROBLEMS. None.

Saccharum officinarum var. *violaceum*

▣ Sunny & Warm, page 44   ▣ Cool & Bright, page 50   ▣ Dark & Damp, page 54   ▣ Dark & Dry, page 56

Salvia
Sage ▣ ▣

HARDINESS VARIES; THOSE LISTED BELOW ARE HARDY TO AT LEAST 25°F

This remarkably diverse group includes some of the showiest plants for the sunny garden, although a few notable species prefer the shade. All salvias are attractive to hummingbirds. Most bloom from early summer to frost, but there are a few that begin to bloom only in late summer in northern gardens.

SPECIES AND CULTIVARS. When we are asked to make just a few recommendations, perhaps no other genus presents us with quite as much of a quandary as that of *Salvia*. Our choices are bound to be arbitrary and fairly personal.

Salvia splendens 'Van-Houttei'

Salvia discolor

We recommend *Salvia cacaliifolia,* with its distinctively triangular leaves and true cobalt flower spikes. The silver foliage and sky blue flowers of *S. chaemedryoides* make it an outstanding choice for many sunny circumstances. Then there is *S. coccinea* 'Brenthurst', a seed-grown strain with rich pink flowers and contrasting silver-raspberry calyces along gray stems. *S. confertiflora* is one of the rare species that prefer moisture and a bit of shade, rewarding the fulfillment of these conditions with large, textured leaves and very fuzzy, rust-red blooms. *S. corrugata* has substantially textured, rich green leaves and paler khaki stems, both covered by fine orange fuzz; its tubular blue flowers appear in winter. *S. discolor* is distinguished by two-toned black-and-gray flowers set against sophisticated, felted silver leaves. The scarlet-flowered *S. greggii,* or autumn sage, is a floriferous species that occurs naturally in southern Texas and Mexico and was named for the Mexican trader J. Gregg, who collected many of them in Texas prior to 1870.

Gardeners only slightly south of us can successfully overwinter the spectacularly cobalt-flowered *S. guaranitica* outdoors. *Salvia* × 'Indigo Spires' is a popular selection, with deep purple spires that are sought out by dried-flower enthusiasts. *S. involucrata* 'Bethellii' is another Mexican native with bright fuchsia flowers and especially shiny leaves. The *S.* × *jamensis* hybrids combine characteristics of *S. microphylla* and *S. greggii;* our favorite might be *S.* × *jamensis* 'San Isidro Moon', which boasts elegant dark gray stems and calyces that clasp luminescent peach and cream flower petals. We named a hybrid some years ago for our older daughter, who was at the time a beginning student of the Spanish language: *Salvia* × *jamensis* 'Señorita Leah'. It has large, clear pink flowers that shade to softer peach tones. Its brilliant cherry red flowers held within dark gray calyces, *S. microphylla* 'Red Velvet' is also a standout. *S. patens* is well known for its large, gentian blue flowers, and makes a decidedly blue statement in the garden. Distinguished by the striking combination of maroon leaves with its brilliant cobalt flowers, *S. sinaloensis* is a diminutive species that is well suited to smaller containters. Producing many wands of large, deep carmine flowers, *S. splendens* 'Van-Houttei' prefers shade and moisture. *S.* 'Waverly' combines glossy foliage with fuzzy white flowers that protrude from violet bracts.

DESIGN IDEAS. There are almost as many ways to use salvia as there are species — many adapt well to planting out in the garden; others, due mainly to their smaller scale, are best viewed closer up in containers. Most, but not all, require good drainage.

OVERWINTERING. Cool and bright, but some gardeners have successfully overwintered salvias in dark, dry conditions. It is worth experimenting with this if there are no other options. *Salvia patens* and *S. guaranitica* can be overwintered as a tuber, in dark and damp conditions. Most salvias should be cut back hard in the fall.

PROPAGATING. For the most part, the species grow easily from seed; cultivars and selections, from cuttings.

COMMON PEST PROBLEMS. In greenhouses, aphids are periodically a problem, but this is a good illustration of how a pest issue that is troublesome when plants are confined indoors will generally clear up quickly when the plants are moved outside. (See Specific Pests and Diseases, page 64.)

Salvia × jamensis 'Señorita Leah'

Santolina 'Lemon Queen'

Santolina
Lemon cotton

HARDY TO AT LEAST 5°F

These aromatic and evergreen members of the daisy family (Compositae) are largely of Mediterranean origin. In order to enjoy their contributions farther north, it is necessary to bring them indoors — not such a hardship, because they make delightful, low-maintenance container plants.

SPECIES AND CULTIVARS. *Santolina chamaecyparissus* is the classic lavender cotton, with its densely tomentose, silver-dotted foliage. In milder climates, it's used to form low herb hedges (especially in knot gardens), but where it won't survive, it's a fine container subject. The cultivar 'Lemon Queen' has very finely toothed, linear, deep green leaves and a compact habit, complemented by pale yellow flowers. Most santolinas are summer blooming.

DESIGN IDEAS. In any combination with plants that have greener leaves, the gray foliage of santolina provides an outstanding contrast. If your climate is not quite a Mediterranean one, you can still have fun with santolinas in containers; they grow into especially handsome topiaries!

OVERWINTERING. Cool and bright. Keep on the dry side. Prune to shape as desired.

PROPAGATING. Cuttings.

COMMON PEST PROBLEMS. None.

Scuttelaria
Skullcap, helmut flower

HARDINESS VARIES; THOSE LISTED BELOW ARE HARDY TO AT LEAST 5°F

The genus contains many hardy species; however, we have also grown and enjoyed these tender ones. *Scuttelaria* species seem to occur everywhere except South Africa.

SPECIES AND CULTIVARS. *Scuttelaria frutescens* has deep rose-pink flowers that open over a long period, and deep green, slightly glossy leaves. 'Cherry Rose' has unusually large flowers for a scuttelaria, and they are vivid pink and rose. Scuttelarias tend to be summer blooming.

DESIGN IDEAS. Scuttelarias should be situated with other plants that like well-drained conditions; fortunately this includes many that make lovely visual combinations. Both *Scuttelaria frutescens* and 'Cherry Rose' mingle well with a wide array of silver-leaved plants, including *Helichrysum* 'Moe's Gold' and *Salvia discolor*.

OVERWINTERING. Cool and bright. These seriously low-maintenance plants will reward any reasonably sunny location with bloom through the winter. Cut back if they appear leggy.

PROPAGATING. We have grown these both from seed and by cuttings.

COMMON PEST PROBLEMS. None.

Scuttelaria frutescens

Sedum
Sedum

HARDINESS VARIES; THOSE LISTED BELOW ARE HARDY TO AT LEAST 5°F

There are more than 300 species of sedum, and those of us who love the hardy ones are just as susceptible to the charms of the tenders. Extremely drought-tolerant, sun-loving plants, they're well adapted to life in both the house and the conservatory. In general, the maintenance of dry growing conditions is more critical to their winter survival than temperature.

SPECIES AND CULTIVARS. *Sedum spathulifolium* 'Cape Blanco', originally found in Cape Blanco, Oregon, is a dense-growing sedum with exceptionally silver-white leaves. With bright yellow flowers, it makes a handsome container subject. *S. makinoi* 'Ogon' has diminutive oval leaves of pale yellow, making it an indispensable ingredient in well-drained container combinations.

DESIGN IDEAS. Just like the hardy ones, tender sedums make outstanding container subjects, requiring little fuss or water. Combine them with each other or with other succulent

Sedum makinoi 'Ogon'

plants. 'Ogon' is handsome with a range of blue- and green-leaved companions, such as pachyphytums, echeverias, and agaves.

OVERWINTERING. Cool and bright. Sedums are also quite content when treated as houseplants, as long as they receive plenty of light. Water sparingly and allow soil to dry out thoroughly between waterings.

PROPAGATING. You do not need a large piece of the plant to propagate a sedum; a leaf will often suffice. They root easily from cuttings.

COMMON PEST PROBLEMS. Aphids. (See Specific Pests and Diseases, page 64.)

Senecio
Natal ivy, orangeglow vine, senecio 🌱

HARDINESS VARIES; THOSE LISTED BELOW ARE HARDY TO AT LEAST 35°F

Variety is the key to this enormous — approximately 1,000 species — genus. Senecios range from vines to 30-foot trees, and seem to occur in almost every part of the world.

SPECIES AND CULTIVARS. The spectacular *Senecio confusus* (recently renamed *Pseudogynoxys chenopodioides*), also called orangeglow vine, twines vigorously and covers with its shiny foliage and fragrant, brilliant orange daisies all summer. The succulent *S. crassissimus* hails from Madagascar and sports flattened, nearly round, glaucous leaves that are rimmed by a fine purple line. *Senecio macroglossus* 'Variegatus', also known as Natal ivy, masquerades as an exceptionally handsome ivy, despite the occasional yellow daisy. Like some unusually gifted dusty miller, *Senecio viravira* presents handsomely felted and finely cut white foliage.

DESIGN IDEAS. We have planted *Senecio viravira* in the garden, where it provides dramatic contrast with anything dark-leaved, like *Capsicum anuum* 'Bellingrath Gardens' or *Amaranthus* 'Prince's Feather'. Other senecios may be at their most engaging in containers — *Senecio macroglossus* 'Variegatus' is wonderful trailing out of pots, either alone or with a few more-subdued companions. *Senecio crassissimus* may be best combined in a large container with other succulent types. It seems a shame not to make the most of the vibrant orange provided by the flowers of *Senecio confusus*; how about mixing it with *Plumbago* 'Powder Blue' and *Solanum* 'Glasnevin' or *Canna* 'Striata' and *Alternanthera* 'Red Thread'?

OVERWINTERING. Cool and bright. Prune to shape as desired.

PROPAGATING. Cuttings.

COMMON PEST PROBLEMS. None.

Senecio confusus

Senecio viravira

🌱 Sunny & Warm, page 44   🌱 Cool & Bright, page 50   🌱 Dark & Damp, page 54   🌱 Dark & Dry, page 56

Serissa foetida

Serissa foetida
Serissa 🌿

HARDY TO AT LEAST 15°F

A hardy evergreen shrub in its native Southeast Asia, the more compact forms of serissa are well adapted to container culture. With its densely branched form and the delicacy of its small leaves, this shrub provides wonderful textural interest both indoors and out.

SPECIES AND CULTIVARS. We have enjoyed growing the cultivar 'Mt. Fuji', which has diminutive, smooth oval leaves that begin dark green but then become variously splashed with cream over time. 'Flore Pleno' is a dwarf form with small, double, roselike white flowers.

DESIGN IDEAS. Best in containers by themselves.

OVERWINTERING. Cool and bright. Serissas rarely need pruning, but you may want to prune lightly to shape plants.

PROPAGATING. Cuttings.

COMMON PEST PROBLEMS. None.

Setaria palmifolia
Palm grass 🌿

HARDY TO AT LEAST 35°F

This tropical Asian relative of foxtail and millet has lovely pleated leaves that emerge from deep maroon stalks. It grows quite happily in containers, whether in full sun or partial shade.

SPECIES AND CULTIVARS. Especially lovely is the cultivar 'Variegata', with an elegant cream stripe along the outer edge of each pleated leaf fold.

DESIGN IDEAS. We have had great results planting setaria in the ground in partial shade, and also enjoy it as a solitary specimen in a pot.

OVERWINTERING. Cool and bright.

PROPAGATING. Division.

COMMON PEST PROBLEMS. Aphids. (See Specific Pests and Diseases, page 64.)

Setaria palmifolia

Sideritis
Sideritis

HARDY TO AT LEAST 25°F

The genus *Sideritis* comprises annuals, perennial herbs, and some shrubs, and is well represented in the Canary Islands, although nearly 50 species also grow in the region between southern Spain and Turkey. Many of these are found in mountainous areas and are collected to make the Turkish herbal tea *ada çay*. Some species, like those mentioned below, are better suited to container culture than others.

SPECIES AND CULTIVARS. *Sideritis cypria* forms a domed mound of large gray-white leaves with pale yellow flowers on tall spikes. *S. dasygnaphala* has an upright habit and yellow-gray leaves; its flower spikes are pale yellow. Both bloom in summer.
DESIGN IDEAS. We plant these in pots by themselves.
OVERWINTERING. Cool and bright. Water sparingly. Prune to shape as desired.
PROPAGATING. Cuttings.
COMMON PEST PROBLEMS. None.

Sideritis cypria

Sinningia
Florist's gloxinia

HARDY TO AT LEAST 45°F

This fascinating South American genus belongs to the same family as African violets (Gesneriaceae), a fact we first made note of when we observed that cold water spilled on the plants' fuzzy leaves tended to leave discolored spots on them. Warmer water, of course, does not cause this problem, something your grandmother could have told you. John Fyfe, the gardener at Rothesay, Bute, England, first raised the florist's gloxinia from a mutant of the Brazilian species *Sinningia speciosa* in 1845. Today, many color forms are raised from seed and available as dormant tubers.

SPECIES AND CULTIVARS. *Sinningia canescens* grows on cliffs in Brazil, where it apparently flowers much of the year. Its silky, felted whitish leaves and tubular, bright pink to orange flowers would be reasons enough to grow this marvelous plant, but it is also easy to grow. Requiring only dry soil conditions in winter, it thrives in dry indoor air. *S. tubiflora* is our favorite, with its modest, fuzzy, gray-green oval leaves and spectacularly fragrant, creamy white flowers. Bloom time is somewhat dependent on when the plant is potted up, but if it is brought out of the basement in the spring, this plant will

Sinningia tubiflora

bloom in late summer to frost. The fragrance is emitted in noticeable waves at twilight, making it a fantastic plant to have near a patio or porch; hummingbirds seem to enjoy it, too.

DESIGN IDEAS. *Sinningia tubiflora* is elegant in a pot by itself. Because of their specific cultural considerations, it is probably best to grow most siningias this way, although you can also plant them in the garden.

OVERWINTERING. Dark and dry. Sinningia's preference for dry winters makes it a trouble-free tender perennial to store. We have put the entire pot down in the cellar for the winter and brought it upstairs in the spring, at which point it revived abruptly with light and water. After exposure to a light frost, cut back sinningia stems before storing for the winter.

PROPAGATING. Most species are easily grown from seed and reach flowering size within a year. The mature plants form tubers, which you can separate when they are dormant. Even the florist's gloxinia is commonly potted up as a tuber in the spring or summer.

COMMON PEST PROBLEMS. Botrytis can become a problem if conditions are too moist.

Solanum pyracanthum with *Lantana* 'Orange'

Solanum
Nightshade 🌿

HARDINESS VARIES; THOSE LISTED BELOW ARE HARDY TO AT LEAST 45°F

This very large genus includes trees and familiar food plants like eggplant, potatoes, and tomatoes. (The majority of solanums, however, produce highly poisonous fruits.) Many nightshades, including those below, are valuable for their ornamental foliage, regardless of whether they produce fruits.

SPECIES AND CULTIVARS. *Solanum* 'Glasnevin' is a very fine selection made at the National Botanic Garden in Dublin, Ireland. It has exquisite pale blue flowers with bright cadmium yellow stamens. *S. laxum* 'Album' is a climber, selected from a species native to Brazil, and it flowers over a long period; there is a popular variegated form, too. *S. pyracanthum* is an arresting species from Madagascar, with leaves that are armed with prominent bright orange spines. Its stems are covered with orange fuzz and its flowers are the usual lavender. The downy, oval white leaves of *S. marginatum,* an African nightshade, hold vicious spikes along their veins and are supported by ghostly white stems. Its smooth white fruits resemble small eggplants. *S. quitoense,* also known as the naranjilla, is a dramatic plant with large and furry, occasionally spiny purple-veined leaves and felty purple-flushed stems. Its woolly purple buds open to large, pinkish-white flowers — which are then transformed into bright orange, tomato-shaped fruits. It makes an easy and enjoyable container plant.

DESIGN IDEAS. The only factors limiting what you combine with solanums are, in some cases, their size and their spines. Once it gets going, *Solanum quitoense* is simply too big to fit with other plants. *S. marginatum* is simply too vicious. But 'Glasnevin' makes a highly desirable candidate for combined containers, associating nicely with orange and yellow shades. Try it with phormiums of the Maori series or *Helichrysum petiolare* 'Limelight'.

OVERWINTERING. Cool and bright. Prune to shape as desired.

PROPAGATING. Species, seeds; cultivars, cuttings.

COMMON PEST PROBLEMS. Few pests want to mess with solanums.

Solanum jasminoides

Solenostemon scutellarioides
Coleus 🗒

HARDY TO AT LEAST 45°F

Native to tropical Africa and Asia, coleus is a perennial plant in those climates. The recent introduction of many gorgeous, cutting-grown named cultivars has positively influenced many gardeners who were formerly prejudiced against this plant. Coleus is one of our favorites for both containers and bedding schemes, especially in partial shade.

SPECIES AND CULTIVARS. There are many coleus cultivars on the market — large-leaved, small-leaved, upright, trailing — and more being hybridized every year. They can be planted in sun or shade, but keep in mind that some may experience color fading if planted in full sun. To keep the plant's energy focused on producing gorgeous foliage, many gardeners cut back coleus flowers. Some of the coleus we plant most often are 'Anini Sunse', 'Coal Mine', 'Dipt in Wine', 'Inky Pink', 'Jungle Love', 'Lemon Frills', and 'Purple Duckfoot'.

DESIGN IDEAS. Once you start thinking about coleus in combination with complementary plants, you won't be able to stop. To achieve the best combinations, always look at the plants by actually placing them side-by-side; don't rely on your memory of the colors. Some of our favorite coleus companions are phormiums, *Ipomoea batatas* hybrids, and, in shady spots, hostas.

OVERWINTERING. Warm and sunny, either as a whole plant or by cuttings. Particularly when grown indoors, coleus will require occasional pruning — do not be afraid to cut off quite a bit to make plants more manageable.

PROPAGATING. Cuttings.

COMMON PEST PROBLEMS. Aphids, scale, whiteflies. (See Specific Pests and Diseases, page 64.)

'Lemon Frills' coleus

'Pineapple Prince' coleus with *Perilla frutescens*

Sollya heterophylla

Sollya heterophylla
Australian bluebell 🌿

HARDY TO AT LEAST 35˚F

This delicate climber from western Australia has charmed many of our visitors with its pendant, bell-like blue flowers in summer, which are followed by the development of shiny blue oval fruits. It is not fussy, and grows quite happily in containers.

DESIGN IDEAS. Here is a plant with flowers of that startling shade of blue that gardeners will die for. It is lovely all by itself, but also looks good with silver leaves like those of *Dichondra argentea* or of *Senecio viravira*.
OVERWINTERING. Cool and bright. Prune lightly, as needed.
PROPAGATING. Seed or cuttings.
COMMON PEST PROBLEMS. None.

Stachys
Betony 🌿

HARDINESS VARIES; THOSE LISTED BELOW ARE HARDY TO AT LEAST 5˚F

These are tender members of the same family as hardier lamb's ears. Although most of these originate in the Mediterranean region, there are species of *Stachys* from many parts of the world.

SPECIES AND CULTIVARS. *Stachys albotomentosa*, with its furry white foliage and stems bearing plump spikes of salmon flowers, is a very lovely tender species. The Mexican *S. coccinea* has the distinction of being the only North American species with red flowers — they're actually bright coral — and has fuzzy green leaves.
DESIGN IDEAS. These are well suited to container combinations with less hirsute companions; try *Euphorbia fulgens* 'Purple Selection' or 'Purple Duckfoot' coleus.
OVERWINTERING. Cool and bright. A hard pruning when you first move the plant inside in the fall is a good idea.
BEST WAY TO PROPOGATE. Cuttings.
COMMON PEST PROBLEMS. None.

Stachys albotomentosa

Stenotaphrum secundatum 'Variegatum'

Stenotaphrum secundatum 'Variegatum'
Variegated St. Augustine grass 🔳

HARDY TO AT LEAST 35°F

This plant may pose a threat in climes where it can survive outdoors — its rate of growth can be somewhat menacing, even when you know that the first frost will get it. But because we know here that its days are seasonally numbered, it's possible to use this vigorous characteristic to our advantage — what a great plant for truly punishing locations! It just adds a few inches to its lovely cream and green length, making a charmingly vigorous container subject reminiscent, in more ways than one, of bamboo.

DESIGN IDEAS. Variegated St. Augustine grass is striking when combined with plants that have dark foliage, like *Euphorbia cotinifolia* or *Colocasia esculenta* 'Black Magic'.
OVERWINTERING. Cool and bright. We are not responsible for the behavior of plants kept in a warm room over the winter. Frequent and vigorous pruning is probably the best policy.
PROPAGATING. We dare you to take just one cutting . . .
COMMON PEST PROBLEMS. None.

Strobilanthes
Persian shield, blue sage 🔳

HARDINESS VARIES; THOSE LISTED BELOW ARE HARDY TO AT LEAST 45°F

There are 250 species of this Acanthus family genus, and they range from perennial herbs to subshrubs. Most are indigenous to Asia.

SPECIES AND CULTIVARS. *Strobilanthes dyeriana,* or Persian shield, is an evergreen subshrub in its native Burma. It has silver and pale blue flowers, but the highly ornamental foliage — marked by white and pink, with an overall iridescent sheen — is what makes this plant so valuable. It can also tolerate partial shade. *Strobilanthes isophyllus,* or blue sage, is indigenous to northeastern India, where it grows into a shrub. Its many finely tapered, linear leaves are a glistening purple-black, with greener new growth. The winter flowers of blue sage are a brilliant shade of deep lavender.
DESIGN IDEAS. *Strobilanthes dyeriana* is exquisite in combination with dark-leaved, contrasting plants like *Ipomoea* 'Ace of Spades' and *Pennisetum* 'Burgundy Giant'. Pink- or white-flowered companions like *Angelonia* 'Serena Rose' or 'White' are another possibility — as are many silver-leaved ones, particularly those with shiny leaves.
OVERWINTERING. Warm and sunny. Cut back before moving plant inside.
PROPAGATING. Cuttings.
COMMON PEST PROBLEMS. None.

Strobilanthes dyeriana

Thunbergia alata

Thunbergia grandiflora

Thunbergia
Black-eyed Susan vine, blue trumpet vine, sky vine, Bengal clock vine, 🎋 🎍

HARDY TO AT LEAST 45°F

These plants originate in Africa, Madagascar, and the warmer portions of Asia, ranging from twining annual and perennial vines to shrubs. Many have the funnel-shaped flowers that we commonly associate with the genus. Most bloom in summer, although in warmer greenhouse conditions, they can be induced to continue bloom through winter.

SPECIES AND CULTIVARS. *Thunbergia alata,* or black-eyed Susan vine, is often grown as an annual in cold climates, but it is actually a true perennial, and can be easily overwintered in a cool greenhouse or on a windowsill. Although a native of tropical Africa, *T. alata* has now naturalized in other locations, including Hong Kong and the Philippines. Situated in the vine's leaf axils, the flowers are generally orange, but can also be yellow or white, with or without the deep purple "eye" that gives it the common name. We are particularly impressed with the recent introduction 'Spanish Eyes', which bears flowers colored in a subtler range, from coppery orange to muted red and terra-cotta.

Blue tumpet vine, Bengal clock vine, sky vine, skyflower, and blue skyflower are all common names for *T. grandiflora,* native from Sikkim and Assam to Burma, Cambodia, Thailand, and even southern China, where it climbs into trees and shrubs at high altitudes. The vine has rough, scalloped leaves and bell-shaped, pale blue flowers with yellow throats, and is popular in gardens on the Cote d'Azur, where it winters outdoors.

Thunbergia mysorensis is a vigorous grower from southern India, where it climbs into forest trees and blooms in winter. Its exotic, pendant yellow and vermilion flowers hang in chains as long as three feet from vines that can reach 30 feet high. When not growing in its native habitat, it is happiest in a warm greenhouse or on a windowsill, and may bloom continuously if it's comfortable.

DESIGN IDEAS. Most thunbergias benefit from some support structure — its size will be determined by the particular species' dimensions. Whereas *Thunbergia mysorensis* and *T. grandiflora* demand large and sturdy supports, *T. alata* can be coaxed to twine around structures that are relatively small and delicate. Thunbergias are adaptable to both garden and container settings, and can be combined with plants that coordinate in some way with either the central zone or the flower-petal color or that echo the shape of their leaves. Try *T. alata* 'Spanish Eyes' on a small tepee with *Ipomoea batatas* 'Blackie' trailing over the side of a container. The black eyes of the standard *T. alata* lend themselves to pairings with all sorts of black- and brown-leaved companions.

Thunbergia mysorensis

OVERWINTERING. Individual species vary in their preferred temperature ranges; for instance, *Thunbergia alata* will thrive in bright, relatively cool environments, as low as 40°F; *T. mysorensis* will not. *T. grandiflora* grows vigorously in a range of conditions from sunny to shaded. It also likes cool temperatures, but is fine with considerable shade; *T. mysorensis* should be kept warm and sunny. Cut plants back hard before moving them indoors in the fall.

PROPAGATING. Some species, such as *Thunbergia alata,* can be started from seed. Others may be easier to grow from cuttings.

COMMON PEST PROBLEMS. None.

Tibouchina urvilleana

Tibouchina
Glory bush, purple glory tree 📷 📷

HARDY TO AT LEAST 45°F

Members of this large genus (350 strong) share several characteristics: large, leathery, conspicuously veined leaves and showy flowers. They are endemic to tropical South America; by far the greatest number of species originate in Brazil.

SPECIES AND CULTIVARS. *Tibouchina urvilleana,* the purple glory tree, with its fuzzy oval leaves and rich purple flowers, is a deservedly popular conservatory plant. Although its greatest period of bloom occurs from spring to fall in a nontropical climate, when grown in warmer conditions, it will continue to bloom sporadically through the year. We were amazed to see it growing happily as part of a hedge in Volcano, Hawaii. We first noticed *T. grandifolia* at Wave Hill, in Bronx, New York, where we were impressed by this plant's densely furred, cupped leaves of significant proportions (up to six inches), which are also distinguished by unusual concentric veins. The violet flowers of *T. grandifolia* are relatively small, but pretty.

DESIGN IDEAS. Tibouchina makes an outstanding container plant; its large size and bold foliage and flower color, however, make it a good candidate for planting out in the garden as well. Try combining it with the similarly purple flowers of *Angelonia* 'Blue Horizon' or the dissimilar purples and pinks of *Tradescantia* 'Purple Queen'. There's no end to the possibilities.

OVERWINTERING. Cool and bright is preferred, although warmer and sunny also works. Cut plants back hard in the fall before moving indoors.

PROPAGATING. Cuttings.

COMMON PEST PROBLEMS. None.

Tradescantia sillamontana

Tradescantia
Spider lily

HARDY TO AT LEAST 45°F

Although there are many perfectly hardy ones, there are also tender members of the tradescantia family that make fantastic bedding plants as well as ideal houseplants; most of these originate in Mexico.

SPECIES AND CULTIVARS. *Tradescantia fluminensis,* a green-leaved Brazilian trailer that roots at its nodes, is a good choice for baskets and ground covering, preferring warm and humid conditions. It has lovely white flowers. *T. pallida* originates in Mexico, and its purple stems and leaves, complemented by pale pink flowers, were a familiar sight in college dorm rooms of a certain era. It is also useful as an element in mixed containers. *T. sillamontana,* also known as white gossamer or white velvet, is another Mexican species. Its oval leaves, green with purple reverse, are covered by long white hairs, and are arranged along the stems in a distinct and curious way. It has bright pink flowers and is well suited to growing in a hanging container. *T. spathacea,* also referred to as *Rhoeo discolor,* is a vigorous, easy-to-grow, semi-succulent plant with sword-shaped leaves that are purple on their reverse and rich green above. Its tiny white flowers are enclosed by boat-shaped purple bracts.

DESIGN IDEAS. In the long run, when they are grown as houseplants, tradescantias may be happiest each in its own container, but you can use them for a season or so as elements in mixed plantings. Their distinctive foliage lends itself to combinations with contrasting leaves like those of various phormiums or *Pennisetum* 'Burgundy Giant'.

OVERWINTERING. Cool and bright will work, as will keeping them at room temperature with less than optimal light — these are tough plants. Cut plants back hard before moving them inside in the fall.

PROPAGATING. Cuttings.

COMMON PEST PROBLEMS. None.

Trichostema
Blue curls

HARDINESS VARIES; THOSE LISTED BELOW ARE HARDY TO AT LEAST 15°F

Most species of this entirely North American genus — they range from annuals to shrubby plants — are aromatic. The Californian species we've grown (see below) are exceptional, drought-tolerant plants, attractive to butterflies and birds as well as to the human eye.

Trichostema lanatum

SPECIES AND CULTIVARS. Thanks to Ginny Hunt, of Seedhunt (see Resources, page 200), we were introduced a few years ago to *Trichostema purpusii,* the handsome and shrubby California native. It has bright fuchsia-pink flowers, reminding us somewhat of a salvia. With its narrow leaves and woolly, royal blue flowers, *T. lanatum* is another California native that's reminiscent of rosemary, both visually and because of its cedarlike fragrance. They are both recommended for warm, well-drained conditions and bloom in summer.

DESIGN IDEAS. *Trichostema purpusii* is handsome planted with a drought-tolerant silver trailer like *Dichondra argentea* or *Lotus berthelotii.* Try *T. lanatum* with *Helichrysum retortum* or *Salvia greggii* 'Pale Yellow'.

OVERWINTERING. Cool and bright; keep them dry. Prune to shape.

PROPAGATING. Seed.

COMMON PEST PROBLEMS. None.

Trifolium repens 'Green Ice'

Trifolium
Clover

HARDY TO AT LEAST 5°F

You may be less than appreciative of those "clovers" growing in your lawn, but the trifoliums have much to offer in the way of leaf interest. They are especially valuable as low-maintenance, single-subject container plants.

SPECIES AND CULTIVARS. The cultivar 'Green Ice' is an elegant, understated study of green on green. The trailing stems are clad in leaves of dull jade, each with a rich emerald center. 'Red Heart' features three-leaved clovers embellished by Nordic sweater patterns in strands of cranberry and white; it has white flowers. Sporting burgundy-centered green leaves, *Trifolium repens* 'Purpurascens' is an exceptionally handsome clover. *T.* 'Wheatfen' is another fine container subject, with small, medium green to purplish leaves that are subtly striated with paler green along its trailing shoots.

DESIGN IDEAS. Many trifoliums will nicely fill a hanging basket or other container by themelves, given time and a little encouragement. They can also be useful ingredients in a mixed planting. Try 'Purpurascens' with the related shades of 'Theatre Velvet' coleus or *Eucomis* 'Sparkling Burgundy'. Or how about 'Green Ice' with *Parahebe perfoliata* and *Centaurea rutifolia*?

OVERWINTERING. Cool and bright, really essential.

PROPAGATING. Cuttings.

COMMON PEST PROBLEMS. None.

Tripogandra
Moses in the bullrushes 🌿

HARDY TO AT LEAST 35°F

Creeping plants that tend to root at their nodes, these natives of tropical South America have abundant small flowers. They have a preference for partial shade and moist, humid air.

SPECIES AND CULTIVARS. *Tripogandra multiflora* has white or occasionally pink flowers throughout the year. *T.* 'Purple Scimitars' is a fine selection of the familiar plant called Moses in the bullrushes, and with its trailing, intensely purple leaves, is well suited to life in a hanging container. An especially lovely foliage subject, *T.* 'False Bromeliad' has long gray-green leaves that are strongly striated by cream markings.
DESIGN IDEAS. All these make happy container subjects, and are especially useful in combinations that highlight their forthright trailing qualities. Try *Tripogandra* 'False Bromeliad' with *Juncus pallidus* and *Iresine herbstii* 'California'.
OVERWINTERING. Cool and bright. Trim to keep the plant manageable.
PROPAGATING. Cuttings.
COMMON PEST PROBLEMS. None.

Tripogandra multiflora

Tulbaghia cominsii

Tulbaghia
Society garlic 🌿

HARDINESS VARIES; THOSE LISTED BELOW ARE HARDY TO AT LEAST 25°F

Its common name refers to the strong, oniony fragrance of society garlic's grasslike foliage and narrow bulbs. A member of the lily family (Liliaceae), these South African perennials make fine container subjects in the conservatory, where their sweet-smelling flowers offer a welcome, as well as surprising, contribution in winter.

SPECIES AND CULTIVARS. *Tulbaghia codii × cepacea* has green leaves and starry orchid flowers. The nocturnally fragrant *T. cominsii* has lovely white flowers and glaucous foliage. *T. natalensis* has fragrant flowers too, but these are generally white tinged with lilac. Forming clumps of glaucous foliage in its rocky habitat, *T. violacea* blooms through the winter with umbels of 12 to 14 soft lavender flowers. Some tulbaghias can survive temperatures as low as 14°F for brief periods.
DESIGN IDEAS. Society garlic is effective potted by itself.
OVERWINTERING. Cool and bright. Cut back spent blooms — occasional trimming of foliage may be a good idea too.
PROPAGATING. Most of the species can be grown from seed, although waiting for them to achieve blooming size requires some patience. After that, there is always division.
COMMON PEST PROBLEMS. None.

Tweedia caerulea
Southern star, tweedia

HARDY TO AT LEAST 35°F

For obscure taxonomic reasons, this member of the milkweed family (Asclepiadaceae) has been the single member of its own genus more than once; in the past it was called *Oxypetalum caeruleum*. By any name, its distinctive, fuzzy, elongated, heart-shaped leaves and starry flowers — which are a surreal and startling shade of turquoise — set this plant apart from other members of the milkweed family. Native to southern Brazil and Uruguay, tweedia is a good candidate for a cool but frost-free greenhouse's sunny windows. It blooms from early spring through fall.

DESIGN IDEAS. The wondrous blue of its flowers makes tweedia a good choice for grounding either in dark shades like those of *Ophiopogon planiscapus* 'Nigrescens' or the metallic shine of any plant with silver foliage, such as *Dichondra argentea* or one of the helichrysums.
OVERWINTERING. Cool and bright. Prune to shape as desired.
PROPAGATING. Just like its cousin *Asclepias syriaca,* the common roadside milkweed, pollinated *Tweedia caerulea* flowers turn into leathery pods full of silk-tasseled seeds; these germinate easily.
COMMON PEST PROBLEMS. Aphids. (See Specific Pests and Diseases, page 64.)

Tweedia caerulea

Uncinia
Uncinia

HARDY TO AT LEAST 25°F

These members of the sedge family (Cyperaceae) are described as "grasslike," which is a fairly accurate appraisal. Tufted small plants of great charm, they grow in much of the Pacific region, although the majority are natives of New Zealand. The species we have grown have a preference for partial shade and moisture.

SPECIES AND CULTIVARS. *Uncinia egmontiana* forms diminutive tufts of copper and gold. *U. rubra* is a dramatic, all-red plant that suggests endless possibilities, especially with silver-leaved companions. Handsome tufts of deep brown to purple leaves make *Uncinia uncinata* a fine addition to mixed containers.
DESIGN IDEAS. Try *Uncinia egmontiana* with *Calocephalus brownii* and *Haloragis* 'Wellington Bronze'. Or plant *U. uncinata* with *Brachyglottis monroi* and *Ipomoea* 'Ace of Spades'.
OVERWINTERING. Cool and bright. Water sparingly. Remove old leaves, but do not trim.
PROPAGATING. Seeds.
COMMON PEST PROBLEMS. None.

Uncinia uncinata

Veltheimia bracteata

Veltheimia
Veltheimia 🔲

HARDY TO AT LEAST 35°F

This relative of the familiar spring-blooming hyacinth consists of only two species — *Veltheimia bracteata* and *V. capensis* — both of which are well suited to pot culture. Veltheimia has a distinctive, tubular inflorescence festively colored in shades of red and green. Although the two species bloom in different seasons, they are both native to South Africa.

SPECIES AND CULTIVARS. In South Africa, *Veltheimia bracteata* grows and blooms in the summer; here in the United States, it's a winter bloomer. Its leaves are dark green and its stems are also dark, verging on black. In warm climates, it prefers some shade. *V. capensis* is a winter grower with undulating glaucous leaves. Its midwinter bloom makes it a valuable guest in the sunny conservatory.
OVERWINTERING. Cool and bright for both species. *Veltheimia capensis* will recuperate after bloom through the spring and much of the summer, and should be kept dry during this period. *V. bracteata* is in active growth all year.
PROPAGATING. Division of bulb offsets or by seed, if flowers are left to set them.
COMMON PEST PROBLEMS. None.

Westringia
Westringia 🔲

HARDY TO AT LEAST 45°F

This group of Australian shrubs is notable for its tolerance of drought and salt winds. In recent years, some particularly ornamental selections have been made.

SPECIES AND CULTIVARS. In its native habitat, *Westringia fruticosa* grows somewhat large for containers, but with its dense, linear green leaves and ever-present small white flowers, it may be worth an occasional pruning to keep indoors through colder winters. *W.* 'Smokey' is a striking, smaller shrub with pointy leaves that are coated in dull silver hairs, making it an excellent subject for both mixed and singular containers.

Westringia 'Smokey'

DESIGN IDEAS. Although they can be moved into the garden for the growing season, westringias are probably best kept in their containers, where they make a handsome statement either alone or in combination with other sun-loving plants.

OVERWINTERING. Cool and bright. Prune to shape as desired.

PROPAGATING. Cuttings.

COMMON PEST PROBLEMS. None.

Xanthosoma
Malanga, tannia, xanthosoma, yautia

HARDY TO AT LEAST 45°F

This native of the West Indies has naturalized through much of South America, and is cultivated throughout the subtropics for both its leaves and tubers, which are edible when young and properly prepared. It grows best in damp, warm settings.

SPECIES AND CULTIVARS. *Xanthosoma sagittifolium* 'Lime Zinger' was our spectacular introduction to the genus, with its giant leaves of neon lime (instead of the species' ordinarily blue-green foliage) and matching bright chartreuse flowers. Other intriguing selections of the species have been made, such as *X. s.* 'Albomarginatum', with glaucous leaves edged and veined in off-white, and *X. s.* 'Maculatum', whose wide, arrow-shaped leaves are a pale green splashed with white. *X. violaceum* is widely grown for its large, starchy, edible tubers, which have a pink interior. This plant's handsome appearance — with green leaves often as wide as 16 inches across and nearly 30 inches long, with purple midribs and veins and supported on thick purple stalks — may be an equally compelling reason to grow it.

Xanthosoma 'Lime Zinger'

DESIGN IDEAS. With its luxuriant tropical appearance, xanthosoma mingles amicably with other sultry types, such as cannas, coleus, colocasias, and oryza.

OVERWINTERING. Warm, sunny, and humid. Trim off old leaves as the plant becomes dormant. The tuber can also be stored in dark and moist conditions, just like a canna. In this case, keep the tuber cool but not cold — above 40°F.

PROPAGATING. Division of offsets.

COMMON PEST PROBLEMS. Perhaps the greatest challenge to cultivating these is providing adequate warmth and humidity. Plants will sulk in less than ideal circumstances, and this can lead to other complications, such as botrytis.

Plant Lists

PLANTS THAT CAN BE PROPAGATED FROM CUTTINGS

Abutilon	Coprosma	Iresine herbstii	Pelargonium
Acaena	Cordyline	Jasminum	Pentas
Acalypha	Cosmos	Juanulloa mexicana	Phygelius
Adromischus	Cotyledon	Kalanchoe	Plecostachys serpyllifolia
Aeonium	Crassula	Kleinia	Plectranthus
Agastache	Cuphea	Lantana	Plumbago
Alonsoa	Diascia	Lavandula	Punica granatum
Aloysia	Dichondra micrantha	Leonotis	Rosa chinensis
Alternanthera	Dicliptera suberecta	Lonicera	Rosmarinus officinalis
Alyogyne	Duranta	Loropetalum chinense f. rubrum	Ruellia
Amicia	Erodium		Saccharum officinarum
Anagallis	Erysimum	Lotus	Salvia
Angelonia	Eucomis	Lupinus albifrons	Santolina
Anisodontea	Eumorphia prostrata	Malvastrum lateritum	Scutelleria
Antirrhinum	Euphorbia	Malvaviscus arboreus	Sedum
Arctotis	Evolvulus pilosus	Mandevilla	Senecio
Argyranthemum	Felicia amelloides	Manihot	Serissa foetida
Aristolochia	Ficus carica	Marrubium	Sideritis
Artemisia	Fuchsia	Michelia figo	Solanum
Ballota	Gardenia	Mussaenda	Solenostemon scutellarioides
Begonia	Gazania	Myoporum	Sollya heterophylla
Brachyglottis	Geranium	Nepeta	Stachys
Brugmansia	Gynura auriantiaca	Nerium oleander	Stenotaphrum secundatum
Buddleia	Haloragis erecta	Nicotiana	Strobilanthes
Calocephalus	Hamelia patens	Ocimum americanum	Thunbergia
Ceanothus	Hebe	Origanum	Tibouchina
Centaurea	Helichrysum	Osamanthus fragrans	Tradescantia
Ceratostigma	Heliotropium arborescens	Osteospermum	Trifolium
Cestrum	Hibiscus	Oxalis	Tripogandra
Cissus	Impatiens	Pachyphytum	Westringia
Citrus	Iochroma	Parahebe	
Convolvulus	Ipomoea	Passiflora	

TENDERS FOR CONTINUOUS BLOOM

Abutilon	Anisodontea × hypomadara	Dicliptera suberecta
Alonsoa	Cestrum	Plumbago
Anagallis	Cuphea	

WINTER BLOOMERS

Abutilon	Diascia	Lupinus albifrons
Alonsoa	Dicliptera suberecta	Malvastrum lateritium
Anisodontea × hypomadara	Euphorbia	Michelia figo
Argyranthemum	Evolvulus pilosus	Monopsis
Buddleia	Felicia amelloides	Osmanthus fragrans
Ceratostigma wilmottianum	Heliotropium arborescens	Plumbago
Cestrum	Jasminum	Scuttelaria
Convolvulus	Kalanchoe	Tulbaghia
Crassula	Loropetalum chinense	Veltheimia
Cuphea	f. rubrum	
Dianella caerulea	Lotus	

PLANTS TO OVERWINTER IN A WARM, SUNNY LOCATION

Acalypha	Colocasia	Kalanchoe	Rhodochiton atrosanguineus
Andromischus	Crassula	Kleinia	Saccharum officinarum
Agave	Echeveria	Lantana	Solenostemom scutellarioides
Aloe	Gasteria	Manihot	Strobilanthes
Alternanthera	Gynura auriantiaca	Musa	Thunbergia
Ananas	Haworthia	Mussaenda	Tibouchina
Aristolochia	Hibiscus	Neoregelia	Xanthosoma
Begonia	Impatiens	Pachyphytum	
Cissus discolor	Juanulloa mexicana	Pentas	

PLANTS TO STORE DARK AND DAMP

Aloysia triphylla	Gunnera manicata
Canna	Ipomoea
Colocasia	Manihot
Cosmos atrosanguineus	Pennisetum setaceum
Dahlia	Xanthosoma
Ficus carica	

PLANTS TO STORE DARK AND DRY

Amorphophallus	Gladiolus
Bessera elegans	Mirabilis
Colocasia	Salvia
Curcuma petiolata	Sinningia

PLANTS TO OVERWINTER IN A COOL, BRIGHT LOCATION

Abutilon	Chondropetalum tectorum	Ipomoea	Phormium
Acaena	Citrus	Iresine herbstii	Phygelius
Aeonium	Convolvulus	Jasminum	Plectostachys serpyllifolia
Agapanthus africanus	Coprosma	Juncus	Plectranthus
Agastache	Cordyline	Kalanchoe	Plumbago
Agave	Cotyledon	Kniphofia	Polianthes tuberosa
Aloe	Crassula	Lavandula	Punica granatum
Alonsoa	Cuphea	Leonotis	Puya
Aloysia triphylla	Datura	Leptinella	Rhodochiton atrosanguineus
Alyogyne	Dianella caerulea	Lonicera	Rosa chinensis
× Amarcrinum	Diascia	Loropetalum chinense f. rubrum	Rosmarinus officinalis
Amicia zygomeris	Dichondra micrantha		Ruellia
Anagallis	Dicliptera suberecta	Lotus	Salvia
Angelonia angustifolia	Duranta	Lupinus albifrons	Santolina
Anigozanthos	Echeveria	Malvastrum lateritum	Scutelleria
Anisodontea × hypomadara	Ephedra	Malvaviscus arboreus	Sedum
Antirrhinum	Erodium	Mandevilla	Senecio
Arctotis × hybrida	Erysimum	Manettia	Serissa foetida
Argyranthemum	Eucomis	Marrubium	Setaria palmifolia
Artemisia × hybrida	Eumorphia prostrata	Melianthus	Sideritis
Arundo	Euphorbia	Michelia figo	Solanum
Asclepias	Evolvulus pilosus	Monopsis	Sollya heterophylla
Astelia	Felicia amelloides	Myoporum	Stachys
Azorina vidalii	Ficus carica	Nepeta	Stenotaphrum secundatum
Ballota	Fuchsia	Nerium oleander	Thunbergia
Begonia	Gardenia	Nicotiana	Tibouchina
Billardiera longiflora	Gasteria	Ocimum americanum	Tradescantia
Bouvardia	Gazania	Ophiopogon planiscapus	Trichostema
Brachyglottis	Geranium	Origanum	Trifolium
Brugmansia	Glaucium	Orthrosanthus chimboracensis	Tripogandra
Buddleia	Gunnera manicata		Tulbaghia
Calocephalus brownii	Haloragis erecta	Osmanthus fragrans	Tweedia caerulea
Capsicum	Haworthia	Osteospermum	Uncinia
Carex	Hebe	Oxalis	Veltheimia
Ceanothus	Helichrysum	Parahebe	Westringia
Centaurea	Heliotropium arborescens	Passiflora	
Ceratostigma wilmottianum	Hibiscus	Pelargonium	
Cestrum	Iochroma	Pentas	

Suggested Reading

Carlile, W. R., and I. Beford. "Plant Growth in Container Media Amended with Calcined Clay," in *Symposium on Horticultural Substates and Their Analysis*. Edited by J. Willumsen. Leuven, Belgium: International Society for Horticultural Science. Can be found on their Web site: *www.actahort.org*

Carruthers, L., and R. Ginns. *Echeverias: A Guide to Cultivation and Identification of the Popular American Succulents*. New York: Arco Publishing, 1973.

Clebsch, Betsy. *A Book of Salvias: A Sage for Every Garden*. Portland, Ore: Timber Press, 1997.

Fernald, Merritt L. *Gray's Manual of Botany*. Discorides Press, 1993.

Graf, Alfred Byrd. *Exotica: Pictorial Cyclopedia of Exotic Plants*. East Rutherford, N.J.: Roehrs Company, 1963.

Griffiths, Mark. *Index of Garden Plants: The New Royal Horticultural Society Dictionary*. Portland, Ore: Timber Press, 1994.

Halpin, Anne M. *The Window Box Book*. New York: Simon & Schuster, 1989.

Hillier, Malcolm. *The Book of Container Gardening*. New York: Simon & Schuster, 1991.

The International Plant Names Index (2004). Published on the Internet: www.ipni.org

L. H. Bailey Hortorium, Cornell University. *Hortus Third: A Concise Dictionary of Plants Cultivated in the United States and Canada*. New York: Macmillan, 1976.

Martin, Tovah. *Once Upon a Windowsill: A History of Indoor Plants*. Portland, Ore: Timber Press, 1988.

Morton, Julia F. *Fruits of Warm Climates*. Miami, Fla.: Florida Flair, 1987.

New England Floriculture, Inc. *New England Greenhouse Floriculture Guide: A Management Guide for Insects, Diseases, Weeds, and Growth Regulators*. Pocasset, Mass.: New England Floriculture, Inc., 2007-2008. Can be ordered through the University of Massachusetts, Amherst, Web site: *www.umass.edu/umext/floriculture*

Nijhuis, Miep, ed. *Fuchsias: The Complete Handbook*. London: Cassell, 1996.

Pavord, Anna. *The Naming of Names: The Search for Order in the World of Plants*. London: Bloomsbury, 2005.

Phillips, Roger and Martin Rix. *Indoor and Greenhouse Plants*. New York: Random House, 1997.

Phillips, Roger and Nicky Foy. *The Random House Book of Herbs*. New York: Random House, 1990.

The Reader's Digest Association. *Container Gardening*. New York: Reader's Digest, 2007.

Wilder, Louise Beebe. *The Fragrant Path*. New York: Macmillan, 1932.

Resources

Some recommended sources for plants and seeds featured in this book:

Annie's Annuals & Perennials
888-266-4370
www.anniesannuals.com

Avant Gardens
508-998-8819
www.avantgardensne.com

Brent and Becky's Bulbs
877-661-2852
www.brentandbeckysbulbs.com

Chiltern Seeds
+44-0-1229-581137
www.chilternseeds.co.uk

Digging Dog Nursery
707-937-1130
www.diggingdog.com

The Fragrant Path
www.fragrantpathseeds.com

Glasshouse Works
740-662-2142
www.exoticplants.com

J. L. Hudson, Seedsman
www.jlhudsonseeds.net

Jelitto Perennial Seeds
502-895-0807
www.jelitto.com

Kartuz Greenhouses
760-941-3613
www.kartuz.com

Logee's
888-330-8038
www.logees.com

Plant Delights Nursery
919-772-4794
www.plantdelights.com

Plant World Seeds
+44-0-1803-872939
www.plant-world-seeds.com

Seedhunt
www.seedhunt.com

Thompson & Morgan
800-274-7333
www.thompson-morgan.com

CELSIUS CONVERSION CHART

°F	°C	°F	°C	°F	°C	°F	°C
0.1	-17.722	7.0	-13.88	22.0	-5.55	37.0	2.77
0.2	-17.666	8.0	-13.33	23.0	-5	38.0	3.33
0.3	-17.611	9.0	-12.77	24.0	-4.44	39.0	3.88
0.4	-17.555	10.0	-12.22	25.0	-3.88	40.0	4.44
0.5	-17.5	11.0	-11.66	26.0	-3.33	41.0	5
0.6	-17.444	12.0	-11.11	27.0	-2.77	42.0	5.55
0.7	-17.388	13.0	-10.55	28.0	-2.22	43.0	6.11
0.8	-17.333	14.0	-10	29.0	-1.66	44.0	6.66
0.9	-17.277	15.0	-9.44	30.0	-1.11	45.0	7.22
1.0	-17.22	16.0	-8.88	31.0	-0.55	46.0	7.77
2.0	-16.66	17.0	-8.33	32.0	0	47.0	8.33
3.0	-16.11	18.0	-7.77	33.0	0.55	48.0	8.88
4.0	-15.55	19.0	-7.22	34.0	1.11	49.0	9.44
5.0	-15	20.0	-6.66	35.0	1.66	50.0	10
6.0	-14.44	21.0	-6.11	36.0	2.22		

Photography Credits

Acknowledgments

IN ADDITION to the formidable knowledge and skills that she brought from two decades of work in the Arnold Arboretum's Herbarium, Ida Hay's eye for botanically accurate detail and her patient resilience and humor in interactions with the public were invaluable to our growing nursery. Maida Goodwin combined an archivist's attention to detail with an infectious enthusiasm for gardening. In addition to their camaraderie through the growing and retail seasons for nearly a decade, both Ida and Maida's editorial and proofreading skills kept me honest each winter as we wrote catalog copy, and we're certain that their scrupulously worded margin notes and good-humored attention to detail helped us to avoid numerous embarrassments in print.

Over the years, we had many other staff members come and go. Of the longest tenures, Ben Silva actually began working for us when he was nine years old; he was part of our original pepper-picking crew back in the years before our daughters were born. Ben was in his twenties by the time he left, but returned periodically to help us re-cover the greenhouses, a job requiring not just agility and carpentry skills, but also a perennial lack of fear concerning heights, which he still, amazingly enough, possesses.

The most senior member of our staff was David Carson, who had moved back to New England in the early nineties after many years in the Carolinas and Florida. We are fortunate that for nearly a decade he shared with us his energy, enthusiasm, and especially his love of moving large stones. His unpretentious familiarity with, and knowledge of, plants in many climates was inspiring to us all.

Part of what made Blue Meadow Farm special was our visitors, many of whom shared both their own gardens and special plants with us. At the risk of inadvertently omitting names, we would like to thank Elsa Bakalar, Bobbi Rosenau, Nell Schwartz, Robert Nicholson, Holly Weir and Bill Pollard, Rich and Gail Sawyer, G. Kristian Fenderson, Sheila Magullion, Ellen McFarland, Gary Koller, Richard Dufresne, Nick Nickou and Carol Hanby, Wayne Winterrowd and Joe Eck, Allan Armitage, Michael Dirr, Wayne Mezitt, Louis Bauer, Tasha Tudor, Helen Dillon, Leo Blanchette, Michael Marcotrigiano, Joanne Stuart, Bunny Williams, Ed Bowen, Carol Stocker, Marco Polo Stufano, Elizabeth Hull, Gordon Hayward, and Bobbi Angell.

We would also like to thank our editor, Carleen Madigan Perkins, without whose patience and encouragement this book might not have become an actuality.

Index

Page references in *italics* indicate photos or illustrations.